# BOOK 3 – EQUITY INVESTMENTS

SCHWESERNOTES™ 2013 CFA LEVEL II BOOK 3: EQUITY INVESTMENTS

©2012 Kaplan, Inc. All rights reserved.

Published in 2012 by Kaplan Schweser.

Printed in the United States of America.

ISBN: 978-1-4277-4245-2 / 1-4277-4245-6

PPN: 3200-2851

# READINGS AND LEARNING OUTCOME STATEMENTS

## READINGS

*The following material is a review of the Equity Investments principles designed to address the learning outcome statements set forth by CFA Institute.*

## STUDY SESSION 10

**Reading Assignments**

*Equity*, CFA Program Curriculum, Volume 4, Level II (CFA Institute, 2013)

## STUDY SESSION 11

**Reading Assignments**

*Equity*, CFA Program Curriculum, Volume 4, Level II (CFA Institute, 2013)

## STUDY SESSION 12

**Reading Assignments**

*Equity*, CFA Program Curriculum, Volume 4, Level II (CFA Institute, 2013)

# LEARNING OUTCOME STATEMENTS (LOS)

## STUDY SESSION 10

*The topical coverage corresponds with the following CFA Institute assigned reading:*

### 30. Equity Valuation: Applications and Processes

The candidate should be able to:

a. Define valuation and intrinsic value, and explain sources of perceived mispricing. (page 9)

b. Explain the going concern assumption and contrast a going concern value to a liquidation value. (page 10)

c. Describe definitions of value, and justify which definition of value is most relevant to public company valuation. (page 10)

d. Describe applications of equity valuation. (page 10)

e. Describe questions that should be addressed in conducting an industry and competitive analysis. (page 12)

f. Contrast absolute and relative valuation models, and describe examples of each type of model. (page 13)

g. Describe sum-of-the-parts valuation, and explain a conglomerate discount. (page 14)

h. Explain broad criteria for choosing an appropriate approach for valuing a given company. (page 15)

*The topical coverage corresponds with the following CFA Institute assigned reading:*

### 31. Return Concepts

The candidate should be able to:

a. Distinguish among realized holding period return, expected holding period return, required return, return from convergence of price to intrinsic value, discount rate, and internal rate of return. (page 21)

b. Calculate and interpret an equity risk premium using historical and forward-looking estimation approaches. (page 23)

c. Estimate the required return on an equity investment using the capital asset pricing model, the Fama–French model, the Pastor–Stambaugh model, macroeconomic multifactor models, and the build-up method (e.g., bond yield plus risk premium). (page 27)

d. Explain beta estimation for public companies, thinly traded public companies, and nonpublic companies. (page 32)

e. Describe strengths and weaknesses of methods used to estimate the required return on an equity investment. (page 34)

f. Explain international considerations in required return estimation. (page 34)

g. Explain and calculate the weighted average cost of capital for a company. (page 35)

h. Evaluate the appropriateness of using a particular rate of return as a discount rate, given a description of the cash flow to be discounted and other relevant facts. (page 35)

## STUDY SESSION 11

*The topical coverage corresponds with the following CFA Institute assigned reading:*

### 32. The Five Competitive Forces That Shape Strategy

The candidate should be able to:

a.  Distinguish among the five competitive forces and explain how they drive industry profitability in the medium and long run. (page 43)

b.  Describe why industry growth rate, technology and innovation, government, and complementary products and services are fleeting factors rather than forces shaping industry structure. (page 46)

c.  Identify changes in industry structure, and forecast their effects on the industry's profit potential. (page 47)

d.  Explain how positioning a company, exploiting industry change, and shaping industry structure may be used to achieve a competitive advantage. (page 48)

*The topical coverage corresponds with the following CFA Institute assigned reading:*

### 33. Discounted Dividend Valuation

The candidate should be able to:

a.  Compare dividends, free cash flow, and residual income as inputs to discounted cash flow models, and identify investment situations for which each measure is suitable. (page 61)

b.  Calculate and interpret the value of a common stock using the dividend discount model (DDM) for single and multiple holding periods. (page 64)

c.  Calculate the value of a common stock using the Gordon growth model, and explain the model's underlying assumptions. (page 67)

d.  Calculate and interpret the implied growth rate of dividends using the Gordon growth model and current stock price. (page 68)

e.  Calculate and interpret the present value of growth opportunities (PVGO) and the component of the leading price-to-earnings ratio (P/E) related to PVGO. (page 69)

f.  Calculate and interpret the justified leading and trailing P/Es using the Gordon growth model. (page 70)

g.  Calculate the value of noncallable fixed-rate perpetual preferred stock. (page 72)

h.  Describe strengths and limitations of the Gordon growth model, and justify its selection to value a company's common shares. (page 73)

i.  Explain the assumptions and justify the selection of the two-stage DDM, the H-model, the three-stage DDM, or spreadsheet modeling to value a company's common shares. (page 74)

j.  Explain the growth phase, transitional phase, and maturity phase of a business. (page 77)

k.  Describe terminal value, and explain alternative approaches to determining the terminal value in a DDM. (page 78)

l.  Calculate and interpret the value of common shares using the two-stage DDM, the H-model, and the three-stage DDM. (page 79)

m.  Estimate a required return based on any DDM, including the Gordon growth model and the H-model. (page 84)

n.  Explain the use of spreadsheet modeling to forecast dividends and to value common shares. (page 87)

o. Calculate and interpret the sustainable growth rate of a company, and demonstrate the use of DuPont analysis to estimate a company's sustainable growth rate. (page 88)

p. Evaluate whether a stock is overvalued, fairly valued, or undervalued by the market based on a DDM estimate of value. (page 90)

## STUDY SESSION 12

*The topical coverage corresponds with the following CFA Institute assigned reading:*

### 34. Free Cash Flow Valuation

The candidate should be able to:

a. Compare the free cash flow to the firm (FCFF) and free cash flow to equity (FCFE) approaches to valuation. (page 108)

b. Explain the ownership perspective implicit in the FCFE approach. (page 109)

c. Explain the appropriate adjustments to net income, earnings before interest and taxes (EBIT), earnings before interest, taxes, depreciation, and amortization (EBITDA), and cash flow from operations (CFO) to calculate FCFF and FCFE. (page 109)

d. Calculate FCFF and FCFE. (page 116)

e. Describe approaches for forecasting FCFF and FCFE. (page 120)

f. Compare the FCFE model and dividend discount models. (page 121)

g. Explain how dividends, share repurchases, share issues, and changes in leverage may affect future FCFF and FCFE. (page 121)

h. Evaluate the use of net income and EBITDA as proxies for cash flow in valuation. (page 121)

i. Explain the single-stage (stable-growth), two-stage, and three-stage FCFF and FCFE models, and select and justify the appropriate model given a company's characteristics. (page 122)

j. Estimate a company's value using the appropriate free cash flow model(s). (page 125)

k. Explain the use of sensitivity analysis in FCFF and FCFE valuations. (page 132)

l. Describe approaches for calculating the terminal value in a multistage valuation model. (page 133)

m. Evaluate whether a stock is overvalued, fairly valued, or undervalued based on a free cash flow valuation model. (page 133)

*The topical coverage corresponds with the following CFA Institute assigned reading:*

### 35. Market-Based Valuation: Price and Enterprise Value Multiples

The candidate should be able to:

a. Distinguish between the method of comparables and the method based on forecasted fundamentals as approaches to using price multiples in valuation, and explain economic rationales for each approach. (page 151)

b. Calculate and interpret a justified price multiple. (page 153)

c. Describe rationales for and possible drawbacks to using alternative price multiples and dividend yield in valuation. (page 153)

d. Calculate and interpret alternative price multiples and dividend yield. (page 153)

e. Calculate and interpret underlying earnings, explain methods of normalizing earnings per share (EPS), and calculate normalized EPS. (page 159)

f. Explain and justify the use of earnings yield (E/P). (page 161)

g.  Describe fundamental factors that influence alternative price multiples and dividend yield. (page 162)
h.  Calculate and interpret the justified price-to-earnings ratio (P/E), price-to-book ratio (P/B), and price-to-sales ratio (P/S) for a stock, based on forecasted fundamentals. (page 162)
i.  Calculate and interpret a predicted P/E, given a cross-sectional regression on fundamentals, and explain limitations to the cross-sectional regression methodology. (page 166)
j.  Evaluate a stock by the method of comparables, and explain the importance of fundamentals in using the method of comparables. (page 168)
k.  Calculate and interpret the P/E-to-growth ratio (PEG), and explain its use in relative valuation. (page 170)
l.  Calculate and explain the use of price multiples in determining terminal value in a multistage discounted cash flow (DCF) model. (page 171)
m.  Explain alternative definitions of cash flow used in price and enterprise value (EV) multiples, and describe limitations of each definition. (page 172)
n.  Calculate and interpret EV multiples, and evaluate the use of EV/EBITDA. (page 174)
o.  Explain sources of differences in cross-border valuation comparisons. (page 176)
p.  Describe momentum indicators and their use in valuation. (page 176)
q.  Explain the use of the arithmetic mean, the harmonic mean, the weighted harmonic mean, and the median to describe the central tendency of a group of multiples. (page 177)
r.  Evaluate whether a stock is overvalued, fairly valued, or undervalued based on comparisons of multiples. (page 168)

*The topical coverage corresponds with the following CFA Institute assigned reading:*
## 36. Residual Income Valuation
The candidate should be able to:
a.  Calculate and interpret residual income, economic value added, and market value added. (page 195)
b.  Describe the uses of residual income models. (page 198)
c.  Calculate the intrinsic value of a common stock using the residual income model, and compare value recognition in residual income and other present value models. (page 198)
d.  Explain fundamental determinants of residual income. (page 201)
e.  Explain the relation between residual income valuation and the justified price-to-book ratio based on forecasted fundamentals. (page 202)
f.  Calculate and interpret the intrinsic value of a common stock using single-stage (constant-growth) and multistage residual income models. (page 202)
g.  Calculate the implied growth rate in residual income, given the market price-to-book ratio and an estimate of the required rate of return on equity. (page 203)
h.  Explain continuing residual income, and justify an estimate of continuing residual income at the forecast horizon, given company and industry prospects. (page 204)
i.  Compare residual income models to dividend discount and free cash flow models. (page 209)
j.  Explain strengths and weaknesses of residual income models, and justify the selection of a residual income model to value a company's common stock. (page 210)

    k. Describe accounting issues in applying residual income models. (page 211)

    l. Evaluate whether a stock is overvalued, fairly valued, or undervalued based on a residual income model. (page 213)

*The topical coverage corresponds with the following CFA Institute assigned reading:*

**37. Private Company Valuation**

The candidate should be able to:

    a. Compare public and private company valuation. (page 227)

    b. Describe uses of private business valuation, and explain applications of greatest concern to financial analysts. (page 229)

    c. Explain various definitions of value, and demonstrate how different definitions can lead to different estimates of value. (page 230)

    d. Explain the income, market, and asset-based approaches to private company valuation and factors relevant to the selection of each approach. (page 231)

    e. Explain cash flow estimation issues related to private companies and adjustments required to estimate normalized earnings. (page 232)

    f. Calculate the value of private company using free cash flow, capitalized cash flow, and/or excess earnings methods. (page 237)

    g. Explain factors that require adjustment when estimating the discount rate for private companies. (page 241)

    h. Compare models used to estimate the required rate of return to private company equity (for example, the CAPM, the expanded CAPM, and the build-up approach). (page 241)

    i. Determine the value of a private company based on market approach methods, and describe advantages and disadvantages of each method. (page 243)

    j. Describe the asset-based approach to private company valuation. (page 249)

    k. Explain and evaluate the effects on private company valuations of discounts and premiums based on control and marketability. (page 249)

    l. Describe the role of valuation standards in valuing private companies. (page 253)

# EQUITY VALUATION: APPLICATIONS AND PROCESSES

Study Session 10

## EXAM FOCUS

This review is simply an introduction to the process of equity valuation and its application. Many of the concepts and techniques introduced are developed more fully in subsequent topic reviews. Candidates should be familiar with the concepts introduced here, including intrinsic value, analyst perception of mispricing, going concern versus liquidation value, and the difference between absolute and relative valuation techniques.

LOS 30.a: Define valuation and intrinsic value, and explain sources of perceived mispricing.

*CFA® Program Curriculum, Volume 4, page 6*

Valuation is the process of determining the value of an asset. There are many approaches and estimating the inputs for a valuation model can be quite challenging. Investment success, however, can depend crucially on the analyst's ability to determine the values of securities.

The general steps in the equity valuation process are:

1. Understand the business.

2. Forecast company performance.

3. Select the appropriate valuation model.

4. Convert the forecasts into a valuation.

5. Apply the valuation conclusions.

When we use the term **intrinsic value** (IV), we are referring to the valuation of an asset or security by someone who has complete understanding of the characteristics of the asset or issuing firm. To the extent that stock prices are not perfectly (informationally) efficient, they may diverge from the intrinsic values.

Analysts seeking to produce positive risk-adjusted returns do so by trying to identify securities for which their estimate of intrinsic value differs from current market price. One framework divides mispricing perceived by the analyst into two sources: the difference between market price and the intrinsic value (actual mispricing) and the difference between the analyst's estimate of intrinsic value and actual intrinsic value (valuation error). We can represent this relation as follows:

$$\text{IV}_{\text{analyst}} - \text{price} = (\text{IV}_{\text{actual}} - \text{price}) + (\text{IV}_{\text{analyst}} - \text{IV}_{\text{actual}})$$

**LOS 30.b: Explain the going concern assumption and contrast a going concern value to a liquidation value.**

*CFA® Program Curriculum, Volume 4, page 7*

The **going concern assumption** is simply the assumption that a company will continue to operate as a business, as opposed to going out of business. The valuation models we will cover are all based on the going concern assumption. An alternative, when it cannot be assumed that the company will continue to operate (survive) as a business, is a firm's **liquidation value**. The liquidation value is the estimate of what the assets of the firm would bring if sold separately, net of the company's liabilities.

**LOS 30.c: Describe definitions of value, and justify which definition of value is most relevant to public company valuation.**

*CFA® Program Curriculum, Volume 4, page 8*

As stated earlier, intrinsic value is the most relevant metric for an analyst valuing public equities. However, other definitions of value may be relevant in other contexts. **Fair market value** is the price at which a hypothetical willing, informed, and able seller would trade an asset to a willing, informed, and able buyer. This definition is similar to the concept of fair value used for financial reporting purposes. A company's market price should reflect its fair market value over time if the market has confidence that the company's management is acting in the interest of equity investors.

**Investment value** is the value of a stock to a particular buyer. Investment value may depend on the buyer's specific needs and expectations, as well as perceived synergies with existing buyer assets.

When valuing a company, an analyst should be aware of the purpose of valuation. For most investment decisions, intrinsic value is the relevant concept of value. For acquisitions, investment value may be more appropriate.

**LOS 30.d: Describe applications of equity valuation.**

*CFA® Program Curriculum, Volume 4, page 9*

*Professor's Note: This is simply a list of the possible scenarios that may form the basis of an equity valuation question. No matter what the scenario is, the tools you will use are the same.*

**Valuation** is the process of estimating the value of an asset by (1) using a model based on the variables the analyst believes influence the fundamental value of the asset or (2) comparing it to the observable market value of "similar" assets. Equity valuation models are used by analysts in a number of ways. Rather than an end unto itself, valuation is a tool that is used in the pursuit of other objectives like those listed in the following paragraphs.

**Stock selection.** The most direct use of equity valuation is to guide the purchase, holding, or sale of stocks. Valuation is based on both a comparison of the intrinsic value of the stock with its market price and a comparison of its price with that of comparable stocks.

**Reading the market.** Current market prices implicitly contain investors' expectations about the future value of the variables that influence the stock's price (e.g., earnings growth and expected return). Analysts can estimate these expectations by comparing market prices with a stock's intrinsic value.

**Projecting the value of corporate actions.** Many market professionals use valuation techniques to determine the value of proposed corporate mergers, acquisitions, divestitures, management buyouts (MBOs), and recapitalization efforts.

**Fairness opinions.** Analysts use equity valuation to support professional opinions about the fairness of a price to be received by minority shareholders in a merger or acquisition.

**Planning and consulting.** Many firms engage analysts to evaluate the effects of proposed corporate strategies on the firm's stock price, pursuing only those that have the greatest value to shareholders.

**Communication with analysts and investors.** The valuation approach provides management, investors, and analysts with a common basis upon which to discuss and evaluate the company's performance, current state, and future plans.

**Valuation of private business.** Analysts use valuation techniques to determine the value of firms or holdings in firms that are not publicly traded. Investors in nonpublic firms rely on these valuations to determine the value of their positions or proposed positions.

**Portfolio management.** While equity valuation can be considered a stand-alone function in which the value of a single equity position is estimated, it can be more valuable when used in a portfolio management context to determine the value and risk of a portfolio of investments. The investment process is usually considered to have three parts: planning, execution, and evaluation of results. Equity valuation is a primary concern in the first two of these steps.

- *Planning.* The first step of the investment process includes defining investment objectives and constraints and articulating an investment strategy for selecting securities based on valuation parameters or techniques. Sometimes investors may not select individual equity positions, but the valuation techniques are implied in the selection of an index or other preset basket of securities. Active investment managers may use benchmarks as indicators of market expectations and then purposely deviate in composition or weighting to take advantage of their differing expectations.
- *Executing the investment plan.* The valuation of potential investments guides the implementation of an investment plan. The results of the specified valuation methods determine which investments will be made and which will be avoided.

**LOS 30.e: Describe questions that should be addressed in conducting an industry and competitive analysis.**

*CFA® Program Curriculum, Volume 4, page 12*

The five **elements of industry structure** as developed by Professor Michael Porter are:

1.  Threat of new entrants in the industry.

2.  Threat of substitutes.

3.  Bargaining power of buyers.

4.  Bargaining power of suppliers.

5.  Rivalry among existing competitors.

The attractiveness (long-term profitability) of any industry is determined by the interaction of these five competitive forces (Porter's five forces).

 *Professor's Note: These factors are covered in detail in the topic review titled "The Five Competitive Forces that Shape Industry."*

There are three generic strategies a company may employ in order to compete and generate profits:

1.  *Cost leadership:* Being the lowest-cost producer of the good.

2.  *Product differentiation:* Addition of product features or services that increase the attractiveness of the firm's product so that it will command a premium price in the market.

3.  *Focus:* Employing one of the previous strategies within a particular segment of the industry in order to gain a competitive advantage.

Once the analyst has identified a company's strategy, she can evaluate the performance of the business over time in terms of how well it executes its strategy and how successful it is.

The basic building blocks of equity valuation come from accounting information contained in the firm's reports and releases. In order for the analyst to successfully estimate the value of the firm, the financial factors must be disclosed in sufficient detail and accuracy. Investigating the issues associated with the accuracy and detail of a firm's disclosures is often referred to as a **quality of financial statement information**. This analysis requires examination of the firm's income statement, balance sheet, and the notes to the financial statements. Studies have shown that the quality of earnings issue is reflected in a firm's stock price, with firms with more transparent earnings having higher market values.

An analyst can often only discern important results of management discretion through a detailed examination of the footnotes accompanying the financial reports. Quality of earnings issues can be broken down into several categories and may be addressed only in the footnotes and disclosures to the financial statements.

*Accelerating or premature recognition of income.* Firms have used a variety of techniques to justify the recognition of income before it traditionally would have been recognized. These include recording sales and billing customers before products are shipped or accepted and bill and hold schemes in which items are billed in advance and held for future delivery. These schemes have been used to obscure declines in operating performance and boost reported revenue and income.

*Reclassifying gains and nonoperating income.* Firms occasionally have gains or income from sources that are peripheral to their operations. The reclassification of these items as operating income will distort the results of the firm's continuing operations, often hiding underperformance or a decline in sales.

*Expense recognition and losses.* Delaying the recognition of expenses, capitalizing expenses, and classifying operating expenses as nonoperating expenses is an opposite approach that has the same effect as reclassifying gains from peripheral sources, increasing operating income. Management also has discretion in creating and estimating reserves that reflect expected future liabilities, such as a bad debt reserve or a provision for expected litigation losses.

*Amortization, depreciation, and discount rates.* Management has a great deal of discretion in the selection of amortization and depreciation methods, as well as the choice of discount rates in determination of pension plan obligations. These decisions can reduce the current recognition of expenses, in effect deferring recognition to later periods.

*Off-balance-sheet issues.* The firm's balance sheet may not fully reflect the assets and liabilities of the firm. Special purpose entities (SPEs) can be used by the firm to increase sales (by recording sales to the SPE) or to obscure the nature and value of assets or liabilities. Leases can be structured as operating, rather than finance, leases in order to reduce the total liabilities reported on the balance sheet.

---

LOS 30.f: Contrast absolute and relative valuation models, and describe examples of each type of model.

---

*CFA® Program Curriculum, Volume 4, page 22*

**Absolute valuation models.** An absolute valuation model is one that estimates an asset's intrinsic value, which is its value arising from its investment characteristics without regard to the value of other firms. One absolute valuation approach is to determine the value of a firm today as the *discounted* or *present value* of all the cash flows expected in the future. *Dividend discount models* estimate the value of a share based on the present value of all expected dividends discounted at the opportunity cost of capital. Many analysts realize that equity holders are entitled to more than just the dividends and so expand the measure of cash flow to include all expected cash flow to the firm that is not payable to senior claims (bondholders, taxing authorities, and senior stockholders). These models include the free cash flow approach and the residual income approach.

Another absolute approach to valuation is represented by *asset-based* models. This approach estimates a firm's value as the sum of the market value of the assets it owns or controls. This approach is commonly used to value firms that own or control natural resources, such as oil fields, coal deposits, and other mineral claims.

**Relative valuation models.** Another very common approach to valuation is to determine the value of an asset in relation to the values of other assets. This is the approach underlying relative valuation models. The most common models use market price as a multiple of an individual financial factor of the firm, such as earnings per share. The resulting ratio, price-to-earnings (P/E), is easily compared to that of other firms. If the P/E is higher than that of comparable firms, it is said to be *relatively* overvalued, that is, overvalued relative to the other firms (not necessarily overvalued on an intrinsic value basis). The converse is also true: if the P/E is lower than that of comparable firms, the firm is said to be relatively undervalued.

---

LOS 30.g: Describe sum-of-the-parts valuation, and explain a conglomerate discount.

---

*CFA® Program Curriculum, Volume 4, page 25*

Rather than valuing a company as a single entity, an analyst can value individual parts of the firm and add them up to determine the value for the company as a whole. The value obtained is called the *sum-of-the-parts value,* or sometimes *breakup value* or *private market value*. This process is especially useful when the company operates multiple divisions (or product lines) with different business models and risk characteristics (i.e., a conglomerate).

*Conglomerate discount* is based on the idea that investors apply a markdown to the value of a company that operates in multiple unrelated industries, compared to the value a company that has a single industry focus. Conglomerate discount is thus the amount by which market value under-represents sum-of-the-parts value.

Three explanations for conglomerate discounts are:

1.  Internal capital inefficiency: The company's allocation of capital to different divisions may not have been based on sound decisions.

2.  Endogenous (internal) factors: For example, the company may have pursued unrelated business acquisitions to hide poor operating performance.

3.  Research measurement errors: Some hypothesize that conglomerate discounts do not exist, but rather are a result of incorrect measurement.

LOS 30.h: Explain broad criteria for choosing an appropriate approach for valuing a given company.

*CFA® Program Curriculum, Volume 4, page 27*

When selecting an approach for valuing a given company, an analyst should consider whether the model:

- Fits the characteristics of the company (e.g., Does it pay dividends? Is earnings growth estimable? Does it have significant intangible assets?).
- Is appropriate based on the quality and availability of input data.
- Is suitable given the purpose of the analysis.

The purpose of the analysis may be, for example, valuation for making a purchase offer for a controlling interest in the company. In this case, a model based on cash flow may be more appropriate than one based on dividends because a controlling interest would allow the purchaser to set dividend policy.

One thing to remember with respect to choice of a valuation model is that the analyst does not have to consider only one. Using multiple models and examining differences in estimated values can reveal how a model's assumptions and the perspective of the analysis are affecting the estimated values.

## KEY CONCEPTS

### LOS 30.a

Intrinsic value is the value of an asset or security estimated by someone who has complete understanding of the characteristics of the asset or issuing firm. To the extent that market prices are not perfectly (informationally) efficient, they may diverge from intrinsic value. The difference between the analyst's estimate of intrinsic value and the current price is made up of two components: the difference between the actual intrinsic value and the market price, and the difference between the actual intrinsic value and the analyst's estimate of intrinsic value:

$$IV_{analyst} - price = (IV_{actual} - price) + (IV_{analyst} - IV_{actual})$$

### LOS 30.b

The going concern assumption is simply the assumption that a company will continue to operate as a business as opposed to going out of business. The liquidation value is the estimate of what the assets of the firm would bring if sold separately, net of the company's liabilities.

### LOS 30.c

Fair market value is the price at which a hypothetical willing, informed, and able seller would trade an asset to a willing, informed and able buyer. Investment value is the value to a specific buyer after including any additional value attributable to synergies. Investment value is an appropriate measure for strategic buyers pursuing acquisitions.

### LOS 30.d

Equity valuation is the process of estimating the value of an asset by (1) using a model based on the variables the analyst believes influence the fundamental value of the asset or (2) comparing it to the observable market value of "similar" assets. Equity valuation models are used by analysts in a number of ways. Examples include stock selection, reading the market, projecting the value of corporate actions, fairness opinions, planning and consulting, communication with analysts and investors, valuation of private business, and portfolio management.

### LOS 30.e

The five elements of industry structure as developed by Professor Michael Porter are:

1. Threat of new entrants in the industry.

2. Threat of substitutes.

3. Bargaining power of buyers.

4. Bargaining power of suppliers.

5. Rivalry among existing competitors.

Quality of earnings issues can be broken down into several categories and may be addressed only in the footnotes and disclosures to the financial statements:
- Accelerating or premature recognition of income.
- Reclassifying gains and nonoperating income.
- Expense recognition and losses.
- Amortization, depreciation, and discount rates.
- Off-balance-sheet issues.

## LOS 30.f

An absolute valuation model is one that estimates an asset's intrinsic value (e.g., the discounted dividend approach). Relative valuation models estimate an asset's investment characteristics compared to the value of other firms (e.g., comparing P/E ratios to those of other firms in the industry).

## LOS 30.g

Sum-of-the-parts valuation is the process of valuing the individual components of a company and then adding these values together to obtain the value of the whole company. Conglomerate discount refers to the amount by which market price is lower than the sum-of-the-parts value. Conglomerate discount is an apparent price reduction applied by the markets to firms that operate in multiple industries.

## LOS 30.h

When selecting an approach for valuing a given company, an analyst should consider whether the model fits the characteristics of the company, is appropriate based on the quality and availability of input data, and is suitable, given the purpose of the analysis.

Study Session 10
**Cross-Reference to CFA Institute Assigned Reading #30 – Equity Valuation: Applications and Processes**

Study Session 10

## CONCEPT CHECKERS

1. Susan Weiber, CFA, has noted that even her best estimates of a stock's intrinsic value can differ significantly from the current market price. The *least likely* explanation is:
   A. differences between her estimate and the actual intrinsic value.
   B. differences between the actual intrinsic value and the market price.
   C. differences between the intrinsic value and the going concern value.

2. An appropriate valuation approach for a company that is going out of business would be to calculate its:
   A. residual income value.
   B. dividend discount model value.
   C. liquidation value.

3. Davy Jarvis, CFA, is performing an equity valuation as part of the planning and execution phase of the portfolio management process. His results will also be useful for:
   A. communication with analysts and investors.
   B. technical analysis.
   C. benchmarking.

4. The five elements of industry structure, as outlined by Michael Porter, include:
   A. the threat of substitutes.
   B. product differentiation.
   C. cost leadership.

5. Tom Walder has been instructed to use absolute valuation models, and not relative valuation models, in his analysis. Which of the following is *least likely* to be an example of an absolute valuation model? The:
   A. dividend discount model.
   B. price-to-earnings market multiple model.
   C. residual income model.

6. Davy Jarvis, CFA, is performing an equity valuation and reviews his notes for key points he wanted to cover when planning the valuation. He finds the following questions:
   - Does the company pay dividends?
   - Is earnings growth estimable?
   - Does the company have significant intangible assets?

   Which of the following general questions is Jarvis trying to answer when planning this phase of the valuation?
   A. Does the model fit the characteristics of the investment?
   B. Is the model appropriate based on the availability of input data?
   C. Can the model be improved to make it more suitable, given the purpose of the analysis?

**Use the following information to answer Questions 7 and 8.**

Sun Pharma is a large pharmaceutical company based in Sri Lanka that manufactures prescription drugs under license from large multinational pharmaceutical companies. Delenga Mahamurthy, CEO of Sun Pharma, is evaluating a potential acquisition of Island Cookware, a small manufacturing company that produces cooking utensils.

Mahamurthy feels that Sun Pharma's excellent distribution network could add value to Island Cookware. Sun Pharma plans to acquire Island Cookware for cash. Several days later, Sun Pharma announces that they have acquired Island Cookware at market price.

7.      Sun Pharma's *most appropriate* valuation for Island Cookware is its:
        A.  sum-of-the-parts value.
        B.  investment value.
        C.  liquidation value.

8.      Upon announcement of the merger, the market price of Sun Pharma drops. This is *most likely* a result of the:
        A.  unrelated business effect.
        B.  tax effect.
        C.  conglomerate discount.

Study Session 10
**Cross-Reference to CFA Institute Assigned Reading #30 – Equity Valuation: Applications and Processes**

Study Session 10

## ANSWERS – CONCEPT CHECKERS

1. **C** The difference between the analyst's estimate of intrinsic value and the current price is made up of two components:

   $$IV_{analyst} - price = (IV_{actual} - price) + (IV_{analyst} - IV_{actual})$$

2. **C** The liquidation value is the estimate of what the assets of the firm will bring when sold separately, net of the company's liabilities. It is most appropriate because the firm is not a going concern and will not pay dividends. The residual income model is based on the going concern assumption and is not appropriate for valuing a firm that is expected to go out of business.

3. **A** Communication with analysts and investors is one of the common uses of an equity valuation. Technical analysis and benchmarking do not require equity valuation.

4. **A** The five elements of industry structure as developed by Professor Michael Porter are:

   1. Threat of new entrants in the industry.

   2. Threat of substitutes.

   3. Bargaining power of buyers.

   4. Bargaining power of suppliers.

   5. Rivalry among existing competitors.

5. **B** Absolute valuation models estimate value as some function of the present value of future cash flows (e.g., dividend discount and free cash flow models) or economic profit (e.g., residual income models). Relative valuation models estimate an asset's value relative to the value of other similar assets. The price-to-earnings market multiple model is an example of a relative valuation model.

6. **A** Jarvis is most likely trying to be sure the selected model fits the characteristics of the investment. Model selection will depend heavily on the answers to these questions.

7. **B** The appropriate valuation for Sun Pharma's acquisition is the investment value, which incorporates the value of any synergies present in the acquisition. Sum-of-the-parts value is not applicable, as the valuation does not require separate valuation of different divisions of Island Cookware. Liquidation value is also not relevant, as Sun Pharma does not intend to liquidate the assets of Island Cookware.

8. **C** Upon announcement of the acquisition, the market price of Sun Pharma should not change if the acquisition was at fair value. However, the market is valuing the whole company at a value less than the value of its parts: this is a conglomerate discount. We are not given any information about tax consequences of the merger and hence a tax effect is unlikely to be the cause of the market price drop. The acquisition of an unrelated business may result in a conglomerate discount, but there is no defined 'unrelated business effect.'

# RETURN CONCEPTS

## EXAM FOCUS

Much of this material builds on concepts covered elsewhere in the Level II curriculum. Be able to distinguish among return concepts such as holding period return, realized return, expected return, required return, and discount rate. Understand the concept of convergence of price to intrinsic value. Be able to explain the equity risk premium, the various methods and models used to calculate the equity risk premium, and the strengths and weaknesses of those methods. The review also covers the weighted average cost of capital (WACC). You must be able to explain and calculate the WACC and be able to select the most appropriate discount rate for a given cash flow stream.

LOS 31.a: Distinguish among realized holding period return, expected holding period return, required return, return from convergence of price to intrinsic value, discount rate, and internal rate of return.

*CFA® Program Curriculum, Volume 4, page 45*

## Holding Period Return

**Holding period return** is the increase in price of an asset plus any cash flow received from that asset, divided by the initial price of the asset. The measurement or *holding period* can be a day, a month, a year, and so on. In most cases, we assume the cash flow is received at the end of the holding period, and the equation for calculating holding period return is:

$$\text{holding period return} = r = \frac{P_1 - P_0 + CF_1}{P_0} = \frac{P_1 + CF_1}{P_0} - 1$$

The subscript 1 simply denotes one period from today. *P* stands for price and *CF* stands for cash flow. For a share of common stock, we might think of this in terms of:

$$r = \frac{CF_1}{P_0} + \frac{P_1 - P_0}{P_0}$$

where:

$\dfrac{CF_1}{P_0}$ = the cash flow yield

$\dfrac{P_1 - P_0}{P_0}$ = the return from price appreciation

If the cash flow is received before the end of the period, then $CF_1$ would equal the cash flow received during the period plus any interest earned on the reinvestment of the cash flow from the time it was received until the end of the measurement period.

In most cases, holding period returns are annualized. For example, if the return for one month is 1% (0.01), then the analyst might report an annualized holding period return of $(1 + 0.01)^{12} - 1 = 0.1268$ or 12.68%. Annualized holding period returns should be scrutinized to make sure that the return for the actual holding period truly represents what could be earned for an entire year.

### Realized and Expected Holding Period Return

A **realized return** is a historical return based on past observed prices and cash flows. An **expected return** is based on forecasts of future prices and cash flows. Such expected returns can be derived from elaborate models or subjective opinions.

### Required Return

An asset's **required return** is the minimum return an investor requires given the asset's risk. A more risky asset will have a higher required return. Required return is also called the *opportunity cost* for investing in the asset. If expected return is greater (less) than required return, the asset is undervalued (overvalued).

### Price Convergence

If the *expected return* is not equal to required return, there can be a "return from convergence of price to intrinsic value." Letting $V_0$ denote the true intrinsic value, and given that price does not equal that value (i.e., $V_0 \neq P_0$), then the return from convergence of price to intrinsic value is $(V_0 - P_0) / P_0$. If an analyst expects the price of the asset to converge to its intrinsic value by the end of the horizon, then $(V_0 - P_0) / P_0$ is also the difference between the expected return on an asset and its required return:

$$\text{expected return} = \text{required return} + \frac{(V_0 - P_0)}{P_0}$$

It is possible that there are chronic inefficiencies that impede price convergence. Therefore, even if an analyst feels that $V_0 \neq P_0$ for a given asset, the convergence yield may not be realized.

### Discount Rate

The **discount rate** is the rate used to find the present value of an investment. While it is possible to estimate a discount rate subjectively, a much sounder approach is to use a market determined rate.

## Internal Rate of Return

For publicly traded securities, the **internal rate of return** (IRR) is a market-determined rate. It is the rate that equates the value of the discounted cash flows to the current price of the security. If markets are efficient, then the IRR represents the required return.

---

LOS 31.b: Calculate and interpret an equity risk premium using historical and forward-looking estimation approaches.

---

*CFA® Program Curriculum, Volume 4, page 50*

The **equity risk premium** is the return in excess of the risk-free rate that investors require for holding equity securities. It is usually defined as the difference between the required return on a broad equity market index and the risk-free rate:

> equity risk premium = required return on equity index – risk-free rate

An estimate of a future equity risk premium, based on historical information, requires the following preliminary steps:

- Select an equity index.
- Select a time period.
- Calculate the mean return on the index.
- Select a proxy for the risk-free rate.

The risk-free return should correspond to the time horizon for the investment (e.g., T-bills for shorter-term and T-bonds for longer-term horizons). The broad market equity risk premium can be used to determine the required return for individual stocks using beta:

> required return for stock j = risk-free return + $\beta_j$ × (equity risk premium)

where:
$\beta_j$ = the "beta" of stock j and serves as the adjustment for the level of systematic risk inherent in the stock.

If the systematic risk of stock j equals that of the market, then $\beta_j$ =1. If systematic risk is greater (less) than that of the market, then $\beta_j$ > 1 (< 1). A more general representation is:

> required return for stock j = risk-free return + (equity risk premium) + other risk premia/discounts appropriate for j

The general model is used in the build-up method (discussed later) and is typically used for valuation of private businesses. It does not account for systematic risk.

Note that an equity risk premium is an estimated value and may not be realized. Also keep in mind that these estimates can be derived in several ways. An analyst reading a report that discusses a "risk premium" should take note to see how the author of the report has arrived at the estimated value.

*Professor's Note: As you work through this topic review, keep in mind that the risk premiums, including the equity risk premium, are differences in rates—typically a market rate minus the risk-free rate.*

### ESTIMATES OF THE EQUITY RISK PREMIUM: STRENGTHS AND WEAKNESSES

There are two types of estimates of the equity risk premium: historical estimates and forward-looking estimates.

### HISTORICAL ESTIMATES

A **historical estimate** of the equity risk premium consists of the difference between the historical mean return for a broad-based equity-market index and a risk-free rate over a given time period. Its strength is its objectivity and simplicity. Also, if investors are rational, then historical estimates will be unbiased.

A weakness of the approach is the assumption that the mean and variance of the returns are constant over time (i.e., that they are stationary). This does not seem to be the case. In fact, the premium actually appears to be countercyclical—it is low during good times and high during bad times. Thus, an analyst using this method to estimate the current equity premium must choose the sample period carefully. The historical estimate can also be upward biased if only firms that have survived during the period of measurement (called **survivorship bias**) are included in the sample.

Other considerations include the method for calculating the mean and which risk-free rate is most relevant to the analysis. Because a geometric mean is less than or equal to the corresponding arithmetic mean, the risk premium will always be lower when the geometric mean is used instead of the arithmetic mean. If the yield curve is upward sloping, the use of longer-term bonds rather than shorter-term bonds to estimate the risk-free rate will cause the estimated risk premium to be smaller.

### FORWARD-LOOKING ESTIMATES

**Forward-looking** or **ex ante estimates** use current information and expectations concerning economic and financial variables. The strength of this method is that it does not rely on an assumption of stationarity and is less subject to problems like survivorship bias. There are three main categories of forward-looking estimates: those based on the Gordon growth model, supply-side models, and estimates from surveys.

### Gordon Growth Model

The **constant growth model** (a.k.a. the **Gordon growth model**) is a popular method to generate forward-looking estimates. The assumptions of the model are reasonable when applied to developed economies and markets, wherein there are typically ample sources of reliable forecasts for data such as dividend payments and growth rates. This method estimates the risk premium as the expected dividend yield plus the expected growth rate minus the current long-term government bond yield.

GGM equity risk premium = (1-year forecasted dividend yield on market index) + (consensus long-term earnings growth rate) – (long-term government bond yield)

Denoting each component by $(D_1 / P)$, $\hat{g}$, and $r_{LT,0}$, respectively, the forward-looking equity risk premium estimate is:

$$(D_1 / P) + \hat{g} - r_{LT,0}$$

A weakness of the approach is that the forward-looking estimates will change through time and need to be updated. During a typical economic boom, dividend yields are low and growth expectations are high, while the opposite is generally true when the economy is less robust. For example, suppose that during an economic boom (bust) dividend yields are 2% (4%), growth expectations are 6% (3%), and long-term bond yields are 6% (3%). The equity risk premia during these two different periods would be 2% during the boom and 4% during the bust. And, of course, there is no assurance that the capital appreciation realized will be equal to the earnings growth rate during the forecast period.

Another weakness is the assumption of a stable growth rate, which is often not appropriate in rapidly growing economies. Such economies might have three or more stages of growth: rapid growth, transition, and mature growth. In this case, another forward-looking estimate would use the required return on equity derived from the IRR from the following equation:

equity index price = $PV_{rapid}(r) + PV_{transition}(r) + PV_{mature}(r)$

where:
$PV_{rapid}$ = present value of projected cash flows during the rapid growth stage
$PV_{transition}$ = present value of projected cash flows during the transitional growth stage
$PV_{mature}$ = present value of projected cash flows during the mature growth stage

The forward-looking estimate of the equity premium would be the *r* from this equality minus the corresponding government bond yield.

## Supply-Side Estimates (Macroeconomic Models)

**Macroeconomic model estimates** of the equity risk premium are based on the relationships between macroeconomic variables and financial variables. A strength of this approach is the use of proven models and current information. A weakness is that the estimates are only appropriate for developed countries where public equities represent a relatively large share of the economy, implying that it is reasonable to believe there should be some relationship between macroeconomic variables and asset prices.

One common model [Ibbotson-Chen (2003)] for a supply-side estimate of the risk premium is:

$$\text{equity risk premium} = [1+\hat{i}]\times[1+\widehat{rEg}]\times[1+\widehat{PEg}]-1+\hat{Y}-\widehat{RF}$$

where:

$\hat{i}$ = expected inflation

$\widehat{rEg}$ = expected real growth in GDP

$\widehat{PEg}$ = expected changes in the P/E ratio

$\hat{Y}$ = the expected yield on the index

$\widehat{RF}$ = the expected risk-free rate

The analyst must determine appropriate techniques with which to compute values for these inputs. For example, a market-based estimate of expected inflation can be derived from the differences in the yields for T-bonds and Treasury Inflation Protected Securities (TIPS) having comparable maturities:

$\hat{i}$ = (YTM of 20-year T-bonds) – (YTM of 20-year TIPS)

 *Professor's Note: TIPS are inflation-indexed securities paying interest every six months and principal at maturity. The coupon and principal are automatically increased by the consumer price index (CPI).*

Growth in GDP can be estimated as the sum of labor productivity growth and growth in the labor supply:

$\widehat{rEg}$ = real GDP growth

$\widehat{rEg}$ = labor productivity growth rate + labor supply growth rate

The $\widehat{PEg}$ would depend upon whether the analyst thought the market was over or undervalued. If the market is believed to be overvalued, P/E ratios would be expected to decrease $(\widehat{PEg}<0)$ and the opposite would be true if the market were believed to be undervalued $(\widehat{PEg}>0)$. If the market is correctly priced, $\widehat{PEg}=0$. The $\hat{Y}$ can be estimated using estimated dividends on the index.

### Survey Estimates

**Survey estimates** of the equity risk premium use the consensus of the opinions from a sample of people. If the sample is restricted to people who are experts in the area of equity valuation, the results are likely to be more reliable. The strength is that survey results are relatively easy to obtain. The weakness is that, even when the survey is restricted to experts in the area, there can be a wide disparity between the consensuses obtained from different groups.

LOS 31.c: Estimate the required return on an equity investment using the capital asset pricing model, the Fama–French model, the Pastor–Stambaugh model, macroeconomic multifactor models, and the build-up method (e.g., bond yield plus risk premium).

*CFA® Program Curriculum, Volume 4, page 62*

## Capital Asset Pricing Model

The **capital asset pricing model** (CAPM) estimates the required return on equity using the following formula:

required return on stock j = risk-free rate + equity risk premium × beta of j

> **Example: Using the CAPM to calculate the required return on equity**
>
> The current expected risk-free rate is 4%, the equity risk premium is 3.9%, and the beta is 0.8. Calculate the required return on equity.
>
> **Answer:**
>
> 7.12% = 4% + (3.9% × 0.8)

## Multifactor Models

**Multifactor models** can have greater explanatory power than the CAPM, which is a single-factor model. The general form of an *n*-factor multifactor model is:

$$\text{required return} = RF + (\text{risk premium})_1 + (\text{risk premium})_2 + \ldots + (\text{risk premium})_n$$

$$(\text{risk premium})_i = (\text{factor sensitivity})_i \times (\text{factor risk premium})_i$$

The factor sensitivity is also called the *factor beta*, and it is the asset's sensitivity to a particular factor, all else being equal. The factor risk premium is the expected return above the risk-free rate from a unit sensitivity to the factor and zero sensitivity to all other factors.

## Fama-French Model

The **Fama-French model** is a multifactor model that attempts to account for the higher returns generally associated with small-cap stocks. The model is:

$$\text{required return of stock j} = RF + \beta_{mkt,j} \times (R_{mkt} - RF) + \beta_{SMB,j} \times (R_{small} - R_{big}) + \beta_{HML,j} \times (R_{HBM} - R_{LBM})$$

where:

$(R_{mkt} - RF)$ = return on a value-weighted market index minus the risk-free rate

$(R_{small} - R_{big})$ = a small-cap return premium equal to the average return on small-cap portfolios minus the average return on large-cap portfolios

$(R_{HBM} - R_{LBM})$ = a value return premium equal to the average return on high book-to-market portfolios minus the average return on low book-to-market portfolios

The baseline value (i.e., the expected value for the variable) for $\beta_{mkt,j}$ is one, and the baseline values for $\beta_{SMB,j}$ and $\beta_{HML,j}$ are zero.

The latter two of these factors corresponds to the return of a zero-net investment in the corresponding assets [e.g., $(R_{small} - R_{big})$ represents the return on a portfolio that shorts large-cap stocks and invests in small-cap stocks]. The goal is to capture the effect of other underlying risk factors. Many developed economies and markets have sufficient data for estimating the model.

---

**Example: Applying the CAPM and the Fama-French Model**

Assume that market data provides the following values for the factors:

$(R_{mkt} - RF)$ = 4.8%

$(R_{small} - R_{big})$ = 2.4%

$(R_{HBM} - R_{LBM})$ = 1.6%

risk-free rate = 3.4%

An analyst estimates that stock j has a CAPM beta equal to 1.3. Stock j is a small-cap growth stock that has traded at a low book to market in recent years. Using the Fama-French model, an analyst estimates the following betas for stock j:

$$\beta_{mkt,j} = 1.2$$

$$\beta_{SMB,j} = 0.4$$

$$\beta_{HML,j} = -0.2$$

Calculate the required return on equity using the CAPM and the Fama-French models:

**Answer:**

CAPM estimate:              required return = 3.4% + (1.3 × 4.8%) = 9.64%

Fama-French model estimate:  required return = 3.4% + (1.2 × 4.8%) + (0.4 × 2.4%) + (−0.2 × 1.6%) = 9.8%

## Pastor-Stambaugh Model

The **Pastor-Stambaugh model** adds a liquidity factor to the Fama-French model. The baseline value for the liquidity factor beta is zero. Less liquid assets should have a positive beta, while more liquid assets should have a negative beta.

**Example: Applying the Pastor-Stambaugh model**

Assume a liquidity premium of 4%, the same factor risk premiums as before, and the following sensitivities for stock k:

$$\beta_{mkt,k} = 0.9$$

$$\beta_{SMB,k} = -0.2$$

$$\beta_{HML,k} = 0.2$$

$$\beta_{liquidity,k} = -0.1$$

Calculate the cost of capital using the Pastor-Stambaugh model.

**Answer:**

cost of capital = 3.4% + (0.9 × 4.8%) + (−0.2 × 2.4%) + (0.2 × 1.6%) + (−0.1 × 4%) = 7.16%

### Macroeconomic Multifactor Models

**Macroeconomic multifactor models** use factors associated with economic variables that can be reasonably believed to affect cash flows and/or appropriate discount rates. The Burmeister, Roll, and Ross model incorporates the following five factors:

1. *Confidence risk*: unexpected change in the difference between the return of risky corporate bonds and government bonds.

2. *Time horizon risk*: unexpected change in the difference between the return of long-term government bonds and Treasury bills.

3. *Inflation risk*: unexpected change in the inflation rate.

4. *Business cycle risk*: unexpected change in the level of real business activity.

5. *Market timing risk*: the equity market return that is not explained by the other four factors.

As with the other models, to compute the required return on equity for a given stock, the factor values are multiplied by a sensitivity coefficient (i.e., beta) for that stock; the products are summed and added to the risk-free rate.

---

**Example: Applying a multifactor model**

Assume the following values for the factors:

| | | |
|---|---|---|
| confidence risk | = | 2.0% |
| time horizon risk | = | 3.0% |
| inflation risk | = | 4.0% |
| business cycle risk | = | 1.6% |
| market timing risk | = | 3.4% |

Assume the following sensitivities for stock j: 0.3, −0.2, 1.1, 0.3, 0.5, respectively. Using the risk-free rate of 3.4%, calculate the required return using a multifactor approach.

**Answer:**

required return = 3.4% + (0.3 × 2%) + (−0.2 × 3%) + (1.1 × 4%) + (0.3 × 1.6%) + (0.5 × 3.4%) = 9.98%

---

### Build-Up Method

The **build-up method** is similar to the risk premium approach. It is usually applied to closely held companies where betas are not readily obtainable. One popular representation is:

required return = RF + equity risk premium + size premium + specific-company premium

The size premium would be scaled up or down based on the size of the company. Smaller companies would have a larger premium.

As before, computing the required return would be a matter of simply adding up the values in the formula. Some representations use an estimated beta to scale the size of the company-specific equity risk premium but typically not for the other factors.

The formula could have a factor for the level of controlling versus minority interests and a factor for marketability of the equity; however, these latter two factors are usually used to adjust the value of the company directly rather than through the required return.

## Bond-Yield Plus Risk Premium Method

The **bond-yield plus risk premium method** is a build-up method that is appropriate if the company has publicly traded debt. The method simply adds a risk premium to the yield to maturity (YTM) of the company's *long-term* debt. The logic here is that the yield to maturity of the company's bonds includes the effects of inflation, leverage, and the firm's sensitivity to the business cycle. Because the various risk factors are already taken into account in the YTM, the analyst can simply add a premium for the added risk arising from holding the firm's equity. That value is usually estimated at 3–5%, with the specific estimate based upon some model or simply from experience.

> **Example: Applying the bond-yield plus risk premium approach**
>
> Company LMN has bonds with 15 years to maturity. They have a coupon of 8.2% and a price equal to 101.70. An analyst estimates that the additional risk assumed from holding the firm's equity justifies a risk premium of 3.8%. Given the coupon and maturity, the YTM is 8%. Calculate the cost of equity using the bond-yield plus risk premium approach.
>
> **Answer:**
>
> cost of equity = 8% + 3.8% = 11.8%

*Professor's Note: Although most of our examples in this section have focused on the calculation of the return using various approaches, don't lose sight of what information the components of each equation might convey. The betas tell us about the characteristics of the asset being evaluated, and the risk premia tell us how those characteristics are priced in the market. If you encounter a situation on the exam where you are asked to evaluate style and/or the overall impact of a component on return, separate out each factor and its beta—paying careful attention to whether there is a positive or negative sign attached to the component—and work through it logically.*

---

LOS 31.d: Explain beta estimation for public companies, thinly traded public companies, and nonpublic companies.

---

*CFA® Program Curriculum, Volume 4, page 63*

### Beta Estimates for Public Companies

Up to this point, we have concerned ourselves with methods for estimating the equity risk premium. Now we turn our attention to the estimation of beta, the measure of the level of systematic risk assumed from holding the security. For a public company, an analyst can compute beta by regressing the returns of the company's stock on the returns of the overall market. To do so, the analyst must determine which index to use in the regression and the length and frequency of the sample data.

Popular choices for the index include the S&P 500 and the NYSE Composite. The most common length and frequency are five years of monthly data. A popular alternative is two years of weekly data, which may be more appropriate for fast-growing markets.

### Adjusted Beta for Public Companies

When making forecasts of the equity risk premium, some analysts recommend adjusting the beta for **beta drift**. Beta drift refers to the observed tendency of an estimated beta to revert to a value of 1.0 over time. To compensate, an often-used formula to adjust the estimate of beta is:

adjusted beta = (2/3 × regression beta) + (1/3 × 1.0)

> **Example: Calculating adjusted beta**
>
> Assume an analyst estimates a beta equal to 0.8 using regression and historical data and adjusts the beta as described previously. Calculate the adjusted beta and use it to estimate a forward-looking required return.

**Answer:**

> adjusted beta = (2/3 × regression beta) + (1/3 × 1.0) = (2/3 × 0.8) + (1/3 × 1.0) = 0.867

Note that this adjusted beta is closer to one than the regression beta.

If the risk-free rate is 4% and the equity risk premium is 3.9%, then the required return would be:

> required return on stock = risk-free rate + (equity risk premium × beta of stock) = 4% + (3.9% × 0.867) = 7.38%

Note that the required return is higher than the 7.12% derived using the unadjusted beta. Naturally, there are other methods for adjusting beta to compensate for beta drift. Statistical services selling financial information often report both unadjusted and adjusted beta values.

 *Professor's Note: Note that some statistical services use reversion to a peer mean rather than reversion to one.*

## Beta Estimates for Thinly Traded Stocks and Nonpublic Companies

*Beta estimation for thinly traded stocks and nonpublic companies* involves a 4-step procedure. If ABC is the nonpublic company the steps are:

*Step 1:* Identify a benchmark company, which is publicly traded and similar to ABC in its operations.

*Step 2:* Estimate the beta of that benchmark company, which we will denote XYZ. This can be done with a regression analysis.

*Step 3:* Unlever the beta estimate for XYZ with the formula:

$$\text{unlevered beta for XYZ} = \left(\text{beta of XYZ}\right) \times \frac{1}{\left[1 + \dfrac{\text{debt of XYZ}}{\text{equity of XYZ}}\right]}$$

*Step 4:* Lever up the unlevered beta for XYZ using the debt and equity measures of ABC to get an estimate of ABC's beta for computing the required return on ABC's equity:

$$\text{estimate of beta for ABC} = \left(\text{unlevered beta of XYZ}\right) \times \left[1 + \frac{\text{debt of ABC}}{\text{equity of ABC}}\right]$$

 *Professor's Note: The unlevering process isolates systematic risk. It assumes that ABC's debt is high grade. It also assumes that the mix of debt and equity in the capital structure stays at the target weights.*

The procedure is the same if ABC is a thinly traded company. With the beta estimate for ABC in hand, the analyst would then use that value in the CAPM.

LOS 31.e: Describe strengths and weaknesses of methods used to estimate the required return on an equity investment.

*CFA® Program Curriculum, Volume 4, page 62*

The CAPM has the advantage of being very simple in that it uses only one factor. The weakness is choosing the appropriate factor. If a stock trades in more than one market, for example, there can be more than one market index, and this can lead to more than one estimate of required return. Another weakness is low explanatory power in some cases.

A strength of multifactor models is that they usually have higher explanatory power, but this is not assured. Multifactor models have the weakness of being more complex and expensive.

A strength of build-up models is that they are simple and can apply to closely held companies. The weakness is that they typically use historical values as estimates that may or may not be relevant to current market conditions.

LOS 31.f: Explain international considerations in required return estimation.

*CFA® Program Curriculum, Volume 4, page 80*

Additional considerations when investing internationally include exchange rate risk and data issues. The availability of good data may be severely limited in some markets. Note that these issues are of particular concern in emerging markets.

International investment, if not hedged, exposes the investor to exchange rate risk. To compensate for anticipated changes in exchange rates, an analyst should compute the required return in the home currency and then adjust it using forecasts for changes in the relevant exchange rate. Two methods for building risk premia into the required return are discussed in the following.

**Country Spread Model**

One method for adjusting data from emerging markets is to use a corresponding developed market as a benchmark and add a premium for the emerging market. One premium to use is the difference between the yield on bonds in the emerging market minus the yield on corresponding bonds in the developed market.

**Country Risk Rating Model**

A second method is the country risk rating model. This model estimates a regression equation using the equity risk premium for developed countries as dependent variable and risk ratings (published by *Institutional Investor*) for those countries as the independent variable. Once the regression model is fitted (i.e., we estimate the regression coefficients), the model is then used for predicting the equity risk premium (i.e., dependent variable) for emerging markets using the emerging markets risk-ratings (i.e., independent variable).

---

LOS 31.g: Explain and calculate the weighted average cost of capital for a company.

*CFA® Program Curriculum, Volume 4, page 81*

The **cost of capital** is the overall required rate of return for those who supply a company with capital. The *suppliers* of capital are equity investors and those who lend money to the company. An often-used measure is the weighted average cost of capital (WACC):

$$\text{WACC} = \frac{\text{market value of debt}}{\text{market value of debt and equity}} \times r_d \times (1 - \text{tax rate}) + \frac{\text{market value of equity}}{\text{market value of debt and equity}} \times r_e$$

In this representation, $r_d$ and $r_e$ are the required return on debt and equity, respectively. In many markets, corporations can take a deduction for interest expense. The inclusion of the term $(1 - \text{tax rate})$ adjusts the cost of the debt so it is on an after-tax basis. Since the measure should be forward-looking, the tax rate should be the marginal tax rate, which better reflects the future cost of raising funds. For markets where interest expense is not deductible, the relevant tax rate would be zero, and the pre- and after-tax cost of debt would be equal.

WACC is appropriate for valuing a total firm. To obtain the value of equity, first use WACC to calculate the value of a firm and then subtract the market value of long-term debt. We typically assume that the market value weights of debt and equity are equal to their target weights. When this is not the case, the WACC calculation should use the target weights for debt and equity.

---

LOS 31.h: Evaluate the appropriateness of using a particular rate of return as a discount rate, given a description of the cash flow to be discounted and other relevant facts.

*CFA® Program Curriculum, Volume 4, page 82*

The discount rate should correspond to the type of cash flow being discounted. Cash flows to the entire firm should be discounted with the WACC. Alternatively, cash flows in excess of what is required for debt service should be treated as cash flows to equity and discounted at the required return to equity.

An analyst may wish to measure the present value of real cash flows, and a real discount rate (i.e., one that has been adjusted for expected inflation) should be used in that case. In most cases, however, analysts discount nominal cash flows with nominal discount rates.

# KEY CONCEPTS

## LOS 31.a

Return concepts:

- Holding period return is the increase in price of an asset plus any cash flow received from that asset, divided by the initial price of the asset. The holding period can be any length. Usually, it is assumed the cash flow comes at the end of the period:

$$\text{holding period return} = r = \frac{P_1 - P_0 + CF_1}{P_0} = \frac{P_1 + CF_1}{P_0} - 1$$

- An asset's required return is the minimum expected return an investor requires given the asset's characteristics.
- If expected return is greater (less) than required return, the asset is undervalued (overvalued). The mispricing can lead to a return from convergence of price to intrinsic value.
- The discount rate is a rate used to find the present value of an investment.
- The internal rate of return (IRR) is the rate that equates the discounted cash flows to the current price. If markets are efficient, then the IRR represents the required return.

## LOS 31.b

The equity risk premium is the return over the risk-free rate that investors require for holding equity securities. It can be used to determine the required return for specific stocks:

required return for stock j = risk-free return + $\beta_j$ × equity risk premium

where:

$\beta_j$ = the "beta" of stock j and serves as the adjustment for the level of systematic risk

A more general representation is:

required return for stock j = risk-free return + equity risk premium + other
adjustments for j

A historical estimate of the equity risk premium consists of the difference between the mean return on a broad-based, equity-market index and the mean return on U.S. Treasury bills over a given time period.

Forward-looking or ex ante estimates use current information and expectations concerning economic and financial variables. The strength of this method is that it does not rely on an assumption of stationarity and is less subject to problems like survivorship bias.

There are three types of forward-looking estimates of the equity risk premium:
- Gordon growth model.
- Macroeconomic models, which use current information, but are only appropriate for developed countries where public equities represent a relatively large share of the economy.
- Survey estimates, which are easy to obtain, but can have a wide disparity between opinions.

The Gordon growth model can be used to estimate the equity risk premium based on expectational data:

GGM equity risk premium = 1-year forecasted dividend yield on market index + consensus long-term earnings growth rate – long-term government bond yield

## LOS 31.c

Models used to estimate the required return on equity:
- CAPM:

$$\text{required return on stock j} = \text{current risk-free return} + (\text{equity risk premium} \times \text{beta of j})$$

- Multifactor model:

$$\text{required return} = RF + (\text{risk premium})_1 + \ldots + (\text{risk premium})_n$$

- Fama-French model:

$$\text{required return of stock j} = RF + \beta_{mkt,j} \times (R_{mkt} - RF) + \beta_{SMB,j} \times (R_{small} - R_{big}) + \beta_{HML,j} \times (R_{HBM} - R_{LBM})$$

where:
$(R_{mkt} - RF)$ = market risk premium
$(R_{small} - R_{big})$ = a small-cap risk premium
$(R_{HBM} - R_{LBM})$ = a value risk premium

- The Pastor-Stambaugh model adds a liquidity factor to the Fama-French model.
- Macroeconomic multifactor models use factors associated with economic variables that would affect the cash flows and/or discount rate of companies.
- The build-up method is similar to the risk premium approach. One difference is that this approach does not use betas to adjust for the exposure to a factor. The bond yield plus risk premium method is a type of build-up method.

**LOS 31.d**

Beta estimation:

- A regression of the returns of a publicly traded company's stock returns on the returns of an index provides an estimate of beta. For forecasting required returns using the CAPM, an analyst may wish to adjust for beta drift using an equation such as:

$$\text{adjusted beta} = (2/3) \times (\text{regression beta}) + (1/3) \times (1.0)$$

- For thinly traded stocks and non-publicly traded companies, an analyst can estimate beta using a 4-step process: (1) identify publicly traded benchmark company, (2) estimate the beta of the benchmark company, (3) unlever the benchmark company's beta, and (4) relever the beta using the capital structure of the thinly traded/nonpublic company.

**LOS 31.e**

Each of the various methods of estimating the required return on an equity investment has strengths and weaknesses.

- The CAPM is simple but may have low explanatory power.
- Multifactor models have more explanatory power but are more complex and costly.
- Build-up models are simple and can apply to closely held companies, but they typically use historical values as estimates that may or may not be relevant to the current situation.

**LOS 31.f**

In making estimates of required return in the international setting, an analyst should adjust the required return to reflect expectations for changes in exchange rates.

When dealing with emerging markets, a premium should be added to reflect the greater level of risk present. Two methods for estimating the size of the risk premium:

- The country spread model uses a corresponding developed market as a benchmark and adds a premium for the emerging market risk. The premium can be estimated by taking the difference between the yield on bonds in the emerging market minus the yield of corresponding bonds in the developed market.
- The country risk rating model estimates an equation for the equity risk premium for developed countries and then uses the equation and inputs associated with the emerging market to estimate the required return for the emerging market.

**LOS 31.g**

The weighted average cost of capital (WACC) is the required return averaged across all suppliers of capital (i.e., the debt and equity holders). The formula for WACC is:

$$\text{WACC} = \frac{\text{market value of debt}}{\text{market value of debt and equity}} \times r_d \times (1 - \text{tax rate}) + \frac{\text{market value of equity}}{\text{market value of debt and equity}} \times r_e$$

where:

$r_d$ and $r_e$ = the required return on debt and equity, respectively

The term (1 – tax rate) is an adjustment to reflect the fact that, in most countries, corporations can take a tax deduction for interest payments. The tax rate should be the marginal rate.

## LOS 31.h

The discount rate should correspond to the type of cash flow being discounted: cash flows to the entire firm at the WACC and those to equity at the required return on equity.

An analyst may wish to measure the present value of real cash flows, and a real discount rate should be used in that case. In most cases, however, analysts discount nominal cash flows with nominal discount rates.

# CONCEPT CHECKERS

1.  A positive return from return from convergence of price to intrinsic value would *most likely* occur if:
    A.  expected return is greater than required return.
    B.  required return is greater than expected return.
    C.  required return equals expected return.

2.  For a particular stock, the required return can be determined by:
    A.  multiplying the equity risk premium times the risk-free rate.
    B.  multiplying an appropriate beta times the equity risk premium and adding a risk-free rate.
    C.  multiplying an appropriate beta times the equity risk premium and subtracting the risk-free rate.

3.  Which of the following is *most appropriate* to use as an estimate of the market risk premium in the capital asset pricing model (CAPM)?
    A.  Geometric mean of historical returns on a market index.
    B.  Arithmetic mean of historical returns on a market index.
    C.  1-year forecasted market index dividend yield plus long-term earnings growth forecast minus long-term government bond yield.

4.  In computing a historical estimate of the equity risk premium, with respect to possible biases, choosing an arithmetic average of equity returns and Treasury bill rates would *most likely*:
    A.  have an indeterminate effect because using the arithmetic average would tend to increase the estimate, and using the Treasury bill rate would tend to decrease the estimate.
    B.  have an indeterminate effect because using the arithmetic average would tend to decrease the estimate, and using the Treasury bill rate would tend to increase the estimate.
    C.  bias the estimate upwards because using the arithmetic average would tend to increase the estimate, and using the Treasury bill rate would tend to increase the estimate.

5.  Which of the following is included in the Pastor-Stambaugh model but not the Fama-French model?
    A.  A liquidity premium.
    B.  A book-to-market premium.
    C.  A market capitalization premium.

6.  An analyst wishes to estimate a beta for a public company and use it to compute a forward-looking required return. The analyst would *most likely*:
    A.  delever the market beta and relever that value for the company.
    B.  regress the returns of the company on returns on an equity market index and adjust the estimated beta for leverage.
    C.  regress the returns of the company on returns on an equity market index and adjust the estimated beta for beta drift.

7.   Consider the following statements with respect to international considerations in determining the cost of capital.

Statement 1:   Exchange rates are an issue.

Statement 2:   The country risk rating model uses a corresponding developed market as a benchmark and adds a premium for the emerging market.

Are the statements correct?
A.  Yes.
B.  No, because exchange rates are not an issue.
C.  No, because the country risk rating model estimates an equation for the equity risk premium for developed countries and then uses the equation and inputs associated with the emerging market to estimate the required return for emerging markets.

8.   An analyst wishes to calculate the WACC for a company. The company's debt is twice that of the equity. The required returns on the company's debt and equity are 8% and 10%, respectively. The company's marginal tax rate is 30%. The WACC is *closest* to:
A.  6.07%.
B.  7.07%.
C.  8.67%.

# ANSWERS – CONCEPT CHECKERS

1. **A** In this case, the asset is underpriced. If market participants recognize the mispricing, the correction in price will generate additional return.

2. **B** Required return for stock j = risk-free return + $\beta_j \times$ (equity risk premium).

3. **C** The Gordon growth model equity risk premium (choice C) is appropriate for estimating the market risk premium. The geometric or arithmetic mean of the *excess* market returns (NOT the actual returns on the market itself, as in choices A and B) is also appropriate.

4. **C** When using the historical method, the other choices are using the geometric average and a long-term bond rate. The geometric mean is less than the arithmetic average, which results in a lower risk premium. The long-term bond rate is usually greater than the Treasury bill rate, which also results in a lower risk premium. So, using the arithmetic average and the shorter-term Treasury bill rate would likely bias the equity risk premium estimate upwards.

5. **A** The Pastor-Stambaugh model adds a liquidity factor to the Fama-French model. The average liquidity premium for equity should be zero. Less liquid assets should have a positive liquidity beta, and more liquid assets should have a negative beta.

6. **C** For a public company, an analyst can usually compute beta by regressing the returns of the company's stock on the returns of an appropriate market index. This requires a choice of the index to use in the regression and the length and frequency of the sample. When making forecasts of the equity risk premium, some analysts recommend adjusting the beta for beta drift. Beta drift refers to the observed tendency of a computed beta to revert to a value of 1.0 over time.

7. **C** Statement 1 is correct; exchange rates are an issue. Statement 2 is incorrect because it explains the country spread model.

8. **B** The first step is to determine the percentage debt and equity in the capital structure. With a debt-to-equity ratio of 2 to 1, there is 2/3 = 66.7% debt and 1/3 = 33.3% equity. Then, WACC = $0.667 \times (1 - 0.3) \times 8\% + 0.333 \times 10\% = 7.07\%$.

# THE FIVE COMPETITIVE FORCES THAT SHAPE STRATEGY

Study Session 11

## EXAM FOCUS

In 1979, Michael Porter introduced the concept of the five forces that shape competitive strategy. A recent update to this influential work shows how the five forces can be employed for strategic analysis. For the exam, know each of the five forces and how these combine to drive industry profitability. Describe why some factors that are commonly used in industry analysis have only a temporary effect on the forces that determine profitability in the long run. Finally, be prepared to show how the five forces can be used to design strategies that will enable a firm to achieve a competitive advantage.

## WARM-UP

The primary goal for any for-profit enterprise is to make money. The firm's competitive strategy is its battle plan for achieving that goal. Two central questions provide the basis for the firm's choice of a competitive strategy:

- **Industry attractiveness.** Is the industry attractive in terms of long-term profit potential?
- **Competitive advantage.** How does the firm create value for buyers (in excess of the cost of creating it), relative to other players in the industry?

There are five key forces that underlie an industry's long-run profitability and, thus, drive the optimal choice of competitive strategy.

LOS 32.a: Distinguish among the five competitive forces and explain how they drive industry profitability in the medium and long run.

*CFA® Program Curriculum, Volume 4, page 99*

### Porter's Five Forces

The attractiveness (long-term profitability) of any industry is determined by the interaction of the following five competitive forces (Porter's Five Forces):

1. Threat of new entrants in the industry.
2. Threat of substitutes.
3. Bargaining power of buyers.
4. Bargaining power of suppliers.
5. Rivalry among existing competitors.

*Professor's Note: You should be able to recite these five forces anytime, anywhere!*

While short-term profitability is largely determined by supply and demand, long-term profitability is determined by industry structure. Industry structure is determined by the competitive forces that characterize the industry. These five forces determine the level of industry profitability over the long term through their collective effect on the distribution of value-added among industry participants, suppliers, and buyers. The key issues and factors that affect each of the five forces are discussed below.

### Force One: The Threat of New Entrants into the Industry

Key Issue: What is the likelihood of new entrants emerging to alter the competitive landscape in a way that reduces the share of the value-added realized by our firm and other existing competitors?

Discussion: The strength of this force, meaning the likelihood of new entrants emerging, depends upon a variety of factors, most or all of which relate to the size of the barriers to entry present. All else being equal, the higher the barriers, the weaker the threat, and, the greater the pricing power of existing participants. Factors affecting this force include:

- Economies of scale that will make it difficult for new entrants to achieve critical mass.
- Product differences and brand identity that will deter customers from switching to new brands without costly inducements.
- Switching costs that the product user will incur if they decide to use the new entrant.
- Capital requirements to construct the facilities and other infrastructure required to enter the industry.
- Access to distribution channels, meaning that existing distributors may be at or near capacity and/or may not be willing to take on the new entrant's products.
- Government policy may require licensing or other approvals to enter the industry, and these could be time-consuming or difficult to secure.
- Cost and/or quality advantages may be enjoyed by incumbent firms, and it may take time for the new entrant to reach the point where these advantages are realized.

### Force Two: The Threat of Substitute Products

Key Issue: Do currently-available (or prospective) alternative products put a ceiling on the price buyers are willing to pay for the industry's current products?

Discussion: Note that this force concerns not only existing potential substitutes, but also those that could become available in the future. This subtle distinction is an important one—not all substitutes must exist to have a pricing impact. Factors that affect the strength of this factor include:

- The relative price performance of substitutes. Can the purported substitute products really do the job that the current products fulfill? If not, this force becomes much weaker.

- Buyer propensity to substitute, or how likely are the current buyers to switch, given a viable alternative. Rupturing a 20-year relationship when the marginal benefits of switching are small is unlikely. However, when the potential benefit to the product buyer is large, the propensity increases.
- Switching costs, meaning what is the cost incurred by the buyer. If production processes need minor retrofitting and the costs are low, the switch is more likely to be made.

## Force Three: The Bargaining Power of Buyers

Key Issue: How strong is the negotiating power of the buyers of the firm's or industry's output, and what is the impact on the distribution of the value-added by the industry?

Discussion: The bargaining power of the buyers of the industry's product can be viewed as coming from two main sources—bargaining leverage and price sensitivity.

- Bargaining leverage relates closely to factors affecting the other forces. Low switching costs and readily available substitutes give the buyers leverage and help to strengthen this force for buyers.
- The buyer's price sensitivity depends upon qualitative factors, such as brand identity, product differences, quality, and performance, as well as quantitative measures such as price relative to total purchases and profitability.

## Force Four: The Bargaining Power of Suppliers

Key Issue: How strong is the negotiating position of the suppliers of production inputs to the industry, and what is the impact on the distribution of the value-added?

Discussion: The stronger the bargaining position of the suppliers, the greater their ability to increase their share of the value-added in the form of higher prices for the inputs they sell to the industry. Some key factors that help to determine the power of the suppliers are:

- Differentiation of inputs that are acceptable to the industry. The greater the potential options, the lower the power of the suppliers.
- Presence of substitute inputs is closely related to the differentiation of inputs. The more actual or prospective substitutes that exist, the lower the supplier power.
- Supplier concentration implies that there are relatively few of them. A small number of suppliers increases their relative power, all else being equal.
- Importance of volume to the supplier. The more the seller seeks high volume, the harder they will work to maintain this volume and the lower their bargaining power.
- The threat of forward integration means that the supplier may be interested in entering the industry. This threat implies that the supplier will share in the value-added directly as an industry participant if they can't get the pricing power they want for their inputs.
- Switching costs. The greater the switching costs, the greater the supplier power.

## Force Five: The Degree of Rivalry Among Existing Competitors

Key Issue: Will existing firms compete away the value-added component through lower prices and higher costs to compete?

Discussion: The main points are two-fold. Do the firms follow sensible pricing policies or engage in price competition that cannot be won? Do the firms engage in non-price competition that increases costs but fails to increase profits? The factors that help to determine the likelihood of excess rivalry among existing competitors include:

- Number of competitors. The more there are, the greater the potential for rivalry.
- Industry growth implies demand for the product is strong, and the need to engage in competition, both price and non-price, is reduced.
- A high degree of operating or financial leverage makes it more likely participants will engage in price competition (or respond to such competition) to defend their market share and to cover fixed costs.
- The greater the participant's commitment to business, the greater the likelihood of competitive behavior, particularly if their existing position is challenged.
- Product differences make it more difficult to compete directly on price and reduce the strength of this force.
- Product shelf life. The shorter the shelf life, the greater the potential for price competition if the end of the shelf life is approaching.
- The existence of exit barriers, meaning that it is costly to leave the industry, will increase the potential for competition.
- The amount of informational complexity can make it difficult for competitors to communicate discretely in ways that can reduce the likelihood of damaging competition.

---

LOS 32.b: Describe why industry growth rate, technology and innovation, government, and complementary products and services are fleeting factors rather than forces shaping industry structure.

---

*CFA® Program Curriculum, Volume 4, page 109*

Various factors may affect an industry on a temporary basis but do not determine industry profitability and structure in the long term. For example:

- **Industry growth rate**. A high growth diminishes rivalry but does not assure profitability if other forces are detrimental to profits.
- **Innovation and technology**. Improved technology does not improve profits if it attracts competitors. Low tech industries can be very profitable if the overall effect of the five forces is positive.
- **Government policies**. These can be good or bad and are prone to change through time. Examples include patent protection, licensing requirements, labor policies, bankruptcy code, etc.
- **Complementary products**. These are products that are used in conjunction with the firm's products (like hot dogs and buns), and these can have a positive or negative effect. Some complements can create or increase barriers to entry and reduce the threat of substitutes, while others can increase industry rivalry to serve the demand generated by purchase of the complement.

Factors such as these should be analyzed in terms of their impact on Porter's Five Forces. For instance, barriers to entry may be reduced by weak patent protection or raised by high R&D in support of technological innovation.

LOS 32.c: Identify changes in industry structure, and forecast their effects on the industry's profit potential.

*CFA® Program Curriculum, Volume 4, page 110*

So far, we have discussed how the five forces drive an industry's structural attractiveness and long-term profitability. However, industry structure is not static—it changes over time, sometimes abruptly. Changes can be caused by specific events inside or outside the industry or by changes in technology, regulation, customer needs, and so forth. Analysts should be on the lookout for changes in the five competitive forces that may alter the industry's attractiveness.

## Changes in Threat of New Entrants

Changes in any of the seven factors affecting the threat of new entrants described earlier can increase or decrease the threat of new entry. For example, distributors may expand capacity, allowing new suppliers to enter the market and take advantage of the spare capacity.

## Changes in Power of Suppliers and Buyers

Events may lead to changes in power of suppliers or buyers. For example, when there is consolidation among suppliers in an industry, the power of those suppliers will increase, putting a squeeze on the margins of the buyers in that industry. Similarly, if the buyers in an industry consolidate, power of buyers will increase.

## Changes in Threat from Substitutes

Changes in technology may cause substitutes to become more (or less) viable. Early laptop computers did not compete well with traditional desktop computers on a price-performance basis. With advances in technology, however, laptops have evolved to become a credible substitute for desktop computers.

## Changes in Rivalry

Changes in the number of competitors or changes in the use of leverage in an industry may make the rivalry within an industry more or less intense. Rivalry usually intensifies over time as an industry matures and generally results in lower profits and the withdrawal of weaker competitors. However, some industries may continue to enjoy superior profitability despite increased rivalry if the overall market grows faster. Additionally, if competitors each focus on a niche, rivalry may not translate into price competition. Eliminating competition through merger or acquisition is tempting but risky, because any resulting increase in profits will only be temporary. Over time, it will simply end up attracting new competitors.

### Strategic Alternatives

Industry attractiveness and a firm's competitive position within the industry are interrelated. It is important for the analyst to be alert for fundamental changes that can affect the strength or weakness of the five forces. When this happens, the firm needs to be in a position to act to capitalize on the change. Here we explore three strategies that can be employed by a firm to use the five forces in its favor.

---

LOS 32.d: Explain how positioning a company, exploiting industry change, and shaping industry structure may be used to achieve a competitive advantage.

---

*CFA® Program Curriculum, Volume 4, page 112*

### Altering the Firm's Existing Position

A firm can improve its attractiveness through its choice of competitive strategy. Managers should attempt to intentionally create changes in Porter's Five Forces by reducing:

- **Customer power.** For example, increasing service or bypassing the middleman and selling directly to end users (as pharmaceutical companies reduced physician power by direct advertising to consumers).
- **Supplier power.** For example, using standardized parts that can be sourced from many vendors or outsourcing labor to more favorable markets (as some health care providers have outsourced reading x-rays to overseas radiologists).
- **Substitutes.** For instance, making the product more widely available or enhancing product features. Cellular telephone makers compete against land lines by adding text messaging, music, photography, and various other features not feasible in wired telephones.
- **Threat of entry.** Raise the barriers to entry, for instance by raising fixed costs (through increased R&D or mechanization) or lobbying regulators (for more restrictive licensing or better patent protection). Certain banks have raised entry barriers by investing in large branch networks that make it difficult for smaller banks to compete.
- **Rivalry.** Rivalry tends to increase over time as industry growth slows and products converge to new industry standards. Companies should avoid price wars and focus on differentiating products and finding or creating new market niches and geographic segments.

### Capitalizing on Changes in the Industry

Industry structure and profitability tend to be very stable. However, change does occur over time, either because of decisions made by firms in the industry or because of changes in external factors. Examples include:

- Forward or backward integration, such as clothing retailers' development of their own designer labels.
- External forces such as improvements in a substitute, like cellular and Internet telephones as alternatives to land lines.
- Sudden and dramatic change like the impact e-mail had on document delivery services.

These types of change offer opportunities to firms that are positioned to capitalize on them. Whether these opportunities are seized by industry leaders, smaller competitors, or new entrants depends upon the nature of the opportunity and the industry structure.

## Creating Changes in the Industry Structure

A firm can move the entire industry in directions that improve industry attractiveness, either by enhancing industry value-added overall (e.g., eliminating inefficiencies in the supply chain or distribution network) or by redistributing the value-added in favor of industry participants (e.g., improving pricing by reducing customer power). Industry leaders are best positioned to reshape the industry because of their ability to absorb the related costs and the fact that they generally benefit most from improved industry conditions.

A firm should try to move the industry in directions that play to its strengths and enhance its competitive advantage (e.g., creating barriers to entry by raising fixed costs and increasing economies of scale if it is the largest competitor). Managers should be careful not to engage in practices that improve their competitive position in the short run but that undermine industry attractiveness in the long run (e.g., price discounting by the low-cost competitor).

 *Professor's Note: The information in this topic review has been from the perspective of an existing, or incumbent, company. While not directly addressed in any LOS for this topic review, many of the points discussed could also apply to investors or analysts. In addition to analyzing financial information, Porter argues that investors should perform a five forces analysis that includes the issues discussed in this topic review.*

## Steps in Using the Forces in an Industry Analysis

There are six steps when using Porter's Five Forces in analyzing an industry:

*Step 1:* Define the industry:
- This should be done in terms of the products/services sold and the geographical area over which the products/services are sold.
- The products should then be examined in the context of the five forces.
- If two products appear similar but have different industry structure in terms of the five forces (e.g., the basic product is the same, but the buyers are vastly different), they should be considered separate industries.

*Step 2:* Identify the participants:
- Competitors.
- Buyers.
- Suppliers.
- Potential entrants.
- Substitutes.

*Step 3:* Determine strength or weakness of each force, what drives it, and why. Be careful to focus on the more important forces and analyze them thoroughly.

*Step 4:* Determine industry structure using an analytical framework and how the five forces come to bear on matters such as pricing and input cost structure. Distinguish between cause (ease of entry) and effect (price competition). Which forces are the most important determinants of profitability?

*Step 5:* Assess current and potential shifts in each force. Distinguish between transient blips and long-term structural changes in the industry and the forces. Make sure to incorporate trends and not use static analysis.

*Step 6:* Decide which forces can be altered in ways that will affect the value of the industry or firm.

## EXAMPLE: ANALYZING THE COMPETITIVE FORCES FOR WAL-MART

### Synopsis

Wal-Mart is the world's largest retailer, selling a wide range of products targeted to consumers and small businesses. The firm serves approximately 150 million customers per week in the Americas, Asia, and the United Kingdom.

Wal-Mart is widely viewed as having the lowest prices on a broad variety of frequently-purchased consumer products.

Principal competitors include other broad-based discount stores, grocery stores, as well as small retailers operating in its geographic region. The smaller specialty retailers and single-location boutiques compete with Wal-Mart in limited product lines.

Wal-Mart has a reputation as a formidable competitor, and many retailers have been forced to change their business models in order to stay profitable once Wal-Mart enters their markets.

A major development in recent years at Wal-Mart has been the deterioration in its market image because of accusations of unfair labor practices. The firm is currently defending several lawsuits involving its employment practices, and these have generated significant and damaging press coverage.

### Competitive Forces and Wal-Mart

**Threat of new entrants.** Wal-Mart's cost advantage arises from a famously efficient distribution system, which requires enormous scale and massive capital investment. The barriers to entry for a broad-based discounter are very high. However, Wal-Mart competes with a large variety of specialized retailers in specific types of products, where barriers to entry may be quite low.

**Threat of substitutes.** The threat of substitutes in the retailing industry arises largely from the potential elimination of brick-and-mortar retailers by Internet-based retailing. To mitigate this threat, Wal-Mart has launched its own Internet-based sales effort.

**Bargaining power of buyers.** The bargaining power of buyers is virtually non-existent. Individual consumers have essentially no bargaining leverage against global corporate retailers, and Wal-Mart does not target corporate customers. Wal-Mart is sufficiently large enough that even its biggest customers account for an infinitesimal proportion of its sales.

**Bargaining power of suppliers.** The bargaining power of suppliers has historically been very low. Wal-Mart is well known for vigorous bargaining with its suppliers of both labor and products. Its enormous presence in the retail sales industry makes it the largest purchaser for many of its suppliers, giving them virtually no bargaining leverage against Wal-Mart. Wal-Mart has also vigorously resisted efforts to unionize its workers, who have historically had very little bargaining power. That is changing somewhat as accusations of unfair labor practices have cost Wal-Mart market prestige and position, giving labor more leverage with the firm. Even so, the bargaining power of suppliers of labor remains quite low.

**Rivalry among existing competitors.** Competition among existing competitors in the retail sales industry is very high. An indication of the competitiveness is in Wal-Mart's global market share, which is approximately 3%. The vast majority of other firms have market share too small to be significant on a global basis. Competition in retailing is focused on geographic region, and Wal-Mart's market position varies widely. In the United States, Wal-Mart is the largest retailer of many items it sells and commands 20% of the grocery market. It has a much smaller presence in markets such as Germany, which it eventually abandoned after achieving only 2% share in foods against Aldi's 19%.

## Conclusion

Wal-Mart drives its competitive strategy through its enormous scale, which provides significant barriers to entry, low supplier bargaining power, and low buyer bargaining power. Substitutes are available for all products Wal-Mart sells but usually at higher prices. Wal-Mart's scale has historically enabled it to enjoy high profits for its industry.

A principal threat to Wal-Mart's long-term profitability is the increase in supplier power in the form of the influence of its suppliers of labor on the court system, the press, and public opinion. Wal-Mart should take action to reduce the impact of these labor difficulties on the firm. In fact, it has made steps to improve its public relations through actions such as increased and more visible charitable giving.

# KEY CONCEPTS

## LOS 32.a

Two central questions provide the basis for the firm's choice of a competitive strategy:

- Industry attractiveness: Is the industry attractive in terms of long-term profitability potential?
- Competitive advantage: What determines a firm's relative competitive position within an industry?

These can be analyzed through Porter's Five Forces:

1. Threat of new entrants.
2. Threat of substitutes.
3. Bargaining power of buyers.
4. Bargaining power of suppliers.
5. Rivalry among existing competitors.

Competitive forces drive industry profitability:

- Threat of new entrants. Will new industry entrants compete away the value-added component of price? The greater the threat of entry, the more pricing pressure there is on current competitors and the lower industry profits are.
- Threat of substitutes. Do alternative products or approaches put a ceiling on the price buyers are willing to pay? The more cost-effective a substitute product is, the more pricing pressure there is on industry competitors.
- Bargaining power of buyers. Will buyers capture the value-added component of price? The more power buyers have, the more pressure they can apply to lower industry prices and profits.
- Bargaining power of suppliers. Will suppliers capture the value-added component of price? The more power suppliers have, the more pressure they can apply to raise industry costs and lower profits.
- Rivalry among existing competitors. Will existing firms compete away the value-added component through lower prices or higher costs? The more rivalry there is among current competitors, the more likely they are to engage in destructive price wars or to raise the cost of competing by increasing marketing, enhancing product features and/or services, or other product attributes.

## LOS 32.b

Not all factors that affect an industry are considered one of Porter's Five Forces. For example, industry growth rate, technology and innovation, government, and complementary products and services are transient factors that do not have a clear-cut impact on profitability. These should be evaluated in terms of their influence on Porter's Five Forces.

## LOS 32.c

Industry structure is not static, and analysts should be on the lookout for changes in the five competitive forces (threat of entry, supplier power, buyer power, substitutes, rivalry). Such changes can exert price and margin pressure on the participants in that industry and may impact their profitability.

## LOS 32.d

Managers should intentionally create changes in the five forces by reducing customer power (increase service, bypass middlemen); supplier power (using standardized parts, outsourcing labor); availability of substitutes (enhance features, add distribution channels); threat of entry (raising fixed costs, lobbying regulators); and reduce rivalry (avoid price wars, differentiate products).

Firms can capitalize on changes in the industry with forward/backward integration and changes in external forces (e.g., the use of cell phones vs. land lines). These opportunities can be taken by leaders, smaller competitors, or new entrants depending upon the nature of the opportunity and the industry structure.

A firm can create changes in the industry structure and improve industry attractiveness by enhancing industry value added overall (e.g., eliminating inefficiencies in the supply chain or distribution network), or by redistributing the value added in favor of industry participants (e.g., improving pricing by reducing customer power). Industry leaders are best positioned to reshape the industry.

# CONCEPT CHECKERS

1.  Which of the following is *least likely* to characterize an industry whose buyers have high bargaining power?
    A.  High fixed costs as a percentage of producer total costs.
    B.  Highly differentiated products.
    C.  Low buyer switching costs.

2.  SunderArrica Emeralds is the world's major producer of emeralds and owns 85% of the world's emerald mines. It does not produce or distribute its own jewelry, but instead sells raw emeralds to jewelry manufacturers. SunderArrica would like to reshape the industry structure to improve the long-term profitability of mining emeralds. Which of the following approaches would be *most likely* to result in long-term improvement in the attractiveness of the emerald mining industry?
    A.  Cutting prices to drive competitors out of the industry.
    B.  Forward integration into the jewelry manufacturing and distribution business.
    C.  Undertaking a major marketing campaign to promote emeralds in engagement rings.

3.  The strategy of eliminating rivals is *best* described as:
    A.  an effective long-term strategy to improve company profits.
    B.  a risky strategy because higher industry profits may attract new competitors.
    C.  only effective in low-growth industries where sales growth has to come from increased market share.

4.  Cuisine Chic is a custom builder specializing in kitchen renovation of single-family homes. Cuisine Chic has experienced price pressure from home builders who have expanded into the home renovation business and would like to raise the barriers to entry in its industry in order to reduce price pressure from new entrants. Which of the following approaches to improving profits would be *least likely* to raise the barriers to entry to the custom kitchen renovation business?
    A.  Focusing on high price luxury renovations.
    B.  Increasing the sales force for kitchen renovations.
    C.  Undertaking a major marketing campaign to increase its brand awareness among single-family homeowners.

5.  Which of the following is not one of the Five Forces according to Porter?
    A.  Bargaining power of suppliers.
    B.  Industry growth rate.
    C.  Rivalry among existing competitors.

6.  GrowGlobal Foods is a major grower of fruits and vegetables with farming activities on four continents. Its large volume enables it to use highly mechanized farming techniques and a low-skilled labor force, so labor represents a much smaller percentage of its product prices compared to industry competitors. However, the firm faces stiff pricing competition from other producers of the same fruits and vegetables. GrowGlobal sells its produce to global food packaging corporations who create branded food products for distribution to restaurants and individual consumers. The production of branded processed foods is the high value-added stage of the value chain in the food industry. Which of the following is *most likely* to be a successful strategy for GrowGlobal to increase its long-term profitability?
    A.  Integrate forward into the food packaging business.
    B.  Employ a higher skilled labor force to increase productivity.
    C.  Enter the beef industry since beef is a higher priced product than fruits and vegetables.

## CHALLENGE PROBLEMS

**Use the following information to answer Questions 7 through 9.**

Vadoom Rentals is the dominant firm in the machinery rental industry, with more than 70% of the Euro-zone market. Vadoom rents heavy equipment to construction companies, household equipment to consumers, and transportation equipment—including trucks, containers, and railroad cars—to the shipping industry. Vadoom provides a wide range of equipment for rental, representing dozens of manufacturers. Many of Vadoom's customers are global corporations that use Vadoom equipment in times of high demand and account for significant percentages of Vadoom's revenues.

Vadoom's new Chief Executive, Dina Burghoffer, is unhappy with the historically thin margins of the machinery rental industry. The enormous capital investment required, and the negligible marginal cost of rental, make fixed costs the determining factor in profitability. The fact that all rental companies provide the same types and brands of equipment makes the decision to rent from one company versus another largely a matter of cost.

Burghoffer has decided that she wants to use Vadoom's position as the industry leader to change the industry structure and make it more attractive. She is particularly concerned about the ability of homeowners to get advice about renovation that would encourage them to rent home remodeling equipment. She is considering the purchase of a home remodeling consulting firm.

7.  Which of Porter's Five Forces has historically caused margins in the machinery rental industry to be thin?
    A.  Bargaining power of suppliers.
    B.  Threat of new entrants.
    C.  Bargaining power of buyers.

8. The *least effective* approach to improving industry structure over the long run would be:
   A. using Vadoom's position as the volume producer to reduce prices and drive smaller firms out of business to reduce rivalry among competitors.
   B. increasing the number of outlets and their operating hours to make Vadoom more convenient for customers.
   C. providing delivery and pickup of equipment for renters.

9. Products such as home remodeling advice would *best* be characterized in a Porter Five Forces framework as:
   A. a factor that influences Porter's Five Forces.
   B. an outside industry characteristic not relevant to a Porter Five Forces analysis.
   C. an example of threat of substitutes.

**Use the following information to answer Questions 10 through 15.**

Bergleaf Offices is a publicly traded manufacturer of office furniture and equipment that sells both directly to major office supply stores and also to small boutique retailers through a range of global distributors. It has production facilities in three countries and sources its materials from more than four dozen different suppliers.

Bergleaf sources approximately 28% of the metal components necessary for its furniture and equipment production from TemperedTech, a manufacturer of steel, aluminum, and other metals. Bergleaf also sources the same metals from five other producers in order to maintain an ongoing relationship with a range of suppliers. The cost of metal represents 40% of the total consumer price of the furniture, so Bergleaf is highly cost conscious in its relationships with its suppliers. The rest of the cost is the fixed cost of maintaining the production facilities.

TemperedTech has recently announced its invention of a new steel production technology that it has brand named TemperPlus. TemperPlus steel is capable of supporting a 72% higher load and weighs 41% less than traditional steel. Consequently, office furniture and equipment produced using TemperPlus steel would weigh much less and support a much higher load than traditional office furniture. This advantage is especially important in the production of office shelving, bookcases, file cabinets, and other furniture used to store heavy materials.

TemperedTech has patented the technology and announced that it will be the only producer of TemperPlus steel for at least the next ten years. The product will become available for sale in the next three months, at which time TemperedTech will announce product specifications, pricing, and delivery options for producers in Asia, North America, and Europe. The product will become available on other continents approximately six months later.

Kay Chester is Chief Executive Officer for Bergleaf Offices. She announced on a recent analyst call that Bergleaf is starting a new line of office furniture and equipment using TemperPlus steel. It will be modular but will use a different design than the usual modular shelving sold by many firms in the industry, which is interchangeable with the products of other producers. Chester says that this will force purchasers to buy only from Bergleaf since the products of other producers will not fit the Bergleaf systems.

This will require a large initial investment by Bergleaf in order to build new production facilities and increase the capital requirements of the firm substantially, but Chester thinks the investment will be worthwhile.

Bergleaf plans to promote the new line as a premium office storage solution and anticipates that it will be able to charge a 25% price premium over more traditional office storage products. Chester pointed out on the call that such products represent 40% of Bergleaf's revenues, and that a significant price hike on such a large proportion of the firm's revenue base will have extremely beneficial effects on top line growth over the next year.

Sami Dusman, an analyst at Welking Securities, is extremely excited about the prospects for Bergleaf's new line of office furniture. He has calculated that a 25% increase in price on 40% of Bergleaf's revenue base translates into additional revenue of $1.42 per share. Since materials costs historically account for 40% of revenues, he has raised his EPS target by $0.85 for the upcoming fiscal year.

Dusman has decided to recommend purchase of Bergleaf stock based on this significant jump in EPS. Dusman writes in his report recommending purchase of Bergleaf, "The increased price resulting from the improvement in product functionality will have a dramatic impact on Bergleaf's profitability over the next year." He has rated the stock a "strong buy" based on expected upward revision to earnings estimates as the new product line is introduced.

10. Chester's decision to change the design of Bergleaf's new premium furniture is *best* described as an attempt to reduce the strength of which of Porter's Five Forces?
    A. Threat of new entrants.
    B. Supplier bargaining power.
    C. Buyer bargaining power.

11. The bargaining power of buyers and of suppliers in the office furniture industry before the introduction of TemperPlus is *best* described as:
    A. low for one and high for the other.
    B. low for both suppliers and buyers.
    C. high for both suppliers and buyers.

12. The anticipated increase in sales at Bergleaf because of the new product line is *best* analyzed in the Porter framework:
    A. by considering it as an outside influence independent of the Porter framework since it is not one of the Five Forces.
    B. as a factor influencing Porter's Five Forces.
    C. as a long-term improvement in industry attractiveness since high-growth industries are more attractive than low-growth ones.

13. Dusman's statement in his report about the impact of the new product line on Bergleaf's profitability is *best* described as:
    A. correct, assuming Chester's forecast that the new furniture product line will command a 25% price premium is accurate.
    B. incorrect, because it doesn't account for bargaining power of buyers.
    C. incorrect, because it doesn't account for bargaining power of suppliers.

14. The increase in capital expenditures that Bergleaf anticipates making to expand its production facilities is *least likely* to increase:
   A. buyer power.
   B. barriers to entry.
   C. rivalry among existing firms in the industry.

15. The *most appropriate* conclusion about the value implied by the premium price for office furniture made from TemperPlus is that it is likely to:
   A. accrue to office furniture makers in the form of higher prices.
   B. accrue to office furniture buyers in the form of improved performance.
   C. be appropriated by TemperedTech.

# ANSWERS – CONCEPT CHECKERS

1.  **B**  Highly differentiated products is one strategy for reducing buyer power. Low switching costs for the buyer and high fixed costs as a percentage of total costs for the producer are both characteristics that tend to increase buyer power in an industry.

2.  **C**  The most effective way to improve the long-term profitability of the emerald mining industry would be to increase demand for emeralds and thus, pricing, by persuading consumers to use emeralds in engagement rings. Cutting prices is likely to be destructive, especially since SunderArrica is unlikely to gain much market share because of its already dominant position in the industry. Forward integration may or may not be a good idea for SunderArrica; we have no information about the value-added at that stage of the value chain. Even if it were a good strategic move for the firm, it does not change the attractiveness of the mining industry.

3.  **B**  Eliminating rivals is a risky strategy because the increase in industry profits may attract new competitors. Consequently, it is not an effective strategy in the long term, even in low-growth markets.

4.  **A**  Focusing on high price luxury renovations may enable Cuisine Chic to charge higher prices and improve profitability, but it does not raise the barriers to entry for new entrants to the industry. Increasing the sales force or the marketing effort would raise barriers to entry by raising the capital requirements for new entrants (to pay for more sales people or more advertising).

5.  **B**  Porter's Five Forces are:

    1. Bargaining power of buyers.
    2. Bargaining power of suppliers.
    3. Threat of new entrants.
    4. Threat of substitutes.
    5. Rivalry among existing competitors.

    Industry growth rate is not one of Porter's Five Forces in determining existing industry competition. It is a fleeting factor that can influence industry profitability through its effect on Porter's Five Forces.

6.  **A**  Integrating forward into the food production industry, which has high value-added, is most likely to improve the firm's long-term profitability. Increasing skilled labor is unlikely to reduce costs much since labor is a very low percentage of costs. Although beef is a higher priced product than fruits and vegetables, it is not a differentiated product and does not represent a high value-added component of the industry value chain.

## ANSWERS – CHALLENGE PROBLEMS

7. **C**   Vadoom's thin margins are most likely the result of bargaining power of buyers. The firm faces high fixed costs, low marginal costs, and deals with buyers who represent a significant proportion of firm revenues, all of which tend to increase bargaining power of buyers. We have no indication that suppliers have significant bargaining power since Vadoom represents many equipment manufacturers. The high capital investment required is likely to deter new entrants.

8. **A**   Price cutting is generally a destructive form of competition. Trying to drive other firms out of business is unlikely to succeed in the long run since improved profits are likely to attract new competitors. Competing on service such as delivery, location, and operating hours is more likely to improve industry attractiveness.

9. **A**   Home remodeling advice is a complementary product for home machinery rental. Complementary products should be considered in a Porter analysis as a factor that influences Porter's Five Forces.

10. **C**   The decision to change the design of the furniture so that it no longer can be used in conjunction with the products of other manufacturers is an example of increasing switching costs to reduce buyer bargaining power. The design change does not affect suppliers or barriers to entry.

11. **A**   The industry is best described as one with low power of suppliers because they produce very similar products, but high power of buyers because the office furniture is modular and interchangeable with furniture of other producers (low switching costs) and fixed costs are a high percentage of total costs.

12. **B**   The increase in growth rate is not one of Porter's Five Forces itself; it is a fleeting factor that affects the industry through its impact on the five forces. Higher growth rates do not necessarily make an industry more attractive.

13. **C**   Dusman's profit estimate is most likely incorrect because it doesn't account for the bargaining power of the supplier of TemperPlus. Since TemperedTech will be the only supplier of the product, it is highly likely that it will charge a substantial price premium for it relative to traditional steel, and Dusman has not accounted for that in his earnings estimates.

14. **B**   The increase in capital expenditures is least likely to increase barriers to entry because potential entrants are not tied to a specific (modular) product line. It is likely to create price pressure in two ways. First, it increases rivalry among existing firms by causing overcapacity and an incentive for firms to cut price in general. Second, it increases buyer power by creating an incentive for producers to cut price for specific buyers as long as producers can cover marginal costs and make some contribution to covering fixed costs.

15. **C**   The fact that TemperedTech's patent will give it a temporary monopoly position as the only supplier of TemperPlus makes it highly likely that TemperedTech will appropriate all the value added by the invention of the product for itself in the form of higher prices to its own customers. Furniture makers and furniture buyers are unlikely to enjoy the benefits of the value added until competition is introduced in the manufacture of the improved steel once the patent has expired.

# DISCOUNTED DIVIDEND VALUATION

## EXAM FOCUS

This topic review presents the use of dividend discount models, one of the classes of models using the present value of future cash flows to determine the value of a firm. Dividend discount models use forecasted dividends as the estimate of cash flow to the shareholder. This material has several important topics that will require careful study. You should be able to choose the appropriate model for the firm to be valued (based on the pattern of expected dividend growth), forecast the future dividends to be discounted, and determine the appropriate discount rate to apply. You should also understand the concept of sustainable growth and be able to estimate a firm's sustainable growth rate.

LOS 33.a: Compare dividends, free cash flow, and residual income as inputs to discounted cash flow models, and identify investment situations for which each measure is suitable.

*CFA® Program Curriculum, Volume 4, page 124*

In stock valuation models, there are three predominant definitions of future cash flows: dividends, free cash flow, and residual income.

**Dividends.** Dividend discount models (DDMs) define cash flow as the dividends to be received by the shareholders. The *primary advantage* of using dividends as the definition of cash flow is that it is theoretically justified. The shareholder's investment today is worth the present value of the future cash flows he expects to receive, and ultimately he will be repaid for his investment in the form of dividends. Even if the investor sells the stock at any time prior to the liquidation of the company, before all the dividends are paid, he will receive from the buyer of the shares the present value of the expected future dividends.

An *additional advantage* of dividends as a measure of cash flow is that dividends are less volatile than other measures (earnings or free cash flow), and therefore the value estimates derived from dividend discount models are less volatile and reflect the long-term earning potential of the company.

The *primary disadvantage* of dividends as a cash flow measure is that it is difficult to implement for firms that don't currently pay dividends. It is *possible* to estimate expected future dividends by forecasting the point in the future when the firm is expected to begin paying dividends. The problem with this approach in practice is the uncertainty associated with forecasting the fundamental variables that influence stock price (earnings, dividend payout rate, growth rate, and required return) so far into the future.

A *second disadvantage* of measuring cash flow with dividends is that it takes the perspective of an investor who owns a minority stake in the firm and cannot control the dividend policy. If the dividend policy dictated by the controlling interests bears a meaningful relationship to the firm's underlying profitability, then dividends are appropriate. However, if the dividend policy is *not* related to the firm's ability to create value, then dividends are not an appropriate measure of expected future cash flow to shareholders.

Dividends are appropriate as a measure of cash flow in the following cases:

- The company has a *history of dividend payments*.
- The dividend policy is clear and *related to the earnings of the firm*.
- The *perspective* is that of a *minority shareholder*.

Firms in the mature stage of the industry life cycle are most likely to meet the first two criteria.

---

### Example: Identifying the appropriate valuation model

Given the financial information on Eastern Consolidated, Inc., in the table, determine whether or not a dividend discount model is the appropriate model to value Eastern Consolidated common stock.

### Earnings and Dividend Data for Eastern Consolidated

|                    | 2007   | 2006   | 2005   | 2004   | 2003   |
|--------------------|--------|--------|--------|--------|--------|
| Earnings per share | $7.50  | $6.25  | $5.85  | $5.40  | $5.00  |
| Dividends per share| $1.25  | $1.25  | $1.25  | $1.25  | $1.25  |

**Answer:**

Earnings have grown at a compound rate of 10.7% over the four years while dividends have been constant, resulting in a decrease in the dividend payout ratio. A dividend discount model is not appropriate in this case because the firm's dividend policy is not consistent with its profitability trend.

---

**Free cash flow.** *Free cash flow to the firm (FCFF)* is defined as the cash flow generated by the firm's operations that is in excess of the capital investment required to sustain the firm's current productive capacity. *Free cash flow to equity (FCFE)* is the cash available to stockholders after funding capital requirements and expenses associated with debt financing.

One advantage of free cash flow models is that they can be applied to many firms, regardless of dividend policies or capital structures. The ability to influence the distribution and application of a firm's free cash flow makes these models more pertinent to a firm's controlling shareholders. Free cash flow is also useful to minority shareholders because the firm may be acquired for a market price equal to the value to the controlling party.

However, there are cases in which the application of a free cash flow model may be very difficult. Firms that have significant capital requirements may have negative free cash flow for many years into the future. This can be caused by a technological revolution in an industry that requires greater investment to remain competitive or by rapid expansion into untapped markets. This negative free cash flow complicates the cash flow forecast and makes the estimates less reliable.

Free cash flow models are most appropriate:

- For firms that do not have a dividend payment history or have a dividend payment history that is not clearly and appropriately related to earnings.
- For firms with free cash flow that corresponds with their profitability.
- When the valuation perspective is that of a controlling shareholder.

 *Professor's Note: See the next topic review for details on free cash flow models.*

**Residual income.** Residual income is the amount of earnings during the period that exceeds the investors' required return. The theoretical basis for this approach is that the required return is the opportunity cost to the suppliers of capital, and the residual income is the amount that the firm is able to generate in excess of this return. The residual income approach can be applied to firms with negative free cash flow and to dividend- and non-dividend-paying firms.

Residual income models can be more difficult to apply, however, because they require in-depth analysis of the firm's accounting accruals. Management discretion in establishing accruals for both income and expense may obscure the true results for a period. If the accounting is not transparent or if the quality of the firm's reporting is poor, the accurate estimation of residual income is likely to be difficult.

The residual income approach is most appropriate for:

- Firms that do not have dividend histories.
- Firms that have negative free cash flow for the foreseeable future (usually due to capital demands).
- Firms with transparent financial reporting and high quality earnings.

 *Professor's Note: Residual income models are addressed in Study Session 12.*

## LOS 33.b: Calculate and interpret the value of a common stock using the dividend discount model (DDM) for single and multiple holding periods.

*CFA® Program Curriculum, Volume 4, page 131*

### One-Period DDM

We can rearrange the holding period formula to solve for the value today of the stock given the expected dividend, the expected price in one year, and the required return:

$$V_0 = \frac{D_1 + P_1}{1 + r}$$

where:
$V_0$ = fundamental value
$D_1$ = dividends expected to be received at end of Year 1
$P_1$ = price expected upon sale at end of Year 1
$r$ = required return on equity

---

**Example: Calculating value for a one-period DDM**

BuyBest shares are expected to pay a dividend at the end of the year of €1.25. The analyst estimates the required return to be 8% and the expected price at the end of the year to be €28.00. The current price is €26.00. Calculate the value of the shares today, and determine whether BuyBest is overvalued, undervalued, or properly valued.

**Answer:**

The current value of the shares according to the DDM is equal to:

$$V_0 = \frac{€1.25 + €28.00}{1.08} = €27.08$$

BuyBest is undervalued. We can draw that conclusion by either:

- Comparing the current price of €26.00 to the fundamental value of €27.08.
- Comparing the expected return (12.5%) calculated previously to the required return (8.0%).

---

## Two-Period DDM

The value of a share of stock using the two-period DDM is the present value of the dividends in years 1 and 2, plus the present value of the expected price in Year 2:

$$V_0 = \frac{D_1}{(1+r)^1} + \frac{D_2 + P_2}{(1+r)^2}$$

where:
$V_0$ = fundamental value
$D_1$ = dividends expected to be received at end of Year 1
$D_2$ = dividends expected to be received at end of Year 2
$P_2$ = price expected upon sale at end of Year 2
$r$ = required return on equity

### Example: Calculating value for a two-period DDM

Machines Unlimited shares are expected to pay dividends of 1.55 Canadian dollars (C\$) and C\$1.72 at the end of each of the next two years, respectively. The investor expects the price of the shares at the end of this 2-year holding period to be C\$42.00. The investor's required rate of return is 14%. Calculate the current value of Machines Unlimited shares.

### Answer:

The value of Machines Unlimited shares can be determined with a two-period DDM as:

$$\frac{C\$1.55}{1.14^1} + \frac{C\$1.72 + C\$42.00}{1.14^2} = C\$35.00$$

## Multi-Period DDM

The DDM can easily be adapted to any number of holding periods by adjusting the discount factor to match the time to receipt of each expected return. With this, the present value becomes the sum of the properly discounted values of all expected cash flows (dividends and terminal value):

$$V_0 = \frac{D_1}{(1+r)^1} + \frac{D_2}{(1+r)^2} + \ldots + \frac{D_n + P_n}{(1+r)^n}$$

where:
$V_0$ = fundamental value
$D_i$ = dividends expected to be received at end of year $i$, $i$ = 1 to $n$
$P_n$ = price expected upon sale at end of year $n$
$r$ = required return on equity
$n$ = length of holding period

For example, if we extend the holding period to three years, we simply extend the formula.

---

**Example: Calculating value for a three-period DDM**

Reliable Motors shares are expected to pay dividends of $1.50, $1.60, and $1.75 at the end of each of the next three years, respectively. The investor expects the price of the shares at the end of this 3-year holding period to be $54.00. The investor's required rate of return is 15%. Calculate the current value of Reliable's shares.

**Answer:**

The value of Reliable Motors shares can be determined with a multi-period DDM as:

$$\frac{\$1.50}{1.15^1} + \frac{\$1.60}{1.15^2} + \frac{\$1.75 + \$54.00}{1.15^3} = \$39.17$$

When we have to calculate the total of three or more discounted cash flows, we can generally save a considerable amount of time (and improve accuracy) by using our financial calculators as shown in the following table:

**Calculating the PV of Multiple Cash Flows With the TI BA II Plus®**

| Key Strokes | Explanation | Display |
|---|---|---|
| [CF]→[2nd]→[CLR WORK] | Clear memory registers | $CF_0 = 0$ |
| [ENTER] | Initial cash outlay | $CF_0 = 0$ |
| [↓]→1.50→[ENTER] | Year 1 cash flow | C01 = 1.50 |
| [↓] | Frequency of cash flow 1 | F01 = 1 |
| [↓]→1.60→[ENTER] | Year 2 cash flow | C02 = 1.60 |
| [↓] | Frequency of cash flow 2 | F02 = 1 |
| [↓]→55.75→[ENTER] | Year 3 cash flow | C03 = 55.75 |
| [↓] | Frequency of cash flow 3 | F03 = 1 |
| [↓][NPV] →15→[ENTER] | 15% discount rate | I = 15 |
| [↓]→[CPT] | Calculate NPV of all CFs | NPV= 39.17 |

## WARM-UP: THE GENERAL DIVIDEND DISCOUNT MODEL

If we extend the holding period indefinitely, the value simply becomes the present value of an infinite stream of dividends, represented by John Burr Williams's (1938) original DDM formula:

$$V_0 = \sum_{t=1}^{\infty} \frac{D_t}{(1+r)^t}$$

While the DDM is theoretically correct, applying it in practice requires the analyst to accurately forecast dividends for many periods, a task for which we rarely can expect to have sufficient information. We can use one of several growth models, including the:

- Gordon *constant* growth model.
- *Two-stage* growth model.
- *H*-model.
- *Three-stage* growth model.

With the appropriate model, we can forecast dividends up to the end of the investment horizon where we no longer have confidence in the forecasts and then forecast a terminal value based on some other method, such as a multiple of book value or earnings. Choosing the appropriate growth model is essential to accurate forecasts.

---

LOS 33.c: Calculate the value of a common stock using the Gordon growth model, and explain the model's underlying assumptions.

---

*CFA® Program Curriculum, Volume 4, page 134*

The **Gordon growth model** (GGM) assumes that *dividends increase at a constant rate indefinitely*. The simplifying factor of the constant growth assumption is that the rate of growth can be expressed per period in the same way that the required return is expressed, allowing the expression to be condensed into a simple formula:

$$V_0 = \frac{D_0 \times (1+g)^1}{(1+r)^1} + \frac{D_0 \times (1+g)^2}{(1+r)^2} + \frac{D_0 \times (1+g)^3}{(1+r)^3} + \ldots + \frac{D_0 \times (1+g)^n}{(1+r)^n}$$

which condenses to:

$$V_0 = \frac{D_0 \times (1+g)}{r-g} = \frac{D_1}{r-g}$$

where:
$V_0$ = fundamental value
$D_0$ = dividend just paid
$D_1$ = dividends expected to be received at end of Year 1
$r$ = required return on equity
$g$ = dividend growth rate

The model assumes that:

- The firm expects to pay a dividend, $D_1$, in one year.
- Dividends grow indefinitely at a constant rate, $g$ (which may be less than zero).
- The growth rate, $g$, is less than the required return, $r$.

A firm's growth rate projections can be compared to the growth rate of the economy to determine if it can continue indefinitely. It is unrealistic to assume that any firm can continue to grow indefinitely at a rate higher than the long-term growth rate in real gross domestic product (GDP) plus the long-term inflation rate. In general, a perpetual dividend growth rate forecast above 5% is suspect.

> **Example: Calculating value with the Gordon growth model**
>
> DownUnder Financial recently paid a dividend of 1.80 Australian dollars (A\$). An analyst has examined the financial statements and historical dividend policy of DownUnder and expects that the firm's dividend rate will grow at a constant rate of 3.5% indefinitely. The analyst also determines DownUnder's beta is 1.5, the risk-free rate is 4%, and the expected return on the market portfolio is 8%. Calculate the current value of DownUnder's shares.
>
> **Answer:**
>
> First use the capital asset pricing model (CAPM) to estimate DownUnder's required return:
>
> $$r = 4\% + [1.5 \times (8\% - 4\%)] = 10\%$$
>
> Then use the Gordon growth model to estimate share value:
>
> $$V_0 = \frac{A\$1.80 \times 1.035}{0.10 - 0.035} = \frac{A\$1.863}{0.10 - 0.035} = A\$28.66$$

*Professor's Note: The dividend to be discounted is the next period dividend, $D_1$, not the dividend from the previous period, $D_0$. Use either $D_0 \times (1 + g)$ or $D_1$ in the numerator, depending on whether you're given the most recent dividend paid ($D_0$) or the expected dividend in one year ($D_1$).*

---

LOS 33.d: Calculate and interpret the implied growth rate of dividends using the Gordon growth model and current stock price.

---

*CFA® Program Curriculum, Volume 4, page 142*

The Gordon growth model includes four variables, so if we know any three of them, we can solve for the fourth. In practice, we can typically observe the price and current dividend for a publicly traded stock. Consequently, we are usually interested in either backing out the implied required return, using an assumed growth rate, or the implied growth rate, using an assumed required return. In this example, we calculate the implied growth rate using an estimated return.

**Example: Calculating the implied growth rate using the Gordon growth model**

Assume that the current price and most recent annual dividend for Aurora Mining (AM) are \$24.25 and \$1.10, respectively. If the required return on Aurora is 8.5%, what is the implied growth rate?

**Answer:**

We can set up the Gordon growth model in its standard form using the information we know:

$$P_0 = \frac{D_0(1+g)}{r-g} = \frac{1.10(1+g)}{(0.085-g)} = \$24.25$$

Rearranging the terms gives us:

$$1.10 + 1.10g = 2.06125 - 24.25g$$
$$25.35g = 0.96125$$
$$g = 0.0379$$

So, assuming that our estimated required return is on target, the implied growth rate for Aurora Mining's dividends is 3.8%.

 *Professor's Note: Also be prepared to solve for the implied required return given the other variables in the model.*

---

LOS 33.e: Calculate and interpret the present value of growth opportunities (PVGO) and the component of the leading price-to-earnings ratio (P/E) related to PVGO.

---

*CFA® Program Curriculum, Volume 4, page 143*

A firm that has additional opportunities to earn returns in excess of the required rate of return would benefit from retaining earnings and investing in those growth opportunities rather than paying out dividends. The fundamental value then represents not only the present value of the future dividends (on a non-growth basis) but also the present value of the growth opportunities (PVGO):

$$V_0 = \frac{E}{r} + PVGO$$

where:
E = no-growth earnings level
r  = required return on equity

*Professor's Note: If the growth rate is zero and the dividend rate is 100%, earnings equal dividends, and earnings are the same every year:*

$$E = D$$
$$E_1 = E_2 = E_3 \dots = E$$

This means the value of a firm's equity has two components:

- The value of its assets in place (E/r), which is the present value of a perpetual cash flow of $E$.
- The present value of its future investment opportunities (PVGO).

A substantial portion of the value of growth companies is in their PVGO. In contrast, companies in slow-growth industries (e.g., utilities) have low PVGO, and most of their value comes from their assets in place.

---

**Example: Calculating PVGO**

Reliable, Inc.'s shares trade at 60.00 Swiss francs (Sf) with expected earnings of Sf 5.00 per share and a required return of 10%. Assume the shares are properly priced, so price is equal to fundamental value. Calculate the PVGO and the portion of the leading P/E related to PVGO.

**Answer:**

$$Sf\,60 = \frac{Sf\,5.00}{0.10} + PVGO \Rightarrow PVGO = Sf\,10.00$$

P/E firm = Sf60/5 = 12x

P/E PVGO = Sf10/5 = 2x

2/12 or 16.7% of the firm's leading P/E ratio is attributable to PVGO.

---

**LOS 33.f: Calculate and interpret the justified leading and trailing P/Es using the Gordon growth model.**

*CFA® Program Curriculum, Volume 4, page 146*

The price-to-earnings (P/E) ratio is the most commonly used relative valuation indicator. An analyst derives a **justified P/E** based on the firm's fundamentals. The two most common forms are the **leading P/E**, which is based on the earnings forecast for the next period, and the **trailing P/E**, which is based on the earnings for the previous period. Both of these can be derived from the DDM:

$$\text{justified leading P/E} = \frac{P_0}{E_1} = \frac{D_1 / E_1}{r - g} = \frac{1 - b}{r - g}$$

$$\text{justified trailing P/E} = \frac{P_0}{E_0} = \frac{D_0 \times (1 + g) / E_0}{r - g} = \frac{(1 - b) \times (1 + g)}{r - g}$$

where:

| | |
|---|---|
| $P_0$ | = fundamental value |
| $D_0$ | = dividends just paid |
| $D_1$ | = dividends expected to be received in one year |
| $E_0$ | = current earnings |
| $E_1$ | = earnings expected in one year |
| b | = retention ratio |
| (1 – b) | = dividend payout ratio |
| g | = dividend growth rate |

*Professor's Note: The notation is tricky here. Because these are justified P/E ratios, the "price" in the numerator is actually the fundamental value of the stock derived from the Gordon growth model. It would be more accurate to label these ratios $V_0 / E_0$ and $V_0 / E_1$, but the common convention is to call them "justified P/Es."*

---

**Example: Calculating justified leading and trailing P/E**

Alliance, Inc., is currently selling for $16.00 on current earnings of $3.00 and a current dividend of $1.50. Dividends are expected to grow at 3.5% per year indefinitely. The risk-free rate is 4%, the market equity risk premium is 6%, and Alliance's beta is estimated to be 1.1. Calculate the justified leading and trailing P/E ratios of Alliance, Inc.

**Answer:**

$$\text{required return} = 4.0\% + (1.1 \times 6.0\%) = 10.6\%$$

$$\text{retention ratio} = b = \frac{\$1.50}{\$3.00} = 0.5$$

$$\text{payout ratio} = 1 - b = 1 - 0.5 = \frac{\$1.50}{\$3.00} = 0.5$$

$$\text{justified leading P / E} = \frac{1-b}{r-g} = \frac{0.5}{0.106 - 0.035} = 7.04$$

$$\text{justified trailing P / E} = \frac{(1-b) \times (1+g)}{r-g} = \frac{0.5 \times 1.035}{0.106 - 0.035} = 7.29$$

or

$$\text{justified trailing P / E} = 7.04 \times (1.035) = 7.29$$

*Professor's Note: Remember that if earnings are expected to grow, $E_1$ will be greater than $E_0$, and the justified leading P/E ($P_0 / E_1$) will be smaller than the justified trailing P/E ($P_0 / E_0$) because you're dividing by a larger number when you are calculating leading P/E. In fact, trailing P/E will be larger than leading P/E by a factor of (1 + g): justified trailing P/E = justified leading P/E × (1 + g).*

---

## LOS 33.g: Calculate the value of noncallable fixed-rate perpetual preferred stock.

*CFA® Program Curriculum, Volume 4, page 140*

A firm that has no additional opportunities to earn returns in excess of the required rate of return should distribute all of its earnings to shareholders in the form of dividends. Under this assumption the growth rate would be zero, and the current value of the firm would be equal to the current dividend divided by the required rate of return. This is exactly the same approach used to determine the value of fixed-rate perpetual preferred shares.

$$\text{value of perpetual preferred shares} = \frac{D_p}{r_p}$$

where:
$D_p$ = preferred dividend (which is assumed not to grow)
$r_p$ = cost of preferred equity

**Example: Calculating the value of fixed-rate perpetual preferred stock**

United Publishing has a fixed-rate perpetual preferred stock outstanding with a dividend of 6% (based on an issue at par of £100). If the investors' required rate of return for holding these shares is 9.5%, calculate the current value of these shares.

**Answer:**

Dividends are not growing because the preferred dividend is based on a fixed rate of 6.0% on a stated par value of £100, so this is comparable to DDM with a fixed dividend in perpetuity.

$$D = 0.06 \times £100.00 = £6.00$$

$$\text{value of preferred shares} = \frac{£6.00}{0.095} = £63.16$$

---

**LOS 33.h: Describe strengths and limitations of the Gordon growth model, and justify its selection to value a company's common shares.**

---

*CFA® Program Curriculum, Volume 4, page 148*

The Gordon growth model (GGM) has a number of characteristics that make it useful and appropriate for many applications. The model:

- Is applicable to stable, mature, dividend-paying firms.
- Is appropriate for valuing market indices.
- Is easily communicated and explained because of its straightforward approach.
- Can be used to determine price-implied growth rates, required rates of return, and value of growth opportunities.
- Can be used to supplement other, more complex valuation methods.

There are also some characteristics that limit the applications of the GGM:

- Valuations are very sensitive to estimates of growth rates and required rates of return, both of which are difficult to estimate with precision.
- The model cannot be easily applied to non-dividend-paying stocks.
- Unpredictable growth patterns of some firms would make using the model difficult and the resulting valuations unreliable.

Next we discuss multistage growth models, which accommodate more realistic growth rate assumptions.

LOS 33.i: Explain the assumptions and justify the selection of the two-stage DDM, the H-model, the three-stage DDM, or spreadsheet modeling to value a company's common shares.

*CFA® Program Curriculum, Volume 4, page 148*

For most companies, the Gordon growth model assumption of constant dividend growth that continues into perpetuity is unrealistic. For example, many companies experience growth rates in excess of the required rate of return for short periods of time as a result of a competitive advantage they have developed. We need more realistic multistage growth models to estimate value for companies with several stages of future growth. The appropriate model is the one that most closely matches the firm's expected pattern of growth. However, whichever multistage model we use, there are two important points to keep in mind:

- We're still just forecasting dividends into the future and discounting them back to today to find intrinsic value.
- Over the long term, growth rates tend to revert to a long-run rate approximately equal to the long-term growth rate in real gross domestic product (GDP) plus the long-term inflation rate. Historically, that number has been between 2% and 5%. Anything higher than 5% as a long-run perpetual growth rate is difficult to justify.

*Professor's Note: The required rate of return applicable to each stage might also be different. For instance, a firm with a supernormal growth rate is probably more risky (should have a higher required return) than a stable, mature firm with a slower growth rate. In most cases on the exam, however, a single required return is applied to all of the stages.*

**Figure 1: Example of a Two-Stage DDM**

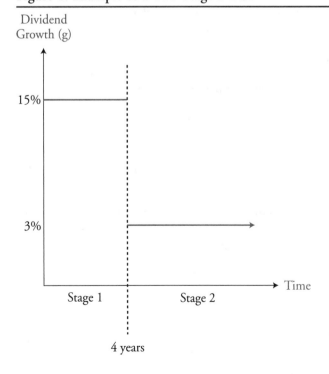

©2012 Kaplan, Inc.

*Two-Stage DDM*: The most basic multistage model is a two-stage DDM in which we assume the company grows at a high rate for a relatively short period of time (the first stage) and then reverts to a long-run perpetual growth rate (the second stage). The length of the high-growth phase is a function of the visibility of the company's operations; in other words, it tells how far into the future the analyst can predict growth rates with a certain degree of confidence. An example in which the two-stage model would apply is a situation in which a company has a patent that will expire. For example, suppose a firm is expected to grow at 15% until patents expire in four years, then immediately revert to a long-run growth rate of 3% in perpetuity. This stock should be modeled by a two-stage model, with dividends growing at 15% before the patent expires and 3% thereafter (see Figure 1).

**Figure 2: Example of an H-Model**

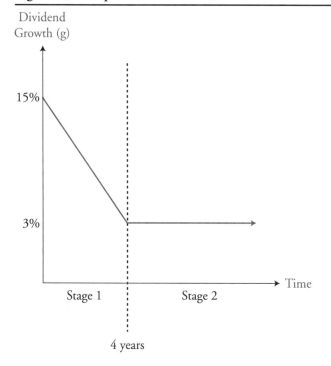

*H-Model*: The problem with the basic two-stage DDM is that it is usually unrealistic to assume that a stock will experience high growth for a short period, then *immediately* fall back to a long-run level. The H-model utilizes a more realistic assumption: the growth rate starts out high and then declines linearly over the high-growth stage until it reaches the long-run average growth rate. For example, consider a firm that generates high profit margins, faces little competition from within its industry, and is currently growing at 15%. We might forecast that the firm's growth rate will decline by 3% per year as competitors enter the market until it reaches 3% at the end of the fourth year, when the industry matures and growth rates stabilize (see Figure 2).

**Figure 3: Example of a Three-Stage DDM**

*Three-stage DDM*: Three-stage models are appropriate for firms that are expected to have three distinct stages of earnings growth. A three-stage model is a slightly more complex refinement of a two-stage model. For example, suppose we forecast that a biotech company will experience supernormal growth of 25% for three years, then 15% growth for five years, and finally slow down to a stable, long-run rate of 3% (see Figure 3).

*Spreadsheet modeling*: The two and three stage models we've discussed so far are really just models in which we've simplified the growth pattern to make the calculations doable. Obviously that's an important consideration on the exam. However, in practice we can use spreadsheets to model any pattern of dividend growth we'd like with different growth rates for each year because the spreadsheet does all the calculations for us. Spreadsheet modeling is applicable to firms about which you have a great deal of information and can project different growth rates for differing periods, such as construction firms and defense contractors with many long-term contracts. Figure 4 is an example of three different spreadsheet models.

**Figure 4: Examples of Spreadsheet Modeling**

| | *Growth Rates* | | | | | | |
|---|---|---|---|---|---|---|---|
| *Year* | *1* | *2* | *3* | *4* | *5* | *6* | *7 and after* |
| Scenario 1 | 20% | 19% | 13% | 5% | 5% | 5% | 5% |
| Scenario 2 | 20% | 19% | 13% | 11% | 5% | 5% | 5% |
| Scenario 3 | 20% | 19% | 13% | 11% | 8% | 7% | 5% |

LOS 33.j: Explain the growth phase, transitional phase, and maturity phase of a business.

*CFA® Program Curriculum, Volume 4, page 149*

While the basic GGM assumes constant growth, most firms go through a pattern of growth that includes several phases:

- An *initial growth phase,* where the firm has rapidly increasing earnings, little or no dividends, and heavy reinvestment.
- A *transition phase,* in which earnings and dividends are still increasing but at a slower rate as competitive forces reduce profit opportunities and the need for reinvestment.
- A *mature phase,* in which earnings grow at a stable but slower rate, and payout ratios are stabilizing as reinvestment matches depreciation and asset maintenance requirements.

The level and pattern of specific fundamental variables during the three phases, as well as the appropriate valuation model to apply in each phase, are shown in Figure 5.

**Figure 5: Growth, Transition, and Maturity Phase**

| Variable | Growth Phase | | |
| --- | --- | --- | --- |
| | Initial Growth | Transition | Maturity |
| *Earnings Growth* | Very high | Above average but falling | Stable at long-run level |
| *Capital Investment* | Significant requirements | Decreasing | Stable at long-run level |
| *Profit Margin* | High | Above average but falling | Stable at long-run level |
| *FCFE* | Negative | May be positive, and growing | Stable at long-run level |
| *ROE vs. Required Return* | ROE > r | ROE approaching r | ROE = r |
| *Dividend Payout* | Low or zero | Increasing | Stable at long-run level |
| *Appropriate Model* | Three-stage | Two-stage | Gordon growth |

This pattern is not predestined because many firms are successful in constantly adapting and entering into new growth opportunities. Mature firms may develop technology that forms the basis for a whole new product and market. The point is that a multistage model is required in order to value many firms. Fortunately, the GGM is easily adaptable to multistage growth.

## LOS 33.k: Describe terminal value, and explain alternative approaches to determining the terminal value in a DDM.

*CFA® Program Curriculum, Volume 4, page 149*

No matter which dividend discount model we use, we have to estimate a terminal value at some point in the future. There are two ways to do this: using the Gordon growth model and using the market multiple approach.

The most common method (on the exam) is to estimate the terminal value with the Gordon growth model. In other words, at some point in the future, we assume dividends will begin to grow at a constant, long-term rate. Then the terminal value at that point is just the value derived from the Gordon growth model.

Many analysts also use market price multiples to estimate the terminal value rather than use the GGM method of discounting dividends. For example, we could forecast earnings and a P/E ratio at the forecast horizon and then estimate the terminal value as the P/E multiplied by the earnings estimate.

---

### Example: Estimating terminal value

Level Partners is expected to have earnings in ten years of $12 per share, a dividend payout ratio of 50%, and a required return of 11%. At that time, the dividend growth rate is expected to fall to 4% in perpetuity, and the trailing P/E ratio is forecasted to be eight times earnings. Estimate the terminal value at the end of ten years using the Gordon growth model and the P/E multiple.

### Answer:

The dividend at the end of ten years is expected to be $6 ($12 multiplied by 50%). The dividend in Year 11 is then $6.00 × 1.04 = $6.24. The terminal value using the Gordon growth model is therefore:

$$\text{terminal value in Year 10 (Gordon growth model)} = \frac{\$6.24}{0.11 - 0.04} = \$89.14$$

The terminal value given forecasted earnings of $12 and a P/E ratio of 8 is:

terminal value in Year 10 (trailing P/E multiple) = $12.00 × 8 = $96.00

*Professor's Note: Remember that terminal value in Year 10 is equal to:*

$$\frac{D_{10} \times (1 + g)}{r - g} = \frac{D_{11}}{r - g}$$

---

## LOS 33.l: Calculate and interpret the value of common shares using the two-stage DDM, the H-model, and the three-stage DDM.

*CFA® Program Curriculum, Volume 4, page 149*

### Valuation Using the Two-Stage Model

The two-stage fixed growth rate model is based on the assumption that the firm will enjoy an initial period of high growth, followed by a mature or stable period in which growth will be lower but sustainable:

$$V_0 = \left[ \sum_{t=1}^{n} \frac{D_0 (1+g_S)^t}{(1+r)^t} \right] + \left[ \frac{D_0 \times (1+g_S)^n \times (1+g_L)}{(1+r)^n \times (r-g_L)} \right]$$

where:
$g_S$ = short-term growth rate
$g_L$ = long-term growth rate
$r$  = required return
$n$  = length of high growth period

---

**Example: Calculating value with a two-stage DDM**

Sea Island Recreation currently pays a dividend of $1.00. An analyst forecasts growth of 10% for the next three years, followed by 4% growth in perpetuity thereafter. The required return is 12%. Calculate the current value per share.

**Answer:**

We could solve the problem by plugging the appropriate numbers into the formula as follows:

$$V_0 = \left[ \sum_{t=1}^{3} \frac{\$1.00 \times (1.10)^t}{(1.12)^t} \right] + \left[ \frac{\$1.00 \times (1.10)^3 \times (1.04)}{(1.12)^3 (0.12 - 0.04)} \right]$$

$$V_0 = \frac{\$1.00 \times (1.10)^1}{(1.12)^1} + \frac{\$1.00 \times (1.10)^2}{(1.12)^2} + \frac{\$1.00 \times (1.10)^3}{(1.12)^3} + \frac{\$1.00 \times (1.10)^3 \times (1.04)}{(1.12)^3 \times (0.12 - 0.04)}$$

$$V_0 = \frac{\$1.10}{(1.12)^1} + \frac{\$1.21}{(1.12)^2} + \frac{\$1.331}{(1.12)^3} + \frac{\$1.3842}{(1.12)^3 \times (0.12 - 0.04)}$$

$$V_0 = \$15.21$$

---

If we were robots instead of humans, this would be fine. However, because we are human beings (and not mindless machines), it might be better to actually try to understand what we are doing, limit the need to remember yet another formula, and reduce the possibility of error. This can be accomplished by drawing a time line and placing the appropriate cash flows on the line, followed by the fairly straightforward computation on our financial calculators that we did earlier (in the multiperiod DDM). The forecasted dividends are shown in the following figure.

**Dividend Cash Flows**

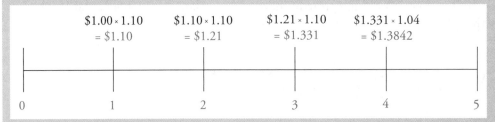

Constant growth at 4% begins after the third year, and we can employ the DDM to determine the value of the stock at time t = 3. Accordingly:

$$V_3 = \frac{D_3 \times (1+g)}{r-g} = \frac{D_4}{r-g} = \frac{\$1.3842}{0.12-0.04} = \$17.30$$

Now the problem is exactly like the three-period DDM we solved in LOS 39.b: we know the dividends in years 1, 2, and 3, the terminal value in Year 3, and the discount rate. The cash flows that we need to solve the problem are shown in the following figure.

**Dividend and Terminal Value Cash Flows**

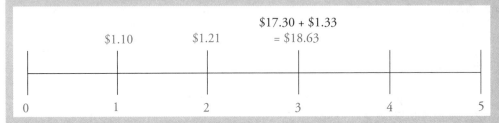

The financial calculator does the hard work for us: CF0 = 0; C01 = 1.10; C02 = 1.21; C03 = 18.63; I = 12; CPT → NPV = 15.21.

We arrived at an estimated value of $15.21 using the calculator, which is exactly the same answer we got with the ugly formula. After a bit of practice, you should find that the calculator method is easier than the complicated formula, and, just as importantly, it will be less prone to error.

The value of a firm that doesn't currently pay a dividend is a simple version of the two-stage DDM, where the firm pays no dividends in the first stage. Therefore, the value of the firm is just the present value of the terminal value computed at the point in time at which dividends are projected to start.

**Example: Valuing a non-dividend-paying stock**

Arena Distributors is a new company and currently pays no dividends. The company recently reported earnings of $1.50 per share and is expected to grow at a 15% rate for the next four years. Beginning in Year 5, Arena is expected to distribute 20% of its earnings in the form of dividends and to have a constant growth rate of 5%. The required rate of return is 12%. Calculate the value of Arena shares today.

**Answer:**

First forecast the earnings in Year 5. Then calculate the dividends in Year 5 as 20% of Year 5 earnings. Applying the Gordon growth model to the Year 5 dividend gives us an estimate of the terminal value in Year 4. The terminal value discounted back four years is the current value of the stock.

$$E_4 = \$1.50 \times (1.15)^4 = \$2.62$$

$$E_5 = \$2.62 \times 1.05 = \$2.75$$

$$D_5 = \$2.75 \times 0.20 = \$0.55$$

$$V_4 = \frac{\$0.55}{0.12 - 0.05} = \$7.86$$

$$V_0 = \frac{\$7.86}{1.12^4} = \$5.00$$

## Valuation Using the H-Model

The earnings growth of most firms does not abruptly change from a high rate to a low rate as in the two-stage model but tends to decline over time as competitive forces come into play. The H-model approximates the value of a firm assuming that an initially high rate of growth declines linearly over a specified period. The formula for this approximation is:

$$V_0 = \frac{D_0 \times (1 + g_L)}{r - g_L} + \frac{D_0 \times H \times (g_S - g_L)}{r - g_L}$$

where:

$H = \left(\dfrac{t}{2}\right)$ = half-life (in years) of high-growth period

$t$ = length of high growth period

$g_S$ = short-term growth rate

$g_L$ = long-term growth rate

$r$ = required return

Note that the first term is what the shares would be worth if there were no high-growth period and the perpetual growth rate was $g_L$. The second term is an approximation of the additional value that results from the high-growth period.

> **Example: Calculating value with the H-model**
>
> Omega Foods currently pays a dividend of €2.00. The growth rate, which is currently 20%, is expected to decline linearly over the next ten years to a stable rate of 5% thereafter. The required return is 12%. Calculate the current value of Omega.
>
> **Answer:**
>
> $$V_0 = \frac{€2.00 \times 1.05}{0.12 - 0.05} + \frac{€2.00 \times \left(\frac{10}{2}\right) \times (0.20 - 0.05)}{0.12 - 0.05} = €30.00 + €21.43 = €51.43$$
>
> Remember that the H-model provides only an approximation of the value of Omega shares. To find the exact answer, we'd have to forecast each of the first ten dividends, applying a different growth rate to each, and then discount them back to the present at 12%. In general, the H-value approximation is more accurate the shorter the high-growth period, $t$, and/or the smaller the spread between the short-term and long-term growth rates, $g_S - g_L$.

## Valuation Using the Three-Stage DDM

A *three-stage model* can be used to estimate the value of a firm that is projected to have three stages of growth with a fixed rate of growth for each stage. The approach is the same as the two-stage model, with the projected dividends and the terminal value of the shares discounted to their present value at the required rate of return. Again, a time line or an equivalent cash flow table will help the intuition. Your speed and accuracy will develop with practice.

> **Example: Calculating value with the three-stage DDM**
>
> R&M has a current dividend of $1.00 and a required rate of return of 12%. A dividend growth rate of 15% is projected for the next two years, followed by a 10% growth rate for the next four years before settling down to a constant 4% growth rate thereafter. Calculate the current value of R&M.

**Answer:**

**Relevant Cash Flows for R&M Example**

| Time | Value | Calculation | $D_t$ or $V_t$ |
|------|-------|-------------|----------------|
| 1 | $D_1$ | $1.00(1.15) | $1.150 |
| 2 | $D_2$ | $1.150(1.15) | $1.323 |
| 3 | $D_3$ | $1.323(1.10) | $1.455 |
| 4 | $D_4$ | $1.455(1.10) | $1.600 |
| 5 | $D_5$ | $1.600(1.10) | $1.760 |
| 6 | $D_6$ | $1.760(1.10) | $1.936 |
| 6 | $V_6$ | [$1.936(1.04)] / (0.12 − 0.04) | $25.168 |

Now we enter the cash flows into our calculator, noting that the total cash flow at Time 6 is $1.936 + $25.168 = $27.104: CF0 = 0; C01 = 1.150; C02 = 1.323; C03 = 1.455; C04 = 1.600; C05 = 1.760; C06 = 27.104; I = 12; CPT → NPV = 18.864.

According to the three-stage model, R&M is worth $18.864 today. This question is tedious, but it is not a question to be feared, as long as your calculator batteries hold up.

**Example: Three-stage growth model with linear growth decline in stage 2**

As an analyst, you have gathered the following information on a company you are tracking. The current annual dividend is $0.75. Dividends are expected to grow at a rate of 12% over the next three years, decline linearly to 4% over the next six years, and then remain at a long-term equilibrium growth rate of 4% in perpetuity. The required return is 9%. Calculate the value of the company.

**Answer:**

Let's start by valuing the last two stages using the H-model. We know that:

$$V_3 = \frac{\left[D_3 \times (1 + g_L)\right] + \left[D_3 \times H(g_S - g_L)\right]}{r - g_L}$$

$D_3 = D_0(1 + g_S)^3 = \$0.75(1.12)^3 = \$1.0537$

It follows that:

$$V_3 = \frac{\left[\$1.0537 \times (1.04)\right] + \left[\$1.0537 \times \frac{6}{2} \times (0.12 - 0.04)\right]}{0.09 - 0.04} = \$26.9747$$

Now we have a series of three cash flows to discount in order to find the current value of the stock, and our financial calculator does the rest of the work.

CF0 = 0; C01 = $D_1$ = $0.75(1.12) = $0.84; C02 = $D_2$= $0.75(1.12)$^2$ = $0.9408;
and C03 = $D_3$ + $V_3$ = $1.0537 + $26.9747 = $28.0284; I = 9;
CPT → NPV = 23.2056.

The price of the stock is $23.2056.

## Valuation Models Using Spreadsheets

If you have been calculating along with the examples, you already recognize that the use of these models can be computationally intensive, though the formulas are straightforward. These characteristics make DDM models ideally suited to being solved with spreadsheet programs. A spreadsheet allows the analyst to easily calculate values based on models with many stages, growth rates, and required rates of return.

---

LOS 33.m: Estimate a required return based on any DDM, including the Gordon growth model and the H-model.

---

*CFA® Program Curriculum, Volume 4, page 161*

We have been using DDMs to determine the value of a stock, assuming that we know the dividends and required rates of return. The models are just as useful in determining the required rate of return, given the current value and dividends of a stock. No matter which model you're using (whether it's a two-stage DDM, an H-model, a three-stage DDM, or a spreadsheet model), in theory this is easy: *Given all the other inputs to the model, we can back into the expected return that makes the present value of the forecasted dividend stream equal to the current market price.*

For example, if the dividend growth rate is constant forever, we can use the Gordon growth model to calculate the implied expected return given the expected dividend, the current market price, and the expected growth rate:

$$r = \frac{D_1}{P_0} + g$$

**Example: Calculating expected return with the Gordon growth model**

Smyth & Weston Explosives' stock is expected to pay a dividend of $1.60, has a current price of $40.00, and has a projected growth rate of 9%. Calculate S&W's implied required return.

**Answer:**

$$r = \frac{\$1.60}{\$40.00} + 0.09 = 0.13 = 13\%$$

The H-model can be rewritten in terms of $r$ and used to solve for $r$ given the other model inputs:

$$r = \left[\left(\frac{D_0}{P_0}\right) \times \left\{(1 + g_L) + [H \times (g_S - g_L)]\right\}\right] + g_L$$

**Example: Solving for expected return with the H-model**

Beluga Fisheries, Inc., just paid a current dividend of $0.75, which has been growing at a rate of 10%. This growth rate is expected to decline to 5% over the next five years and then remain at 5% indefinitely. Calculate the implied required return for Beluga based on the current price of $30.00.

**Answer:**

$$r = \left(\frac{\$0.75}{\$30.00}\right) \times \left\{(1 + 0.05) + \left[\left(\frac{5}{2}\right) \times (0.10 - 0.05)\right]\right\} + 0.05 = 0.0794 = 7.94\%$$

Using the general two-stage model is more difficult because we have to solve for $r$ with an iterative process because there is no closed-form solution. Here is an example of how to approach the problem using the two-stage DDM.

**Example: Solving for expected return with the two-stage DDM**

Ozone Laboratories, Inc., recently paid a dividend of $1.00. Dividends are expected to grow at a rate of 11% for the next two years and 8% thereafter. Calculate the implied required return for Ozone based on the current price of $36.00.

**Answer:**

Our financial calculators will only provide marginal help here because we cannot specify all the cash flows precisely. In effect, we have to solve for the rate in the following expression:

$$\frac{\$1.00 \times 1.11}{1+r} + \frac{\$1.00 \times 1.11^2}{(1+r)^2} + \left(\frac{\$1.00 \times 1.11^2 \times 1.08}{r-0.08}\right)\left(\frac{1}{(1+r)^2}\right) = \$36.00$$

One way to proceed is to estimate the required return in order to begin the iteration process. If we assume that the present values of the first two dividends are going to be worth about $1.00 each, we're left with $34.00 for the terminal value. Based on this "guess" we can estimate the required return:

$$\text{terminal value in Year 2 estimate} = \$34.00 = \frac{D_3}{r_{guess}-0.08} = \frac{(\$1.00) \times (1.11)^2 \times (1.08)}{r_{guess}-0.08}$$

$$= \frac{\$1.331}{r_{guess}-0.08} \Rightarrow r_{guess} \approx 0.119 \approx 11.9\%$$

We can then discount the first two dividends and the terminal value at this rate to determine their value:

$$PV(D_1) = \frac{\$1.11}{1.119} = \$0.99$$

$$PV(D_2) = \frac{\$1.23}{1.119^2} = \$0.98$$

$$PV(P_2) = \frac{\left(\frac{\$1.331}{0.119-0.08}\right)}{1.119^2} = \$27.26$$

The total value at a required rate of return of 11.9% would be $0.99 + $0.98 + $27.26 = $29.23. The required rate of return must be less than 11.9% because the discounted cash flows have to add up to $36.00 instead of $29.23. We could repeat the process, increasing or decreasing the assumed return each time, until we arrive at a return that makes the present value exactly equal to the price of $36.00. If you do all the work, the answer turns out to be approximately 11.2%.

*Professor's Note: The solver function in Excel can be used to solve for r in a two-stage model. Unfortunately, you can't take your laptop with you into the exam. The good news is that the LOS does not ask you to be able to calculate the required return using the two-stage model, but you are held accountable for being able to explain how it can be done.*

---

LOS 33.n: Explain the use of spreadsheet modeling to forecast dividends and to value common shares.

*CFA® Program Curriculum, Volume 4, page 160*

We have previously noted that, in practice, financial analysts are much more likely to use a spreadsheet than any of the stylized models present here when valuing equity securities. The reason for this is the inherent flexibility and computational accuracy of spreadsheet modeling.

A firm's dividends (or cash flows) often do not grow at a smooth rate for an extended period. When changes in dividends can be predicted, there can obviously be more than two or three stages of change involved. Moreover, there are often idiosyncratic events that, even if they can be predicted, do not fit neatly into any of the patterns required by these models. Using a spreadsheet is relatively straightforward and can accommodate nearly any pattern that the analyst can imagine.

*Step 1:* Establish the base level of cash flows or dividends. In the case of dividends, this would ordinarily be either the amount paid over the preceding year or some normalized level based upon projected firm earnings.

*Step 2:* Estimate changes in the firm's dividends for the foreseeable future (also known as the supernormal growth period) and project future cash dividends on the basis of these estimates. Because the spreadsheet can be programmed in a virtually infinite series of combinations, any dividend pattern desired can be achieved.

*Step 3:* Because an equity security has an infinite life, the analyst needs to estimate what normalized level of growth will occur at the end of the supernormal growth period. This allows for an estimate of a terminal value, representing the cash flow (i.e., the firm's value if sold at this time) to be received at the end of the supernormal growth period.

*Step 4:* Discount all projected dividends and the terminal value back to today to obtain an estimate of the firm's current value.

The last step is where the use of the spreadsheet really pays off. The analyst is in position to conduct detailed scenario analyses wherein the model inputs can be altered to see how changes in the pattern of future dividends, interest rates, and firm risk affect firm valuation estimates.

The bottom line is that performing the above analysis for a period of 10 or 20 years is relatively easy with a spreadsheet but would be all but impossible with any of the stylized models presented.

## LOS 33.o: Calculate and interpret the sustainable growth rate of a company, and demonstrate the use of DuPont analysis to estimate a company's sustainable growth rate.

*CFA® Program Curriculum, Volume 4, page 164*

The sustainable growth rate (SGR) is the rate at which earnings (and dividends) can continue to grow indefinitely, assuming that the firm's debt-to-equity ratio is unchanged and it doesn't issue new equity. SGR is a simple function of the earnings retention ratio and the return on equity:

$$SGR = b \times ROE$$

where:
b = earnings retention rate = 1 – dividend payout rate
ROE = return on equity

The SGR is important because it tells us how quickly a firm can grow with internally generated funds.

---

**Example: Calculating SGR**

Biotechnica, Inc., is growing earnings at an annual rate of 9%. It currently pays out dividends equal to 20% of earnings. Biotechnica's ROE is 15%. Calculate its SGR.

**Answer:**

$$g = (1 - 0.20) \times (15\%) = 12\%$$

---

A firm's rate of growth is a function of both its earnings retention and its return on equity. ROE can be estimated with the DuPont formula, which presents the relationship between margin, sales, and leverage as determinants of ROE:

$$ROE = \frac{\text{net income}}{\text{stockholders' equity}} = \left(\frac{\text{net income}}{\text{sales}}\right) \times \left(\frac{\text{sales}}{\text{total assets}}\right) \times \left(\frac{\text{total assets}}{\text{stockholders' equity}}\right)$$

If the other factors remain constant, we can see that the growth of a firm's earnings (and dividends) is a function of its ROE and its retention rate:

$$g = \left(\frac{\text{net income} - \text{dividends}}{\text{net income}}\right) \times \left(\frac{\text{net income}}{\text{sales}}\right) \times \left(\frac{\text{sales}}{\text{total assets}}\right) \times \left(\frac{\text{total assets}}{\text{stockholders' equity}}\right)$$

This has also been called the *PRAT* model, where SGR is a function of the profit margin (P), the retention rate (R), the asset turnover (A), and financial leverage (T). Two of these factors are functions of the firm's financing decisions (leverage and earnings retention), and two are functions of performance (return on assets equals profit margin multiplied by asset turnover). These factors can be used as building blocks in developing an estimate of a firm's growth. If the actual growth rate is forecasted to be greater than SGR, the firm will have to issue equity unless the firm increases its retention ratio, profit margin, total asset turnover, or leverage.

 *Professor's Note: Technically, the correct way to calculate sustainable growth rate is with ROE based on beginning shareholders' equity. However, it is often done with average equity as an approximation. On the exam, use whichever method is specified in the question.*

**Example: Calculating ROE and SGR**

Halo Construction has been successful in a mature industry. Over the last three years, Halo has averaged a profit margin of 10%, a total asset turnover of 1.8, and a leverage ratio of 1.25. Assuming Halo continues to distribute 40% of its earnings as dividends, calculate its long-term SGR.

**Answer:**

$$g = P \times R \times A \times T$$

$$g = 0.10 \times (1 - 0.4) \times 1.8 \times 1.25 = 0.135 = 13.5\%$$

 *Professor's Note: Sustainable growth rate is a very, very important topic. Make sure you know how to calculate ROE and SGR given a balance sheet and an income statement, as in the following example.*

**Example: Calculating ROE and SGR**

Given the following partial balance sheets and income statement for Far Horizons Company, calculate three components of the ROE (using the DuPont model) and the sustainable growth rate for 2008 based on beginning balance sheet values. Assume the dividend payout ratio is 30%. All values are in millions of USD.

**Far Horizons Income Statement**

| Income statement for fiscal year 2008 | |
| --- | --- |
| Sales | $40.0 |
| Net income | $1.8 |

**Far Horizons Balance Sheet**

| | Balance sheet fiscal year end 2007 and 2008 | | | | | |
| | 2007 | 2008 | | | 2007 | 2008 |
|---|---|---|---|---|---|---|
| Assets | $30.0 | $50.0 | Liabilities | | $10.0 | $20.0 |
| | | | Equity | | 20.0 | 30.0 |
| Total | $30.0 | $50.0 | Total | | $30.0 | $50.0 |

**Answer:**

$$\text{profit margin} = \frac{\$1.80}{\$40.00} = 0.045 = 4.5\%$$

$$\text{asset turnover} = \frac{\$40.00}{\$30.00} = 1.333$$

$$\text{financial leverage} = \frac{\$30.00}{\$20.00} = 1.5$$

$$\text{ROE} = (0.045) \times (1.333) \times (1.5) = 0.09 = 9.0\%$$

$$g = \text{ROE} \times b = 9.0\% \times (1 - 0.30) = 6.3\%$$

LOS 33.p: Evaluate whether a stock is overvalued, fairly valued, or undervalued by the market based on a DDM estimate of value.

*CFA® Program Curriculum, Volume 4, page 155*

If a stock is trading at a price (market price) higher than the price implied by a dividend discount model (model price), the stock is considered to be **overvalued**. Similarly, if the market price is lower than the model price, the stock is considered to be **undervalued**, and if the model price is equal to the market price, the stock is considered to be **fairly valued**.

# KEY CONCEPTS

## LOS 33.a

In stock valuation models, there are three predominant definitions of future cash flows: dividends, free cash flow, and residual income.

Dividends are appropriate when:
- The company has a history of dividend payments.
- The dividend policy is clear and related to the earnings of the firm.
- The asset is being valued from the position of a minority shareholder.

Free cash flow is appropriate when:
- The company does not have a dividend payment history or has a dividend payment history that is not related to earnings.
- The free cash flow corresponds with the firm's profitability.
- The asset is being valued from the position of a controlling shareholder.

Residual income is most appropriate for firms that:
- Do not have dividend payment histories.
- Have negative free cash flow for the foreseeable future.
- Have transparent financial reporting and high-quality earnings.

## LOS 33.b

Stock valuation can be approached using DDMs for single periods, two periods, and multiple holding periods. No matter what the holding period, the stock price is the present value of the forecasted dividends plus the present value of the estimated terminal value, discounted at the required return.

## LOS 33.c

The Gordon growth model assumes that:
- Dividends grow at a constant growth rate.
- Dividend policy is related to earnings.
- Required rate of return $r$ is greater than the long-term constant growth rate $g$.

$$V_0 = \frac{D_0 \times (1+g)}{r-g} = \frac{D_1}{r-g}$$

## LOS 33.d

If $P_0$ is fairly priced:

$$P_0 = V_0 = D_1 / (r - g)$$

$$g = r - (D_1 / P_0)$$

LOS 33.e
The value of an asset is equal to the current earning stream divided by the required return, plus the present value of growth opportunities (PVGO):

$$\text{value} = \frac{\text{earnings}}{\text{required return}} + \text{PVGO}$$

LOS 33.f
The Gordon growth model can also be used to estimate justified leading and trailing P/E ratios based on the fundamentals of the firm:

$$\text{justified leading P/E} = \frac{P_0}{E_1} = \frac{1-b}{r-g}$$

$$\text{justified trailing P/E} = \frac{P_0}{E_0} = \frac{(1-b) \times (1+g)}{r-g}$$

LOS 33.g
The value of a fixed-rate perpetual preferred stock is equal to the dividend divided by the required return:

$$\text{value of perpetual preferred shares} = \frac{D_p}{r_p}$$

LOS 33.h
The GGM has a number of characteristics that make it useful and appropriate for many applications:
- Very applicable to stable, mature dividend-paying firms.
- Can be applied to indices very easily.
- Easily communicated and explained because of its straightforward approach.
- Useful in determining price-implied growth rates, required rates of return, and value of growth opportunities.
- Can be added to other more complex valuations.

There are also some characteristics that limit the applications of the Gordon model:
- Valuations are very sensitive to estimates of growth rates and required rates of return, both of which are difficult to estimate with precision.
- The model cannot be easily applied to non-dividend-paying stocks.
- Unpredictable growth patterns of some firms would make using the model difficult.

LOS 33.i,l
Multistage growth models have a number of strengths and a few limitations.

Strengths:
- Multiple-stage DDMs are flexible.
- The models can be used to estimate values given assumptions of growth and required return or to derive required returns and projected growth rates implied by market prices.
- The models enable the analyst to review all of the assumptions built into the models and to consider the impact of different assumptions.
- The models are very easily constructed and computed with the use of spreadsheet software.

Limitations:
- The estimates are only as good as the assumptions and projections used as inputs.
- A model must be fully understood in order for the analyst to arrive at accurate estimates. Without a clear understanding of the model, the effects of assumptions cannot be determined.
- The estimates of value are very sensitive to the assumptions of growth and required return.
- Formulas and data input can lead to errors that are difficult to identify.

There are several multistage growth models, with the most appropriate being the one that most closely matches the firm's actual growth pattern. The terminal value for multistage models is estimated using the Gordon growth model or market price multiples.
- The two-stage model has two distinct stages with a stable rate of growth during each stage.
- The H-model also has two stages but assumes that the growth rate declines at a constant linear rate during the first stage and is stable in the second stage:

$$V_0 = \frac{D_0 \times (1 + g_L)}{r - g_L} + \frac{D_0 \times H \times (g_S - g_L)}{r - g_L}$$

- The three-stage model can either have stable growth rates in each of the three stages or have a linearly declining rate in the second stage.
- The spreadsheet model can incorporate any number of stages with specified rates of growth for each stage. This is most easily modeled with a computer spreadsheet.

## LOS 33.j

Most firms go through a pattern of growth that includes three stages:
- An initial growth stage, where the firm has rapidly increasing earnings, little or no dividends, and heavy reinvestment.
- A transition stage, in which earnings and dividends are still increasing but at a slower rate as competitive forces reduce profit opportunities and the need for reinvestment.
- A mature stage, in which earnings grow at a stable but slower rate, and payout ratios are stabilizing as reinvestment matches depreciation and asset maintenance requirements.

## LOS 33.k

No matter which dividend discount model we use, we have to estimate a terminal value using either the Gordon growth model or the market multiple approach. The Gordon growth model assumes that in the future, dividends will begin to grow at a constant, long-term rate. Then the terminal value at that point is just the value derived from the Gordon growth model.

Using market price multiples to estimate the terminal value involves, for example, forecasting earnings and a P/E ratio at the forecast horizon and then estimating the terminal value as the P/E multiplied by the earnings estimate.

LOS 33.m
Given all of the other inputs to the Gordon growth model or H-model, we can rearrange the formula to back into the expected return that makes the present value of the forecasted dividend stream equal to the current market price:

GGM:

$$r = \frac{D_1}{P_0} + g$$

H-Model:

$$r = \left[ \left( \frac{D_0}{P_0} \right) \times \left\{ (1 + g_L) + \left[ H \times (g_S - g_L) \right] \right\} \right] + g_L$$

LOS 33.n
In practice, financial analysts are much more likely to use a spreadsheet than any of the stylized models present here when valuing equity securities. The reason for this is the inherent flexibility and computational accuracy of spreadsheet modeling. Steps include:
*   Establish the base level of cash flows or dividends.
*   Estimate changes in the firm's dividends for the foreseeable future.
*   Estimate what normalized level of growth will occur at the end of the supernormal growth period, allowing for an estimate of a terminal value.
*   Discount and sum all projected dividends and the terminal value back to today.

LOS 33.o
The SGR is defined as the rate that earnings (and dividends) can continue to grow indefinitely, assuming that a firm's debt-to-equity ratio is unchanged and it doesn't issue any new equity. It can be derived from the relationship between the firm's retention rate and ROE as determined by the DuPont formula:

$$g = \left( \frac{\text{net income} - \text{dividends}}{\text{net income}} \right) \times \left( \frac{\text{net income}}{\text{sales}} \right) \times \left( \frac{\text{sales}}{\text{total assets}} \right) \times \left( \frac{\text{total assets}}{\text{stockholders' equity}} \right)$$

This has also been called the PRAT model, where SGR is a function of the profit margin (P), the retention rate (R), the asset turnover (A), and the degree of financial leverage (T). Use beginning-of-period balance sheet values unless otherwise instructed.

LOS 33.p
If the model price is lower than (higher than, equal to) the market price, the stock is considered overvalued (undervalued, fairly valued).

## CONCEPT CHECKERS

1.  JCI Incorporated pays an annual dividend of 5.00 Canadian dollars (C$). The company is expected to continue paying this dividend with no future growth in dividends. Investors require a 9% rate of return on this investment. The current risk-free rate is 4%. The current stock value of JCI Incorporated is *closest* to:
    A.  C$55.56.
    B.  C$100.00.
    C.  C$125.00.

2.  The current stock price of MCD is $89.00. The current dividend for MCD is $2.50, and dividends are expected to grow at a constant rate of 8%. The implied required return for MCD is *closest* to:
    A.  3%.
    B.  8%.
    C.  11%.

3.  An analyst has determined that the required rate of return for an equity investment in shares of Global Partners is 10.5%. If the risk-free rate is 6% and Global's beta is 1.2, the current equity risk premium is *closest* to:
    A.  3.75%.
    B.  4.50%.
    C.  9.75%.

4.  Restoration Software is a growth stock that has never paid a dividend. Free cash flow is forecasted to be negative for the next five years because of Restoration's aggressive expansion plans. Restoration has always received an unqualified opinion from its auditors and is generally considered to have high-quality earnings. Which of the following models is *most appropriate* to value Restoration?
    A.  Free cash flow to the firm model.
    B.  Free cash flow to equity model.
    C.  Residual income model.

5.  CFCRegs, Inc., just paid a dividend of $2.00 per share. The required return is 13%, and the stock is currently trading at $30.28 per share. The growth rate implied by the Gordon growth model is *closest* to:
    A.  4%.
    B.  6%.
    C.  8%.

6.  Aerosail Company exhibits the following fundamental characteristics:
    *   Profit margins are higher than the industry average but have fallen over the last four years from 45% to 32%.
    *   Free cash flow to equity is positive and has grown 18% in the last two years.
    *   Dividend payout has increased from 5% to 15% in the last three years.

    What phase of the life cycle is Aerosail *most likely* in, and which dividend discount model is *most appropriate* to value the company's common stock?

    | | Phase | Model |
    |---|---|---|
    | A. | Transition | Gordon growth |
    | B. | Transition | Multistage |
    | C. | Growth | Gordon growth |

7.  An analyst forecasts dividends over the next three years for Aerosail Company of $1.00, $2.00, and $2.50. He forecasts a terminal value in three years of $52.00. Aerosail is currently selling for $39.71. The implied required return based on the analyst forecast is *closest* to:
    A. 10.2%.
    B. 13.5%.
    C. 14.8%.

**Use the information below to answer Questions 8 through 12.**

Jamie Johnson, CFA, has been asked by her supervisor to evaluate the value of two stocks in the recreational vehicle industry, AAA Motorhomes (AAA) and Three Star Travelers (TST). Johnson compiled analyst information for the two companies in Table 1. The market is expected to earn 11% in the next period, and the risk-free rate is 4%. Johnson's supervisor has requested that Johnson focus on dividends in estimating the value of the two firms.

| TABLE 1 | AAA | TST |
|---|---|---|
| Current ROE | 0.30 | 0.22 |
| Current EPS | $2.50 | $4.60 |
| Retention Ratio | 0.40 | 0.30 |
| Beta | 1.2 | 0.9 |

| TABLE 2 | Risk Premiums | Factor Sensitivities AAA | TST |
|---|---|---|---|
| Confidence Risk | 0.048 | 0.63 | 0.42 |
| Time Horizon Risk | 0.031 | 0.47 | 0.39 |
| Inflation Risk | 0.045 | 0.70 | 0.51 |
| Business Cycle Risk | 0.038 | 0.98 | 0.91 |
| Market Timing Risk | −0.018 | 0.05 | 0.21 |

8.  The sustainable growth rates for each firm are *closest* to:

    | | AAA | TST |
    |---|---|---|
    | A. | 18.0% | 6.6% |
    | B. | 12.0% | 6.6% |
    | C. | 12.0% | 15.4% |

9.  Johnson decides to start by estimating the value of the two stocks using the constant growth dividend discount model and estimating the required rate of returns using the capital asset pricing model (CAPM). Both firms are expected to grow at their sustainable growth rates. The estimated values are *closest* to:

    | | AAA | TST |
    |---|---|---|
    | A. | $273.54 | $92.77 |
    | B. | $273.54 | $48.57 |
    | C. | $420.00 | $92.77 |

10. Johnson believes the estimate for TST using the constant dividend discount model (DDM) is appropriate. However, she believes that AAA is expected to grow at a higher rate of 20% for the next four years and then grow at a rate of 7% after that. Using the two-stage model, the current value of AAA is *closest* to:
    A.  $45.69.
    B.  $58.00.
    C.  $61.62.

11. After further consideration, Johnson feels the growth rates of AAA and TST are more likely to gradually decline over the next four years and therefore considers the H-model. She estimates TST growth will decline from current 15% to long-term 5% and AAA growth will decline from current 20% to long-term 7%. Johnson estimates the required rate of return for AAA and TST to be 15.3% and 12.6%, respectively. Johnson's estimated values of AAA and TST using the H-model are *closest* to:

    | | AAA | TST |
    |---|---|---|
    | A. | $15.35 | $52.96 |
    | B. | $24.04 | $35.58 |
    | C. | $24.04 | $52.96 |

12. Johnson's supervisor also requested a calculation of the justified leading P/E ratios for the two firms using the capital asset pricing model (CAPM) to estimate the required returns. Assuming a worst-case scenario where the earnings and dividends will grow only at the long-term growth rate for each firm, the justified leading P/E ratios are *closest* to:

    | | AAA | TST |
    |---|---|---|
    | A. | 11.11 | 12.87 |
    | B. | 11.11 | 13.21 |
    | C. | 11.89 | 13.21 |

# CHALLENGE PROBLEMS

13.  EBEE is expected to grow at a rate of 30% for the next five years. After that, competition is expected to lower EBEE's growth to a constant 7% indefinitely. The market risk premium is 6%, and the risk-free rate is 5%. EBEE's beta is 1.2, and the company just paid a dividend of $2.50. The current stock value of EBEE is *closest* to:
A.  $127.28.
B.  $154.57.
C.  $191.00.

14.  Beta Forever, Inc., manufactures and distributes a line of VCRs. The company has fallen on hard times and although it will pay a $4 dividend in the next period, it expects dividends to decline by 3% per year thereafter. If the discount rate for the company is 9%, the current value of one share of Beta's common stock is *closest* to:
A.  $33.33.
B.  $44.44.
C.  $66.67.

15.  Titan Industries is not expected to pay a dividend until ten years from now, at which time it is expected to pay a dividend of $1.25 and increase the dividend at a rate of 4% thereafter. If the required rate of return is 12%, the current value of Titan is *closest* to:
A.  $5.64.
B.  $12.78.
C.  $15.63.

16.  Viking Insurance forecasts earnings next year of $4.50 per share. Viking has a dividend payout ratio of 40%. The required return is 15%. Return on equity is 8.33%. The present value of growth opportunities and the value of the stock based on the Gordon growth model are *closest* to:

| | PVGO | Share value |
|---|---|---|
| A. | $ 4.00 | $34.00 |
| B. | –$21.00 | $ 9.00 |
| C. | –$12.00 | $18.00 |

**Use the following information to answer Questions 17 and 18.**

Sally Curten, CFA, has gathered the following information on Jameston Fiber Optics, Inc., (JFOI) and industry norms.

Selected Financial Data for JFOI (in millions)

| | | |
|---|---|---|
| Total sales: | $2,044 | (fiscal year 2007) |
| Total assets: | $1,875 | (FYE 2006) |
| Net income: | $322 | (fiscal year 2007) |
| Total debt: | $1,465 | (FYE 2006) |

| | | |
|---|---|---|
| Industry ratios: | Net profit margin | = 15.7% |
| | Total asset turnover | = 1.1 |
| | Return on equity | = 40.5% |

17. The return on equity for JFOI is *closest* to:
    A. 17.2%.
    B. 37.4%.
    C. 78.5%.

18. Using DuPont analysis, Curten determines that the *most influential* factor(s) that management used to increase the ROE for JFOI compared to the industry is (are):
    A. asset efficiency.
    B. profitability.
    C. leverage.

**Use the following information to answer Questions 19 and 20.**

Lisa Design pays a current annual dividend of €2.00 and is currently growing at a rate of 20%. This rate is expected to decline to 10% over four years and remain at that level indefinitely. The required rate of return for an investment in Lisa Design is 18%.

19. The current estimated value of Lisa Design using the H-model is *closest* to:
    A. €24.22.
    B. €29.78.
    C. €32.50.

20. Suppose instead that the 20% growth rate is expected to persist for four years and then decline immediately to 10%, at which level it will remain indefinitely. The current estimated value of Lisa Design is *closest* to:
    A. €31.99.
    B. €32.50.
    C. €37.78.

21.  Jill Smart is an analyst with Allenton Partners. Jill is reviewing the valuation of three companies (P, Q, and R) using the dividend discount model (DDM) and their corresponding current market prices.

The information below summarizes the findings:

|              | Stock | | |
|--------------|----|----|----|
|              | P  | Q  | R  |
| Market price | 35 | 40 | 38 |
| DDM price    | 40 | 35 | 38 |

Based on the above information, which statement best describes the market's valuation of P, Q, and R?
A.  P is overvalued, Q is undervalued, and R is fairly valued.
B.  P is undervalued, Q is fairly valued, and R is overvalued.
C.  P is undervalued, Q is overvalued, and R is fairly valued.

## ANSWERS – CONCEPT CHECKERS

1. **A** The value of a perpetuity (equal payments forever) is equal to annual cash flow divided by required return:

$$V = \frac{C\$5.00}{0.09} = C\$55.56$$

2. **C** The constant DDM can be used to solve for the required rate of return:

$$r = \frac{D_0 \times (1+g)}{P_0} + g = \frac{\$2.50 \times 1.08}{\$89} + 0.08 = 0.110 = 11.0\%$$

3. **A** We are reversing the usual use of the CAPM equation to solve for the equity premium applicable to the market or index, given the beta. Usually we assume a beta and an equity market premium and solve for a required rate of return.

$$r = r_{\text{risk free}} + \beta(\text{equity risk premium})$$

$$0.105 = 0.06 + 1.2(\text{equity risk premium})$$

equity risk premium = 0.0375 = 3.75%

4. **C** Residual income models are the best valuation method if the firm does not pay dividends, has negative free cash flow over the forecast horizon, and has transparent financial reporting and high earnings quality.

5. **B** Solve the following equation for *g*:

$$30.28 = \frac{2(1+g)}{0.13-g}$$

30.28(0.13 – g) = 2(1 + g)

3.9364 – 30.28g = 2 + 2g

1.9364 = 32.28g

g = 6%

6. **B** Based on its fundamentals, Aerosail is most appropriately categorized as being in the transition phase. Multistage models are most appropriate for firms in the transition phase.

7. **B** Solve for the internal rate of return of the expected cash flows.
   CF0 = –39.71
   C01 = 1.00
   C02 = 2.00
   C03 = 54.50 = 52.00 + 2.50
   CPT → IRR 13.5%

8. **B** Sustainable growth is equal to return on equity multiplied by retention ratio:

$$SGR(AAA) = 0.30 \times 0.40 = 0.120 = 12.0\%$$

$$SGR(TST) = 0.22 \times 0.30 = 0.066 = 6.6\%$$

9. **C** The required returns for the two companies based on the CAPM are calculated below.

AAA: r = 0.04 + 1.2(0.11 − 0.04) = 0.04 + 0.084 = 0.124

TST: r = 0.04 + 0.9(0.11 − 0.04) = 0.04 + 0.063 = 0.103

The current values of the two stocks using the constant DDM are calculated next.

Sustainable growth is equal to return on equity multiplied by retention ratio:

$$SGR(AAA) = 0.30 \times 0.40 = 0.120 = 12.0\%$$

$$SGR(TST) = 0.22 \times 0.30 = 0.066 = 6.6\%$$

Current dividend is current EPS multiplied by payout ratio:

$$D_0(AAA) = \$2.50 \times (1 - 0.4) = \$1.50$$

$$D_0(TST) = \$4.60 \times (1 - 0.3) = \$3.22$$

Value is calculated with the Gordon constant growth model:

$$P_0(AAA) = \frac{\$1.50 \times 1.12}{0.124 - 0.12} = \$420.00$$

$$P_0(TST) = \frac{\$3.22 \times 1.066}{0.103 - 0.066} = \$92.77$$

10. **A** AAA's stock price today can be calculated using the two-stage model. Start by finding the value of the dividends during the high growth period of five years.

$D_0$ = (current EPS)(1 − retention ratio) = \$2.50 × (1 − 0.40) = \$1.50

$D_1 = D_0(1 + g)^1 = \$1.50(1.2)^1 = \$1.800$

$D_2 = D_0(1 + g)^2 = \$1.50(1.2)^2 = \$2.160$

$D_3 = D_0(1 + g)^3 = \$1.50(1.2)^3 = \$2.592$

$D_4 = D_0(1 + g)^4 = \$1.50(1.2)^4 = \$3.110$

Next, find the value of the stock at the beginning of the constant growth period using the constant dividend discount model: $P_4 = \dfrac{D_5}{r - g}$

CAPM: r = 0.04 + (1.2 × 0.07) = 0.124

$$D_5 = D_4 \times (1+g) = \$3.11 \times 1.07 = \$3.3277$$

$$P_4 = \frac{D_5}{r-g} = \frac{\$3.3277}{0.124 - 0.07} = \$61.624$$

The easiest way to proceed is to use the NPV function in the financial calculator.

$CF_0 = 0$; $CF_1 = 1.8$; $CF_2 = 2.16$; $CF_3 = 2.592$; $CF_4 = 3.110 + 61.624 = 64.734$

$I = 12.4$; $NPV = 45.69$

The value of the firm today is $45.69 per share.

11. **C**   The estimated value of AAA using the H-model is calculated as follows:

$$V_0 = \frac{(\$1.50 \times 1.07) + \left[\$1.50 \times \frac{4}{2} \times (0.20 - 0.07)\right]}{0.153 - 0.07} = \$24.04$$

The estimated value of TST using the H-model is calculated as follows:

$$V_0 = \frac{(\$3.22 \times 1.05) + \left[\$3.22 \times \frac{4}{2} \times (0.15 - 0.05)\right]}{0.126 - 0.05} = \$52.96$$

12. **B**   The CAPM-required returns and the current dividends for both stocks are from the answer to Problem 10.

$$\text{Justified leading P/E (AAA)} = \frac{1-b}{r-g} = \frac{0.6}{0.124 - 0.07} = 11.11$$

$$\text{Justified leading P/E (TST)} = \frac{1-b}{r-g} = \frac{0.7}{0.103 - 0.05} = 13.21$$

# ANSWERS – CHALLENGE PROBLEMS

13. **A**   EBEE's stock price today can be calculated using the two-stage model. Start by finding the value of the dividends during the high-growth period of five years.

$D_1 = D_0(1+g)^1 = \$2.50(1.30)^1 = \$3.25$

$D_2 = D_0(1+g)^2 = \$2.50(1.30)^2 = \$4.225$

$D_3 = D_0(1+g)^3 = \$2.50(1.30)^3 = \$5.493$

$D_4 = D_0(1+g)^4 = \$2.50(1.30)^4 = \$7.140$

$D_5 = D_0(1+g)^5 = \$2.50(1.30)^5 = \$9.282$

(Alternatively, you could use your financial calculator to solve for the future value to find $D_1$, $D_2$, $D_3$, $D_4$, and $D_5$.)

Next find the value of the stock at the beginning of the constant growth period using the constant dividend discount model: $P_5 = \dfrac{D_6}{r - g}$

CAPM: $r = 0.05 + (1.2 \times 0.06) = 0.122$

$D_6 = D_5 \times (1 + g) = \$9.282 \times 1.07 = \$9.932$

$P_5 = \dfrac{D_6}{r - g} = \dfrac{\$9.932}{0.122 - 0.07} = \$191.00$

The easiest way to proceed is to use the NPV function on the financial calculator.

$CF_0 = 0$; $CF_1 = 3.25$; $CF_2 = 4.225$; $CF_3 = 5.493$; $CF_4 = 7.140$;
$CF_5 = 9.282 + 191.00 = 200.282$

$I = 12.2$; NPV = 127.28

The value of the firm today is $127.28 per share.

14. **A**  The growth rate is –3%. Therefore, stock value $= \dfrac{D_1}{r - g} = \dfrac{\$4.00}{0.09 - (-0.03)} = \$33.33$.

15. **A**  We calculate the value of the expected cash flows at nine years because the formula uses the value of the dividend of $t + 1$ and then discounts that value to the present at the required rate of return of 12%.

$V_9 = \dfrac{\$1.25}{0.12 - 0.04} = \$15.63$

$V_0 = \dfrac{\$15.63}{1.12^9} = \$5.64$

16. **C**  The PVGO must be less than zero because the ROE is less than the required return, but the firm is still retaining and reinvesting its cash flow. That means it is destroying value!

$D_1 = \$4.50 \times 0.40 = \$1.80$

$g = 0.0833 \times (1 - 0.4) = 0.05 = 5\%$

$V_0 = \dfrac{\$1.80}{0.15 - 0.05} = \$18.00$

$V_0 = \dfrac{E}{r} + PVGO$

$PVGO = V_0 - \dfrac{E}{r} = \$18.00 - \dfrac{\$4.50}{0.15} = \$18.00 - \$30.00 = -\$12.00$

17. **C**  $ROE = \dfrac{\$322}{\$1,875 - \$1,465} = 78.5\%$

18. C    The higher ROE for JFOI is largely due to higher leverage. Assets-to-equity for the industry is calculated as:

$0.405 = 0.1570 \times 1.1 \times (\text{assets/equity}) \Rightarrow (\text{assets/equity}) = 2.35$

The ratios for JFOI are calculated as:

$$(\text{NI/sales}) = \frac{\$322}{\$2,044} = 0.1575$$

$$(\text{sales/assets}) = \frac{\$2,044}{\$1,875} = 1.09$$

$$(\text{assets/equity}) = \frac{\$1,875}{\$1,875 - \$1,465} = \frac{\$1,875}{\$410} = 4.57$$

The comparison of DuPont equations for JFOI and the industry are shown below.

ROE = profitability × asset efficiency × leverage

ROE = NI/sales × sales/assets × assets/equity

Industry: $0.405 = 0.1570 \times 1.1 \times 2.35$

JFOI: $0.785 = 0.1575 \times 1.09 \times 4.57$

Therefore, the higher leverage resulted in a larger ROE for JFOI relative to the industry.

19. C    The H-model uses a half-life factor equal to one-half of the declining stage in years. This approach values the dividend growth at the long-term rate and adds an estimate for the additional value of the supernormal growth during the first stage.

$$V = \frac{\left[ €2.00 \times (1.10) \right] + \left[ €2.00 \times \left( \frac{4}{2} \right) \times (0.20 - 0.10) \right]}{(0.18 - 0.10)} = €32.50$$

20. C    Intuitively, we know that the two-stage model will generate a higher estimate of value than €32.50 because the higher growth rate of stage one is expected to last throughout the stage rather than declining as in the H-model. That means C is the only possible answer.

21. C    Stock P has model price higher than the market price and hence is undervalued by the market. Stock Q has model price lower than the market price and hence is overvalued. Stock R has model price equal to the market price and hence is fairly valued.

# FREE CASH FLOW VALUATION

## EXAM FOCUS

This topic review introduces the concept of free cash flow. The value of a firm's stock is calculated by forecasting free cash flow to the firm (FCFF) or free cash flow to equity (FCFE) and discounting these cash flows back to the present at the appropriate required rate of return. FCFF or FCFE are the appropriate models to use when (1) the firm doesn't pay dividends at all or pays out fewer dividends than dictated by its cash flow, (2) free cash flow tracks profitability, or (3) the analyst takes a corporate control perspective. Make sure you see the parallels between the free cash flow framework and the discounted dividend framework (i.e., the basic free cash flow model is analogous to the Gordon growth model). Memorize the formulas for FCFF and FCFE. This is a very important test topic, as many analysts prefer free cash flow models to dividend discount models.

## WARM-UP: FREE CASH FLOW

Forget about all the complicated financial statement relationships for a minute and simply picture the firm as a cash *processor*. Cash flows into the firm in the form of revenue as it sells its product, and cash flows out as it pays its cash operating expenses (e.g., salaries and taxes, but not interest expense, which is a financing and not an operating expense). The firm takes the cash that's left over and makes short-term net investments in working capital (e.g., inventory and receivables) and long-term investments in property, plant, and equipment (PP&E). The cash that remains is available to pay out to the firm's investors: bondholders and common shareholders (let's assume for the moment that the firm has not issued preferred stock). That pile of remaining cash is called **free cash flow to the firm** (FCFF) because it's *free* to pay out to the firm's investors (see Figure 1). The formal definition of FCFF is the cash available to all of the firm's investors, including stockholders and bondholders, after the firm buys and sells products, provides services, pays its cash operating expenses, and makes short- and long-term investments.

 *Professor's Note: Taxes paid are included in the definition of cash operating expenses for purposes of defining free cash flow, even though taxes aren't generally considered a part of operating income.*

What does the firm do with its FCFF? First, it takes care of its bondholders because common shareholders are paid after all creditors. So it makes interest payments to bondholders and borrows more money from them or pays some of it back. However, making interest payments to bondholders has one advantage for common shareholders: it reduces the tax bill.

The amount that's left after the firm has met all its obligations to its other investors is called **free cash flow to equity** (FCFE), as can be seen in Figure 1. However, the board of directors still has discretion over what to do with that money. It could pay it all out in dividends to its common shareholders, but it might decide to only pay out some of it and put the rest in the bank to save for next year. That way, if FCFE is low the next year, it won't have to cut the dividend payment. So FCFE is the cash available to common shareholders after funding capital requirements, working capital needs, and debt financing requirements.

 *Professor's Note: You need to know these general definitions. We will explore how these two cash flow measures are estimated using accounting data, and in the process we'll throw a lot of formulas at you. It's much easier to remember these formulas and repeat them on the exam if you have a conceptual understanding of what FCFF and FCFE represent. That way if, for example, you happen to forget the FCFE formula on exam day, you still have a chance to reconstruct it by thinking through what FCFE really is.*

**Figure 1: FCFF and FCFE**

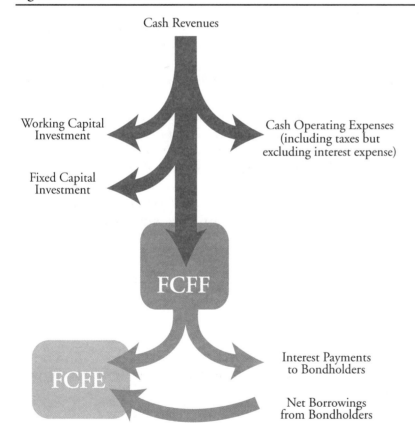

**LOS 34.a: Compare the free cash flow to the firm (FCFF) and free cash flow to equity (FCFE) approaches to valuation.**

*CFA® Program Curriculum, Volume 4, page 192*

We will use the typical discounted cash flow technique for free cash flow valuation, in which we estimate value today by discounting expected future cash flows at the appropriate required return. What makes this complicated is that we'll end up with two values we want to estimate (firm value and equity value), two cash flow definitions (FCFF and FCFE), and two required returns [weighted average cost of capital (WACC) and required return on equity]. The key to this question on the exam is knowing which *cash flows* to discount at which *rate* to estimate which *value*.

The value of the *firm* is the present value of the expected future *FCFF* discounted at the *WACC* (this is so important we're going to repeat it as a formula):

firm value = FCFF discounted at the WACC

The weighted average cost of capital is the required return on the firm's assets. It's a weighted average of the required return on common equity and the after-tax required return on debt. The formula is presented later in this topic review.

 *Professor's Note: Technically, what we've called firm value is actually the value of the operating assets (the assets that generate cash flow). Significant nonoperating assets, such as excess cash (not total cash on the balance sheet), excess marketable securities, or land held for investment should be added to this estimate to calculate total firm value. Most of the time, the value of these assets is small in relation to the present value of the FCFFs, so we don't lose much by ignoring it. If you are asked to calculate the value of the firm using the FCFF approach, calculate the present value of the FCFFs and then look for any additional information in the problem that specifically says "excess cash and marketable securities" or "land held for investment."*

The value of the firm's *equity* is the present value of the expected future *FCFE* discounted at the *required return on equity*:

equity value = FCFE discounted at the required return on equity

Given the value of the firm, we can also calculate equity value by simply subtracting out the market value of the debt:

equity value = firm value – market value of debt

Details of the calculations are discussed later in this topic review. However, this is an extremely important concept, so memorize it now.

*Professor's Note: A very common mistake is to use the wrong discount rate or the wrong cash flow definition. Remember, always discount FCFF at the WACC to find firm value and FCFE at the required return on equity to estimate equity value.*

The differences between FCFF and FCFE account for differences in capital structure and consequently reflect the perspectives of different capital suppliers. FCFE is easier and more straightforward to use in cases where the company's capital structure is not particularly volatile. On the other hand, if a company has negative FCFE and significant debt outstanding, FCFF is generally the best choice. We can always estimate equity value indirectly by discounting FCFF to find firm value and then subtracting out the market value of debt to arrive at equity value.

---

LOS 34.b: Explain the ownership perspective implicit in the FCFE approach.

*CFA® Program Curriculum, Volume 4, page 192*

The ownership perspective in the free cash flow approach is that of an acquirer who can change the firm's dividend policy, which is a control perspective, or for minority shareholders of a company that is *in-play* (i.e., it is a takeover target with potential bidders). The ownership perspective implicit in the dividend discount approach is that of a minority owner who has no direct control over the firm's dividend policy. If investors are willing to pay a premium for control of the firm, there may be a difference between the values of the same firm derived using the two models.

Analysts often prefer to use free cash flow rather than dividend-based valuation for the following reasons:

- Many firms pay no, or low, cash dividends.
- Dividends are paid at the discretion of the board of directors. It may, consequently, be poorly aligned with the firm's long-run profitability.
- If a company is viewed as an acquisition target, free cash flow is a more appropriate measure because the new owners will have discretion over its distribution (control perspective).
- Free cash flows may be more related to long-run profitability of the firm as compared to dividends.

---

LOS 34.c: Explain the appropriate adjustments to net income, earnings before interest and taxes (EBIT), earnings before interest, taxes, depreciation, and amortization (EBITDA), and cash flow from operations (CFO) to calculate FCFF and FCFE.

*CFA® Program Curriculum, Volume 4, page 197*

You may feel overwhelmed by the formulas in this topic review. We'll show you the ones you need to know for this LOS without showing you the derivations. The basic idea is that we can arrive at FCFF by starting with one of four different financial statement items (net income, EBIT, EBITDA, or cash flow from operations [CFO]) and then making the appropriate adjustments. Then we can calculate FCFE from FCFF or by starting with net income or CFO.

**Calculating FCFF from net income.** FCFF is calculated from net income as:

$$FCFF = NI + NCC + \left[ Int \times (1 - tax\ rate) \right] - FCInv - WCInv$$

where:
NI = net income
NCC = noncash charges
Int = interest expense
FCInv = fixed capital investment (capital expenditures)
WCInv = working capital investment

Notice that net income does not represent free cash flows defined as FCFF, so we have to make four important adjustments to net income to get to FCFF: noncash charges, fixed capital investment, working capital investment, and interest expense.

*Noncash charges.* Noncash charges are added back to net income to arrive at FCFF because they represent expenses that reduced reported net income but didn't actually result in an outflow of cash. The most significant noncash charge is usually depreciation. Here are some other examples of noncash charges that often appear on the cash flow statement:

- Amortization of intangibles should be added back to net income, much like depreciation.
- Provisions for restructuring charges and other noncash losses should be added back to net income. However, if the firm is accruing these costs to cover future cash outflows, then the forecast of future free cash flow should be reduced accordingly. Gains or losses on sale of long-term assets are also removed (they would be accounted for under fixed capital investment).
- Income from restructuring charge reversals and other noncash gains should be subtracted from net income.
- The amortization of a bond discount should be added back to net income, and the accretion of the bond premium should be subtracted from net income to calculate FCFF.
- Deferred taxes, which result from differences in the timing of reporting income and expenses for accounting versus tax purposes, must be carefully analyzed. Over time, differences between book and taxable income should offset each other and have no significant effect on overall cash flows. If, however, the analyst expects deferred tax liabilities to continue to increase (i.e., not reverse), increases in deferred tax liabilities should be added back to net income. Increases in deferred tax assets that are not expected to reverse should be subtracted from net income.

*Fixed capital investment.* Investments in fixed capital do not appear on the income statement, but they do represent cash leaving the firm. That means we have to subtract them from net income to estimate FCFF. Fixed capital investment is a net amount: it is equal to the difference between capital expenditures (investments in long-term fixed assets) and the proceeds from the sale of long-term assets:

FCInv = capital expenditures – proceeds from sales of long-term assets

Both capital expenditures and proceeds from long-term asset sales (if any) are likely to be reported on the firm's statement of cash flows. If no long-term assets were sold during the year, then capital expenditures will also equal the change in the gross PP&E account from the balance sheet.

So what is the Level II candidate supposed to do on exam day to calculate FCInv? Let's examine two cases: first, if no long-term assets were sold during the year, and second, if the company did sell long-term assets.

*If no long-term assets were sold during the year*, then FCInv is simply equal to the change in the gross PP&E account:

FCInv = capital expenditures = ending gross PP&E – beginning gross PP&E

or

FCInv = ending net PP&E – beginning net PP&E + depreciation

*If long-term assets were sold during the year*, then:

- Determine capital expenditures from either (1) an item in the statement of cash flows called something like "purchase of fixed assets" or "purchases of PP&E," or (2) data provided in the vignette.
- Determine proceeds from sales of fixed assets from either (1) an item in the statement of cash flows called something like "proceeds from disposal of fixed assets," or (2) data provided in the vignette.
- Calculate FCInv = capital expenditures – proceeds from sale of long-term assets.
- If capital expenditures or sales proceeds are not given directly, find gain (loss) on asset sales from the income statement and PP&E figures from balance sheet. Calculate FCInv = ending gross PP&E – beginning gross PP&E – gain on sale, or FCInv = ending net PP&E – beginning net PP&E + depreciation – gain on sale. If there is a loss on sale of assets, add that instead of deducting it.

---

**Example: Calculating FCInv with no long-term asset sales**

Airbrush, Inc. financial statements for 2009 include the following information:

**Selected Financial Data**

|  | 2009 | 2008 |
|---|---|---|
| Gross PP&E | $5,000 | $4,150 |
| Accumulated depreciation | $1,500 | $1,200 |
| Net PP&E | $3,500 | $2,950 |

There were no sales of PP&E during the year; depreciation expense was $300. Calculate Airbrush's FCInv for 2009.

**Answer:**

FCInv = capital expenditures = ending gross PP&E – beginning gross PP&E
= $5,000 – $4,150 = $850

---

**Example: Calculating FCInv with long-term asset sales**

Use the same information for Airbrush, Inc. as in the previous example, but now also suppose that the company reports capital expenditures of $1,400, long-term asset sales of $600, and depreciation expense of $850. The long-term assets sold were fully depreciated. Calculate Airbrush's revised FCInv for 2009.

**Answer:**

revised FCInv = capital expenditures – proceeds from sales of long-term assets
= $1,400 – $600 = $800

---

*Working capital investment.* The investment in net working capital is equal to the change in working capital, *excluding cash, cash equivalents, notes payable, and the current portion of long-term debt.* Note that there would be a + sign in front of a *reduction* in working capital; we would add it back because it represents a cash inflow.

*Interest expense.* Interest was expensed on the income statement, but it represents a financing cash flow to bondholders that is available to the firm *before* it makes any payments to its capital suppliers. Therefore, we have to add it back. However, we don't add back the entire interest expense, only the after-tax interest cost because paying interest reduces our tax bill. For example, if the marginal tax rate is 30%, every dollar of interest paid reduces the tax bill by 30 cents. The net effect on free cash flow is an increase in the after-tax interest cost of 70 cents.

Unfortunately, you have to memorize a number of free cash flow formulas to be fully prepared for the exam. However, we can use the statement of cash flows (as it is required to be reported under U.S. GAAP) as a framework to provide some intuition concerning the free cash flow formulas and perhaps make it a little easier to remember these formulas.

Given our conceptual discussion of FCFF and FCFE, it would make sense to define them as shown in the first column of Figure 2.

**Figure 2: Calculating FCFF and FCFE Using the Statement of Cash Flows**

| *Statement of Cash Flows* | *FCFF and FCFE* | |
|---|---|---|
| Net income (NI) <br> + Noncash charges (NCC) <br> <u>– WCInv</u> | Net income (NI) <br> + Noncash charges (NCC) <br> <u>– WCInv</u> | |
| Cash flow from operations (CFO) <br><br> <u>– FCInv</u> | Cash flow from operations (CFO) <br> + Int (1 – tax rate) <br> <u>– FCInv</u> | After-tax interest expense is classified as financing outflow rather than operating outflow |
| (Almost) FCFF <br> + Net borrowing | **(Actual) FCFF** <br> + Net borrowing <br> <u>– Int (1 – tax rate)</u> | |
| FCFE <br> – Dividends <br> <u>+/– Common stock issues (repurchases)</u> | **FCFE** <br> – Dividends <br> <u>+/– Common stock issues (repurchases)</u> | |
| Net change in cash | Net change in cash | |

Free cash flow to the firm is the operating cash flow left after the firm makes working capital and fixed capital investment. Therefore, we can get close to the actual calculation by using the first column in Figure 2:

$$\text{(Almost) FCFF} = (NI + NCC - WCInv) - FCInv$$
$$= CFO - FCInv$$

We're not quite there, however, because of one unique feature of the statement of cash flows: interest expense is considered an operating cash flow, whereas we'd like to call it a financing cash flow. Because interest is tax deductible, the after-tax interest expense [interest × (1 – tax rate)] reduces net income; but, we want to add it back to net income and then subtract it out as a financing cash outflow. By doing that, we go from our (almost) definition to the actual formula for FCFF (as shown in the second column in Figure 2):

$$\text{(Actual) FCFF} = (NI + NCC - WCInv) + Int(1 - \text{tax rate}) - FCInv$$
$$= CFO + Int(1 - \text{tax rate}) - FCInv$$

We can also use the second column format to calculate FCFE directly from FCFF:

$$FCFE = FCFF - Int(1 - \text{tax rate}) + \text{net borrowing}$$

Notice that any financial decisions that affect cash flows below FCFE (e.g., dividends, share repurchases, and share issues) do not affect FCFF or FCFE.

**Calculating FCFF from EBIT.** FCFF can also be calculated from earnings before interest and taxes (EBIT):

$$FCFF = \left[ EBIT \times (1 - tax\ rate) \right] + Dep - FCInv - WCInv$$

where:
EBIT = earnings before interest and taxes
Dep = depreciation

If we start with earnings before interest and taxes (EBIT), we have to add back depreciation because it was subtracted out to get to EBIT. However, because EBIT is before interest and taxes, we don't have to take out interest (remember that it's a financing cash flow). We do have to adjust for taxes, though, by computing after-tax EBIT, which is EBIT multiplied by one minus the tax rate. We also make the same adjustments as we did before by subtracting out fixed capital and working capital investment.

> *Professor's Note: Because many noncash adjustments occur on the income statement below EBIT, we don't need to adjust for them when calculating free cash flow if we start with EBIT. We assume that the only noncash charge that appears above EBIT is depreciation in the equation "FCFF from EBIT." In general, however, the rule is to adjust for any noncash charge that appears on the income statement above the income statement item with which you're starting.*

**Calculating FCFF from EBITDA.** We can also start with earnings before interest, taxes, depreciation, and amortization (EBITDA) to arrive at FCFF:

$$FCFF = \left[ EBITDA \times (1 - tax\ rate) \right] + (Dep \times tax\ rate) - FCInv - WCInv$$

where:
EBITDA = earnings before interest, taxes, depreciation, and amortization

Remember that EBITDA is before depreciation, so we only have to add back the depreciation tax shield, which is depreciation multiplied by the tax rate. Even though depreciation is a noncash expense, the firm reduces its tax bill by expensing it, so the free cash flow available is increased by the taxes saved.

**Calculating FCFF from CFO.** Finally, FCFF can also be estimated by starting with cash flow from operations (CFO) from the statement of cash flows:

$$FCFF = CFO + \left[ Int \times (1 - tax\ rate) \right] - FCInv$$

where:
CFO = cash flow from operations

Cash flow from operations is equal to net income plus noncash charges less working capital investment. We have to add back to CFO the after-tax interest expense to get to FCFF because interest expense (and the resulting tax shield) was reflected on the income statement to arrive at net income. We also have to subtract out fixed capital investment since CFO only includes changes in working capital investment.

 *Professor's Note: Which formula should you use on the exam? I suggest that, at a minimum, you memorize the first one (that starts with net income) and the last one (that starts with cash flow from operations). That way, given either an income statement or a cash flow statement, you can calculate FCFF. However, don't be surprised if you're required to know the other two as well.*

**Calculating FCFE from FCFF.** Calculating FCFE is easy once we have FCFF:

$$FCFE = FCFF - \left[ Int \times (1 - tax\ rate) \right] + net\ borrowing$$

where:
net borrowing = long- and short-term new debt issues –
                long- and short-term debt repayments

If we start with FCFF, we have to adjust for the two cash flows to bondholders to calculate FCFE: the after-tax interest expense and any new long- or short-term borrowings. We only subtract the after-tax interest expense because paying interest reduces the firm's tax bill and reduces the cash available to the shareholders by the interest paid minus the taxes saved.

**Calculating FCFE from net income.** We can also calculate FCFE from net income by making some of the usual adjustments. The two differences between this "FCFE from net income" formula and the "FCFF from net income formula" are (1) after-tax interest expense is not added back and (2) net borrowing is added back.

$$FCFE = NI + NCC - FCInv - WCInv + net\ borrowing$$

**Calculating FCFE from CFO.** Finally, we can calculate FCFE from CFO by subtracting out fixed capital investment (which reduces cash available to shareholders) and adding back net borrowing (which increases the cash available to shareholders).

$$FCFE = CFO - FCInv + net\ borrowing$$

## Free Cash Flow With Preferred Stock

The FCFF and FCFE formulas assume that the company uses only debt and common equity to raise funds. The use of preferred stock requires the analyst to revise the FCFF and FCFE formulas to reflect the payment of preferred dividends and any issuance or repurchase of such shares. *Remember to treat preferred stock just like debt, except preferred dividends are not tax deductible.*

Specifically, any preferred dividends should be added back to the FCFF, just as after-tax interest charges are in the net income approach to generating FCFF. This approach assumes that *net income* is net income to common shareholders after preferred dividends have been subtracted out. The WACC should also be revised to reflect the percent of total capital raised by preferred stock and the cost of that capital source. The only adjustment to FCFE would be to modify net borrowing to reflect new debt borrowing and net issuances by the amount of the preferred stock. Keep in mind that relatively few firms issue preferred stock.

 *Professor's Note: See Questions 6 through 10 in the Concept Checkers at the end of this topic review for specific examples in which we calculate free cash flow for a firm with preferred stock.*

---

LOS 34.d: Calculate FCFF and FCFE.

*CFA® Program Curriculum, Volume 4, page 197*

Let's try an example to see if all these formulas really work.

### Example: Calculating FCFF and FCFE

Anson Ford, CFA, is analyzing the financial statements of Sting's Delicatessen. He has a 2009 income statement and balance sheet, as well as 2010 income statement, balance sheet, and cash flow from operations forecasts (as shown in the tables below). Assume there will be no sales of long-term assets in 2010. Calculate forecasted free cash flow to the firm (FCFF) and free cash flow to equity (FCFE) for 2010.

**Sting's Income Statement**

| Income Statement | | |
| --- | --- | --- |
| | 2010 Forecast | 2009 Actual |
| Sales | $300 | $250 |
| Cost of goods sold | 120 | 100 |
| Gross profit | 180 | 150 |
| SG&A | 35 | 30 |
| Depreciation | 50 | 40 |
| EBIT | 95 | 80 |
| Interest expense | 15 | 10 |
| Pre-tax earnings | 80 | 70 |
| Taxes (at 30%) | 24 | 21 |
| Net income | $56 | $49 |

## Sting's Balance Sheet

| Balance Sheet | | |
| --- | --- | --- |
| | 2010 Forecast | 2009 Actual |
| Cash | $10 | $5 |
| Accounts receivable | 30 | 15 |
| Inventory | 40 | 30 |
| Current assets | $80 | $50 |
| Gross property, plant, and equipment | 400 | 300 |
| Accumulated depreciation | (190) | (140) |
| Total assets | $290 | $210 |
| | | |
| Accounts payable | $20 | $20 |
| Short-term debt | 20 | 10 |
| Current liabilities | $40 | $30 |
| Long-term debt | 114 | 100 |
| Common stock | 50 | 50 |
| Retained earnings | 86 | 30 |
| Total liabilities and owners' equity | $290 | $210 |

## Sting's Cash Flow From Operations Forecast

| Cash Flow From Operations Forecast for 2010 | |
| --- | --- |
| Net income | $56 |
| + depreciation | 50 |
| – WCInv | 25 |
| Cash flow from operations | $81 |

**Answer:**

Fixed capital investment is equal to capital expenditures (because there are no asset sales), which is equal to the change in gross PP&E:

$$\text{FCInv} = 400 - 300$$
$$= 100$$

Working capital investment is the change in the working capital accounts, excluding cash and short-term borrowings:

$$\text{WCInv} = (\text{AcctsRec}_{2010} + \text{Inv}_{2010} - \text{AcctsPay}_{2010}) -$$
$$(\text{AcctsRec}_{2009} + \text{Inv}_{2009} - \text{AcctsPay}_{2009})$$

$$\text{WCInv} = (30 + 40 - 20) - (15 + 30 - 20) = 50 - 25 = 25$$

Given that depreciation is the only noncash charge, we can calculate FCFF from net income:

$$\text{FCFF} = \text{NI} + \text{NCC} + [\text{Int} \times (1 - \text{tax rate})] - \text{FCInv} - \text{WCInv}$$
$$= 56 + 50 + [15 \times (1 - 0.3)] - 100 - 25 = -8.5$$
$$= 56 + 50 + 10.5 - 100 - 25 = -8.5$$

It's entirely possible that FCFF can be negative in the short term. We'll talk more later about how to value firms with negative FCFF.

Net borrowing is the difference between the long-term and short-term debt accounts:

$$\text{net borrowing} = (114 + 20) - (100 + 10) = 24$$

$$\text{FCFE} = \text{FCFF} - [\text{Int}(1 - \text{tax rate})] + \text{net borrowing}$$
$$= -8.5 - 10.5 + 24 = 5$$

**Example: Calculating FCFF and FCFE with the other formulas**

Calculate FCFF starting with EBIT, EBITDA, and CFO, and calculate FCFE starting with NI and CFO.

**Answer:**

$$\text{FCFF} = [\text{EBIT} \times (1 - \text{tax rate})] + \text{Dep} - \text{FCInv} - \text{WCInv}$$
$$= [95 \times (1 - 0.3)] + 50 - 100 - 25 = -8.5$$

$$\text{FCFF} = [\text{EBITDA} \times (1 - \text{tax rate})] + (\text{Dep} \times \text{tax rate}) - \text{FCInv} - \text{WCInv}$$
$$= [145 \times (1 - 0.3)] + (50 \times 0.3) - 100 - 25 = -8.5$$

$$\text{FCFF} = \text{CFO} + [\text{Int} \times (1 - \text{tax rate})] - \text{FCInv}$$
$$= 81 + [15 \times (1 - 0.3)] - 100 = -8.5$$

$$\text{FCFE} = \text{NI} + \text{Dep} - \text{FCInv} - \text{WCInv} + \text{net borrowing}$$
$$= 56 + 50 - 100 - 25 + 24 = 5$$

$$\text{FCFE} = \text{CFO} - \text{FCInv} + \text{net borrowing}$$
$$= 81 - 100 + 24 = 5$$

**Example: Calculating FCFF and FCFE using the statement of cash flows**

In order to see how all these formulas fit together, reconstruct the framework from Figure 2 using the actual numbers from the previous example.

**Answer:**

| | | |
|---|---|---|
| Net income | $56.0 | |
| + noncash charges | + 50.0 | |
| − WCInv | − 25.0 | |
| Cash flow from operations | | $81.0 |
| + Int (1 − tax rate) | + 10.5 | |
| − FCInv | − 100.0 | |
| **FCFF** | | −$8.5 |
| + net borrowing | + 24.0 | |
| − Int (1 − tax rate) | − 10.5 | |
| **FCFE** | | +$5.0 |

 *Professor's Note: For a more complicated problem that requires a calculation of FCFE with an unusual gain on the sale of equipment, see Challenge Problem 22.*

An analyst may also be concerned about the uses of cash flow. Typically, this is done to verify the FCFF calculation, as FCFF sources must always equal FCFF uses, and FCFE sources must always equal FCFE uses.

Uses FCFF =  changes in cash balances
                    + net payments to debt providers
                    + net payments to equity stakeholders

Uses FCFE =  changes in cash balances
                    + net payments to equity stakeholders

---

## LOS 34.e: Describe approaches for forecasting FCFF and FCFE.

*CFA® Program Curriculum, Volume 4, page 217*

Two approaches are commonly used to forecast future FCFF and FCFE.

The first method is to calculate *historical free cash flow* and apply a growth rate under the assumptions that growth will be constant and fundamental factors will be maintained. For example, we could calculate free cash flow in the most recent year and then forecast it to grow at 8% for four years and 4% forever after that. This is the same method we used for dividend discount models. Note that the growth rate for FCFF is usually different than the growth rate for FCFE.

The second method is to forecast the underlying *components of free cash flow* and calculate each year separately. This is a more realistic, more flexible, and more complicated method because we can assume that each component of free cash flow is growing at a different rate over some short-term horizon. This often ties sales forecasts to future capital expenditures, depreciation expenses, and changes in working capital. Importantly, capital expenditures have two dimensions: outlays that are needed to maintain *existing capacity* and marginal outlays that are needed to support *growth*. Thus, the first type of outlay is related to the current level of sales, and the second type depends on the predicted sales growth.

In forecasting FCFE with the second method, it is common to assume that the firm maintains a *target debt-to-asset ratio* for net new investment in fixed capital and working capital. For example, if the target debt ratio is 40% and fixed capital investment is $60 million, $24 million (0.40 multiplied by $60 million) is assumed to be financed with debt and $36 million with equity. Thus, net borrowing may be expressed without having to specifically forecast underlying debt issuance or repayment. This implies that we can forecast FCFE with the following formula:

$$FCFE = NI - [(1 - DR) \times (FCInv - Dep)] - [(1 - DR) \times WCInv]$$

where:
DR = target debt-to-asset ratio

## LOS 34.f: Compare the FCFE model and dividend discount models.

*CFA® Program Curriculum, Volume 4, page 221*

The free cash flow to equity approach takes a control perspective that assumes that recognition of value should be immediate. Dividend discount models take a minority perspective, under which value may not be realized until the dividend policy accurately reflects the firm's long-run profitability.

## LOS 34.g: Explain how dividends, share repurchases, share issues, and changes in leverage may affect future FCFF and FCFE.

*CFA® Program Curriculum, Volume 4, page 224*

This is a deceptively simple LOS. The short answer is that dividends, share repurchases, and share issues have *no effect* on FCFF and FCFE; changes in leverage have only a minor effect on FCFE and no effect on FCFF.

The reason is very straightforward. FCFF and FCFE represent cash flows available to investors and shareholders, respectively, before any financing decisions. Dividends, share repurchases, and share issues, on the other hand, represent *uses* of those cash flows; as such, these financing decisions don't affect the level of cash flow *available*. Changes in leverage will have a small effect on FCFE. For example, a decrease in leverage through a repayment of debt will decrease FCFE in the current year and increase forecasted FCFE in future years as interest expense is reduced.

## LOS 34.h: Evaluate the use of net income and EBITDA as proxies for cash flow in valuation.

*CFA® Program Curriculum, Volume 4, page 222*

*Net income is a poor proxy for FCFE.* We can see that by simply examining the formula for FCFE in terms of NI.

Once again, we have not burdened you with the derivation:

$$FCFE = NI + NCC - FCInv - WCInv + \text{net borrowing}$$

Net income includes noncash charges like depreciation that have to be added back to arrive at FCFE. In addition, it ignores cash flows that don't appear on the income statement, such as investments in working capital and fixed assets as well as net borrowings.

*EBITDA is a poor proxy for FCFF.* We can also see this from the formula relating FCFF to EBITDA (which you've already seen):

$$FCFF = [EBITDA \times (1 - \text{tax rate})] + (Dep \times \text{tax rate}) - FCInv - WCInv$$

EBITDA doesn't reflect the cash taxes paid by the firm, and it ignores the cash flow effects of the investments in working capital and fixed capital.

---

LOS 34.i: Explain the single-stage (stable-growth), two-stage, and three-stage FCFF and FCFE models, and select and justify the appropriate model given a company's characteristics.

---

*CFA® Program Curriculum, Volume 4, page 226*

**Single-Stage FCFF Model**

The single-stage FCFF model is analogous to the Gordon growth model discussed in the previous topic review on dividend valuation models. The single-stage FCFF model is useful for stable firms in mature industries. The model assumes that (1) FCFF grows at a constant rate (*g*) forever, and (2) the growth rate is less than the weighted average cost of capital (WACC).

The formula should look familiar; it's the Gordon growth model with FCFF replacing dividends and WACC replacing required return on equity.

$$\text{value of the firm} = \frac{\text{FCFF}_1}{\text{WACC} - g} = \frac{\text{FCFF}_0 \times (1 + g)}{\text{WACC} - g}$$

where:
$\text{FCFF}_1$ = expected free cash flow to the firm in one year
$\text{FCFF}_0$ = starting level of FCFF
$g$ = constant expected growth rate in FCFF
$\text{WACC}$ = weighted average cost of capital

The WACC is the weighted average of the rates of return required by each of the capital suppliers (usually just equity and debt) where the weights are the proportions of the firm's total market value from each capital source:

$$\text{WACC} = \left( w_e \times r_e \right) + \left[ w_d \times r_d \times (1 - \text{tax rate}) \right]$$

where :
$$w_e = \frac{\text{market value of equity}}{\text{market value of equity} + \text{market value of debt}}$$

$$w_d = \frac{\text{market value of debt}}{\text{market value of equity} + \text{market value of debt}}$$

It is assumed that payments to stockholders are *not* tax deductible, and payments to debtholders are tax deductible. Thus, the after-tax cost of debt is the before-tax rate of return on debt multiplied by one minus the firm's marginal tax rate. WACC will change over time as the firm's capital structure changes. Therefore, analysts usually use target capital structure weights rather than actual weights. On the exam, use target weights if they are given in the problem; otherwise use actual market-value weights.

## Single-Stage FCFE Model

The single-stage constant-growth FCFE valuation model is analogous to the single-stage FCFF model, with FCFE instead of FCFF and required return on equity instead of WACC:

$$\text{value of equity} = \frac{\text{FCFE}_1}{r - g} = \frac{\text{FCFE}_0 \times (1 + g)}{r - g}$$

where:
$\text{FCFE}_1$ = expected free cash flow to equity in one year
$\text{FCFE}_0$ = starting level of FCFE
$g$ = constant expected growth rate in FCFE
$r$ = required return on equity

*Professor's Note: It's quite likely that a firm's growth rate in FCFF will be different than its FCFE growth rate.*

The single-stage FCFE model is often used in international valuation, especially for companies in countries with high inflationary expectations when estimation of nominal growth rates and required returns is difficult. In those cases, real (i.e., inflation-adjusted) values are estimated for the inputs to the single-stage FCFE model: FCFE, the growth rate, and the required return.

## Multistage Models: How Many Variations Are There?

This is where things get a little complicated. If we analyze every possible permutation of multistage free cash flow models that might appear on the exam, you would be overwhelmed. There are at least three important ways that these models can differ. Let's take them one at a time, but keep in mind the basic valuation principle at work here: *value is always estimated as the present value of the expected future cash flows discounted at the appropriate discount rate.*

*FCFF versus FCFE*: Remember that the value of the firm is the present value of the FCFF discounted at the WACC; the value of equity is the present value of the FCFE discounted at the required return on equity.

*Two-stage versus three-stage models*: We can model the future growth pattern in two stages or three. There are several variations of each approach depending on how we model growth within the stages.

*Forecasting growth in total free cash flow (FCFF or FCFE) versus forecasting the growth rates in the components of free cash flow*: The simple free cash flow model, in which we forecast total FCFE or FCFF, looks a lot like the multistage dividend discount models. The benefit of using free cash flow models, however, is when we refine our approach by forecasting the values and/or growth rates in the components of free cash flow over the first stage and then calculate free cash flow in each year using one of our formulas. There are even variations of this approach in which we start with earnings per share instead of sales.

## Model Assumptions and Firm Characteristics

The assumptions for the two- and three-stage free cash flow models are simply the assumptions we make about the projected pattern of growth in free cash flow. We would use a two-stage model for a firm with two stages of growth: a short-term supernormal growth phase and a long-term stable growth phase. For example, a firm with a valuable patent that expires in seven years might experience a high growth rate for seven years and then immediately drop to a long-term, lower growth rate beginning in the eighth year. We would use a three-stage model for a firm that we expect to have three distinct stages of growth (e.g., a growth phase, a mature phase, and a transition phase).

## Examples of Two-Stage Models

Let's discuss some examples of two-stage models. We're going to wait until the next LOS, however, to start doing the number crunching. For now, concentrate on the differences in the assumptions: FCFF versus FCFE, growth pattern in the first stage, and forecasting total free cash flow versus forecasting its components.

We could analyze a:

- Two-stage FCFF model in which FCFF is projected to grow at 20% for the first four years and then 4% every year thereafter.
- Two-stage FCFE model in which FCFE declines from 20% to 4% over four years and then stays at 4% forever.
- Two-stage FCFE model in which sales grow at 20% for four years, the net profit margin is constant at 8%, fixed capital investment is equal to 60% of the dollar increase in sales, working capital investment is equal to 25% of the dollar increase in sales, and the debt ratio is 50%. Given a starting value for sales, we have all we need to forecast FCFE for the first four years.

Remember that we also need a terminal value at the end of the first growth stage for each of these examples. The most common method for estimating terminal value is to apply a single-stage free cash flow model at the point in time when growth settles down to its long-run level. This is the same method we used in the last topic review with dividend discount models.

## Examples of Three-Stage Models

Three-stage models have all the complications of the two-stage models, with an additional growth stage to consider. Keep in mind, however, that what we're trying to do is forecast FCFF or FCFE over some interim period with three distinct stages of growth, estimate the terminal value, and then estimate the value of the firm or the value of the equity today as the present value of those cash flows discounted at the appropriate required return. For example, we could analyze a:

- Three-stage FCFE model in which FCFE grows at 30% for two years (stage 1), 15% for four years (stage 2), and then 5% forever (stage 3).
- Three-stage FCFF model in which FCFF grows at 25% for three years (stage 1), declines to 4% over next the five years (stage 2), then stays at 4% forever (stage 3).
- Three-stage FCFE model in which we forecast the components of FCFE over three different stages.

LOS 34.j: Estimate a company's value using the appropriate free cash flow model(s).

*CFA® Program Curriculum, Volume 4, page 226*

We've already discussed free cash flow models, so now let's get to the hard work: actually calculating value using these models. We won't go through every different possible example, but we will give you a range of examples that cover nearly every important concept.

## Single-Stage FCFF Model

The first example is a basic single-stage FCFF model where we first calculate WACC as the appropriate required return.

> **Example: Calculating firm value with a single-stage FCFF model**
>
> Knappa Valley Winery's (KVW) most recent FCFF is $5,000,000. KVW's target debt-to-equity ratio is 0.25. The market value of the firm's debt is $10,000,000, and KVW has 2,000,000 shares of common stock outstanding. The firm's tax rate is 40%, the shareholders require a return of 16% on their investment, the firm's before-tax cost of debt is 8%, and the expected long-term growth rate in FCFF is 5%. Calculate the value of the firm and the value per share of the equity.
>
> **Answer:**
>
> Note that the problem gives the FCFF in the most recent year ($FCFF_0$). Therefore, you need to increase $FCFF_0$ at the growth rate by one year (at the 5% rate) to get $FCFF_1$.
>
> Let's calculate the WACC. The target debt-to-equity ratio is 0.25. This implies that for every $1 of debt, there is $4 of equity, for total capital of $5. Since total assets equals total capital, it follows that the target debt-to-asset ratio is 1/5, or 20%, and the target equity-to-asset ratio is 4/5, or 80%. The WACC is:
>
> $$WACC = (0.8 \times 0.16) + [0.20 \times 0.08(1 - 0.40)] = 0.1376 = 13.76\%$$

We can now calculate the value of the firm as:

$$\text{value of firm} = \frac{\$5,000,000 \times 1.050}{0.1376 - 0.050} = \$59,931,507$$

Given that debt is worth $10,000,000, the implied total value of the equity is:

value of equity = $59,931,507 – $10,000,000 = $49,931,507

With 2,000,000 shares outstanding, the value of the equity per share is:

$$\frac{\$49,931,507}{2,000,000} = \$24.97$$

Notice that the actual debt-to-equity ratio (10,000,000 / 49,931,507 = 0.20) does not equal the target ratio of 0.25. There is nothing inconsistent in this example. WACC is usually calculated using target capital weights.

### Single-Stage FCFE Model

**Example: Calculating value with a single-stage FCFE model**

Ridgeway Construction has an FCFE of 2.50 Canadian dollars (C$) per share and is currently operating at a target debt-to-equity ratio of 0.4. The expected return on the market is 9%, the risk free rate is 4%, and Ridgeway has a beta of 1.5. The expected growth rate of FCFE is 4.5%. Calculate the value of Ridgeway stock.

**Answer:**

Begin by computing the required return on equity with the CAPM:

r = 0.04 + [1.50 × (0.09 – 0.04)] = 0.115 = 11.5%

Note that the problem gives FCFE in the most recent year ($FCFE_0$). The model calls for the FCFE *next* year, which is $FCFE_1$. Therefore, you need to multiply $FCFE_0$ by one plus the growth rate to get $FCFE_1$. The equity value per share is:

$$\text{equity value per share} = \frac{\text{C\$}2.50 \times 1.045}{0.115 - 0.045} = \text{C\$}37.32$$

*Professor's Note: In the first example, we calculated total value and then equity value per share by dividing total value by the number of shares. In the second example we were given FCFE per share, so we could calculate value per share directly. Read the questions on the exam carefully to make sure you use the correct approach given the information in the problem.*

## Two-Stage FCFF Model

The first two-stage example requires the FCFF model and a forecast of the components of FCFF during the high-growth stage.

### Example: Calculating value with a two-stage FCFF model

The Prentice Paint Company earned a net profit margin of 20% on revenues of $20 million this year. Fixed capital investment was $2 million, and depreciation was $3 million. Working capital investment equals 7.5% of sales every year. Net income, fixed capital investment, depreciation, interest expense, and sales are expected to grow at 10% per year for the next five years. After five years, the growth in sales, net income, fixed capital investment, depreciation, and interest expense will decline to a stable 5% per year. The tax rate is 40%, and Prentice has 1 million shares of common stock outstanding and long-term debt paying 12.5% interest trading at its par value of $32 million. Calculate the value of the firm and its equity using the FCFF model if the WACC is 17% during the high-growth stage and 15% during the stable stage.

### Answer:

The components of FCFF are calculated in the following table.

### FCFF for Years 0 Through 6 (in per-share amounts of $)

|  | 0 | 1 | 2 | 3 | 4 | 5 | 6 |
|---|---|---|---|---|---|---|---|
| Sales ($) | 20.00 | 22.00 | 24.20 | 26.62 | 29.28 | 32.21 | 33.82 |
| Net Income | 4.00 | 4.40 | 4.84 | 5.32 | 5.86 | 6.44 | 6.76 |
| Interest (1 – T) | 2.40 | 2.64 | 2.90 | 3.19 | 3.51 | 3.87 | 4.06 |
| Depreciation | 3.00 | 3.30 | 3.63 | 3.99 | 4.39 | 4.83 | 5.07 |
| FCInv | 2.00 | 2.20 | 2.42 | 2.66 | 2.93 | 3.22 | 3.38 |
| WCInv | 1.50 | 1.65 | 1.82 | 2.00 | 2.20 | 2.42 | 2.54 |
| FCFF | $5.90 | $6.49 | $7.13 | $7.84 | $8.63 | $9.50 | $9.97 |

Let's demonstrate the calculation of the FCFF in Year 0:

| | |
|---|---|
| net income | $= \$20.00 \times 0.20 = \$4.00$ |
| interest | $= \$32.00 \times 0.125 = \$4.00$ |
| interest(1 – T) | $= \$4.00 \times (1 - 0.40) = \$2.40$ |
| WCInv | $= \$20.00 \times 0.075 = \$1.50$ |
| FCFF | $= \$4.00 + \$2.40 + \$3.00 - \$2.00 - \$1.50 = \$5.90$ |

In Year 1, sales grow by 10% to $22.00 per share. Following five years of 10% growth, the growth of each component falls to 5%.

The terminal value (as of Year 5, discounted at the stable WACC of 15%) is:

$$\text{terminal value} = \frac{FCFF_6}{WACC - g} = \frac{\$9.97}{0.15 - 0.05} = \$99.70$$

We can place the cash flows to be evaluated on a time line, such as the one in the following figure, to get a clearer picture of what we need to evaluate.

**FCFF Timeline**

Notice that the WACC in the high-growth stage (17%) is different than the stable stage (15%).

We calculated terminal value in Year 5 using 15%, but we'll calculate the present value today of the high-growth cash flows and the terminal value at 17%. The total of the firm today is:

$$\text{value of firm} = \frac{\$6.49}{1.17^1} + \frac{\$7.13}{1.17^2} + \frac{\$7.84}{1.17^3} + \frac{\$8.63}{1.17^4} + \frac{\$109.20}{1.17^5} = \$70.06$$

Since, in all likelihood, we would want to use our financial calculators to perform this calculation more quickly and accurately, the appropriate keystrokes are:

$CF_0 = 0$; $C01 = 6.49$; $C02 = 7.13$; $C03 = 7.84$; $C04 = 8.63$; $C05 = 109.20$
$I = 17$; $CPT \rightarrow NPV = 70.06$

Thus, given that the value of the firm's debt is $32 per share, the value of equity per share is $70.06 − $32.00 = $38.06.

It is uncommon for growth rates to drop as drastically and quickly from stage 1 to stage 2 as shown in the previous example. It is more likely to find a gradual decline in the growth rate as a company matures and attracts more competition that will decrease its profit margin and its sustainable growth rate. This next two-stage example is an FCFE model with declining growth rates in stage 1 and constant growth in stage 2.

Study Session 12

**Example: Two-stage FCFE model with declining growth in stage 1**

Consider a rival to the Prentice Paint Company presented in the previous example. Assume that Sioux Falls Decor also has revenues of $20 million this year. However, we assume that its future performance will be tracked relative to sales as follows:

- Sales growth and the net profit margin are projected by year as shown in the following table:

**Sales and Net Margin Forecasts**

| Year | 1 | 2 | 3 | 4 | 5 | 6 |
|---|---|---|---|---|---|---|
| Sales growth | 30% | 25% | 20% | 15% | 10% | 5% |
| Net profit margin | 8.0% | 7.5% | 7.0% | 6.0% | 5.5% | 5.0% |

- Fixed capital investment *net of depreciation* is projected to be 30% of the sales increase in each year.
- Working capital requirements are 7.0% of the projected dollar increase sales in each year.
- Debt will finance 40% of the investments in net capital and working capital.
- The company has a 12% required rate of return on equity.
- The firm has 1 million shares of common stock outstanding.

Calculate the value of the equity of Sioux Falls using the two-stage FCFE model.

**Answer:**

Recognize that the target debt-to-asset ratio (DR) is 0.40. The following table shows the FCFE for years 1 through 6 ($ amounts are per share).

**Calculating FCFE for Years 1 Through 6:**

| Year | 1 | 2 | 3 | 4 | 5 | 6 |
|---|---|---|---|---|---|---|
| Sales growth | 30% | 25% | 20% | 15% | 10% | 5% |
| Net profit margin | 8.0% | 7.5% | 7.0% | 6.0% | 5.5% | 5.0% |
| Sales | $26.00 | $32.50 | $39.00 | $44.85 | $49.335 | $51.802 |
| Net income | 2.08 | 2.44 | 2.73 | 2.691 | 2.71 | 2.59 |
| FCInv – Dep | 1.80 | 1.95 | 1.95 | 1.755 | 1.346 | 0.74 |
| WCInv | 0.42 | 0.455 | 0.455 | 0.4095 | 0.314 | 0.171 |
| Debt financing | 0.888 | 0.962 | 0.962 | 0.864 | 0.664 | 0.364 |
| FCFE | $0.748 | $0.997 | $1.287 | $1.391 | $1.714 | $2.043 |

Let's demonstrate the calculation of the cash flow components in Year 1:

$$\text{sales} = \$20.00 \times 1.30 = \$26.00$$

$$\text{net income} = \$26.00 \times 0.08 = \$2.08$$

$$\text{net FCInv} = (\$26.00 - \$20.00) \times 0.30 = \$1.80$$

$$\text{WCInv} = (\$26.00 - \$20.00) \times 0.07 = \$0.42$$

$$\text{FCFE} = NI - \big[(1 - DR) \times (FCInv - Dep)\big] - \big[(1 - DR) \times WCInv\big]$$
$$= \$2.08 - \big[(1 - 0.4) \times \$1.80\big] - \big[(1 - 0.4) \times \$0.42\big] = \$0.748$$

Terminal value (as of Year 5, assuming 5% stable long-term growth) is equal to:

$$\text{terminal value} = \frac{\$2.043}{0.12 - 0.05} = \$29.186$$

Total current value of equity:

$$\text{value of equity} = \frac{\$0.748}{1.12^1} + \frac{\$0.997}{1.12^2} + \frac{\$1.287}{1.12^3} + \frac{\$1.391}{1.12^4} + \frac{\$1.714 + \$29.186}{1.12^5} = \$20.80$$

As usual, we would rely on the cash flow keys of our financial calculator to perform the above calculation:

$CF_0 = 0$; $C01 = 0.748$; $C02 = 0.997$; $C03 = 1.287$; $C04 = 1.391$; $C05 = 30.90$

$I = 12$; $CPT \rightarrow NPV = 20.80$

### Three-Stage FCFE Model

The following example of a three-stage FCFE model is a little different than the last two examples because we're given growth in total FCFE in each of three stages, rather than the growth rates in the components. Growth in the first and third stage is constant, while growth in the second stage is declining. There is one tricky feature to this problem—the required return in each of the three growth stages is different.

**Example: Three-stage FCFE model with forecast growth in total FCFE**

Medina Classic Furniture, Inc. is expected to experience growth in three distinct stages in the future. Its most recent FCFE is 0.90 Canadian dollars (C$) per share. The following information has been compiled:

*High-growth period:*

- Duration = 3 years.
- FCFE growth rate = 30%.
- Shareholders' required return = 20%.

*Transitional period:*

- Duration = 3 years.
- FCFE growth will decline by 9% per year down to the indicated stable growth rate.
- Shareholders' required return = 15%.

*Stable-growth period:*

- FCFE growth rate = 3%.
- Shareholders' required return = 10%.

Calculate the value of the firm's equity using the three-stage FCFE model.

**Answer:**

The annual FCFE and the associated present value are presented in the table:

**FCFE and PV**

| High-Growth Period | Year 1 | Year 2 | Year 3 |
|---|---|---|---|
| Growth rate | 30% | 30% | 30% |
| FCFE | C$1.170 | C$1.521 | C$1.977 |
| PV (@ 20%) | C$0.975 | C$1.056 | C$1.144 |

| Transitional Period | Year 4 | Year 5 | Year 6 |
|---|---|---|---|
| Growth rate | 21% | 12% | 3% |
| FCFE | C$2.393 | C$2.680 | C$2.760 |
| PV | C$1.204 | C$1.173 | C$1.050 |

The transitional present values are computed using a combination of the 20% initial discount rate and the transitional 15% rate. For example, the present value of $FCFE_5$ is computed as:

$$C\$1.173 = \frac{C\$2.680}{1.20^3 \times 1.15^2}$$

We can calculate the terminal value of the stock as of Year 6 using the FCFE projected for Year 7. Notice that we use the stage 3 required return of 10%.

$$\text{terminal value} = \frac{\$2.760 \times 1.03}{0.10 - 0.03} = \$40.611$$

The value of Medina stock is:

$$\text{value per share} = 0.975 + 1.056 + 1.144 + 1.204 + 1.173 + 1.050 + \left( \frac{40.611}{1.20^3 \times 1.15^3} \right)$$

$$= C\$22.055$$

The changing discount rates were important here for a couple of reasons. First, the terminal value in Year 6 had to be discounted for three years at 20% and for three years at 15%. Second, due to the changing discount rates, our financial calculator was not as helpful as it was in other multiple cash flow calculations. It simply cannot handle the changing discount rates in one easy set of calculations.

---

LOS 34.k: Explain the use of sensitivity analysis in FCFF and FCFE valuations.

---

*CFA® Program Curriculum, Volume 4, page 228*

**Sensitivity analysis** shows how sensitive an analyst's valuation results are to changes in each of a model's inputs. Some variables have a greater impact on valuation results than others. The importance of various forecasting errors can be assessed through comprehensive sensitivity analysis.

*Professor's Note: On the exam, you are unlikely to be asked to conduct a comprehensive sensitivity analysis that includes numerous calculations. However, a few key calculations and/or an interpretation of a sensitivity analysis are quite possible.*

There are two major sources of error in valuation analysis:

- Estimating the future *growth* in FCFF and FCFE. Growth forecasts depend on a firm's future profitability, which in turn depends on sales growth, changes in profit margin, position in the life cycle, its competitive strategy, and the overall profitability of the industry.

- The chosen *base years* for the FCFF or FCFE growth forecasts. A representative base year must be chosen, or all of the subsequent analysis and valuation will be flawed.

For example, suppose an analyst is conducting a sensitivity analysis on the value of a beverage stock using the FCFE approach. She provides high and low estimates of the following variables consistent with their forecasted ranges in her model: FCFE, beta, risk-free rate of return, equity risk premium, and the FCFE growth rate. This produces a series of value estimates that reveal the sensitivity of her valuation estimate to variations in her underlying inputs.

LOS 34.l: Describe approaches for calculating the terminal value in a multistage valuation model.

*CFA® Program Curriculum, Volume 4, page 230*

There are two basic approaches for calculating terminal value: using a single-stage model or a multiple approach. All of our examples used the first approach, in which we forecasted an FCFF or FCFE at the point in time at which cash flows begin to grow at the long-term, stable growth rate, and then we estimated terminal value using a single-stage model.

The other way to do this is to use valuation multiples (like P/E ratios) to estimate terminal value. The terminal value in year *n* in terms of P/E, for example, would be expressed as:

terminal value in year n = (trailing P/E) × (earnings in year n)
terminal value in year n = (leading P/E) × (forecasted earnings in year n+1)

---

**Example: Estimating terminal value with a P/E multiple**

An analyst estimates the EPS of Polar Technology in five years to be $2.10, the EPS in six years to be $2.32, and the median trailing industry P/E to be 35. Calculate the terminal value in Year 5.

**Answer:**

terminal value in Year 5 = Year 35 × $2.10 = $73.50

---

LOS 34.m: Evaluate whether a stock is overvalued, fairly valued, or undervalued based on a free cash flow valuation model.

*CFA® Program Curriculum, Volume 4, page 230*

If a stock is trading at a price (market price) higher than the price implied by a free cash flow valuation model (model price), the stock is considered to be **overvalued**. Similarly, if the market price is lower than the model price, the stock is considered to be **undervalued**, and if the model price is equal to the market price, the stock is considered to be **fairly valued**.

# KEY CONCEPTS

## LOS 34.a

FCFF is the cash available to all of the firm's investors, including stockholders and bondholders, after the firm buys and sells products, provides services, pays its cash operating expenses, and makes short- and long-term investments. FCFE is the cash available to common shareholders after funding capital requirements, working capital needs, and debt financing requirements.

The value of the firm is the present value of the expected future FCFF discounted at the WACC. The value of the firm's equity is the present value of the expected future FCFE discounted at the required return on equity.

FCFE is easier and more straightforward to use in cases where the company's capital structure is not particularly volatile. On the other hand, if a company has negative FCFE and significant debt outstanding, FCFF is generally the best choice.

## LOS 34.b

Analysts prefer to use either FCFF or FCFE as a measure of value if:
- The firm does not pay dividends.
- The firm pays dividends, but the dividends do not reflect the company's long-run profitability.
- The analyst takes a control perspective.

Thus, in valuation, the use of free cash flows reflects a control perspective while the use of dividends reflects a minority common stockholder's perspective. The ownership perspective in the free cash flow approach is that of an acquirer who can change the firm's dividend policy, which is a control perspective.

## LOS 34.c,d

FCFF and FCFE may be calculated starting either from net income, cash flows from operations, EBIT, or EBITDA. You need to know how to calculate the following measures using financial data:

$$FCFF = NI + NCC + \left[ Int \times (1 - tax\ rate) \right] - FCInv - WCInv$$

$$FCFF = \left[ EBIT \times (1 - tax\ rate) \right] + Dep - FCInv - WCInv$$

$$FCFF = \left[ EBITDA \times (1 - tax\ rate) \right] + (Dep \times tax\ rate) - FCInv - WCInv$$

$$FCFF = CFO + \left[ Int \times (1 - tax\ rate) \right] - FCInv$$

$$FCFE = FCFF - \left[ Int \times (1 - tax\ rate) \right] + net\ borrowing$$

$$FCFE = NI + NCC - FCInv - WCInv + net\ borrowing$$

$$FCFE = CFO - FCInv + net\ borrowing$$

**LOS 34.e**
For forecasting FCFE, use:

$$\text{FCFE} = \text{NI} - \big[(1-\text{DR}) \times (\text{FCInv} - \text{Dep})\big] - \big[(1-\text{DR}) \times \text{WCInv}\big]$$

**LOS 34.f**
The free cash flow to equity approach takes a control perspective, which assumes that recognition of value should be immediate. Dividend discount models take a minority perspective, under which value may not be realized until the dividend policy accurately reflects the firm's long-run profitability.

**LOS 34.g**
Dividends, share repurchases, and share issues have no effect on FCFF and FCFE; changes in leverage have only a minor effect on FCFE and no effect on FCFF.

**LOS 34.h**
**Net income is a poor proxy for FCFE.** Net income includes noncash charges (e.g., depreciation) that have to be added back to arrive at FCFE. In addition, it ignores cash flows that don't appear on the income statement, such as investments in working capital and fixed assets as well as net borrowings. This can be seen by simply examining the formula for FCFE in terms of NI:

$$\text{FCFE} = \text{NI} + \text{NCC} - \text{FCInv} - \text{WCInv} + \text{net borrowing}$$

**EBITDA is a poor proxy for FCFF.** The following equation makes this point clear:

$$\text{FCFF} = \text{EBITDA}(1 - \text{tax rate}) + (\text{Dep} \times \text{tax rate}) - \text{FCInv} - \text{WCInv}$$

EBITDA doesn't reflect the cash taxes paid by the firm, and it ignores the cash flow effects of the investments in working capital and fixed capital.

**LOS 34.i,j**
The single-stage free cash flow models are useful for stable firms in mature industries. The models assume free cash flows grow at a constant rate, $g$, forever and that the growth rate is less than the required return (WACC for FCFF models and required return on equity for FCFE models).

$$\text{value of the firm} = \frac{\text{FCFF}_1}{\text{WACC} - g}$$

$$\text{value of equity} = \frac{\text{FCFE}_1}{r - g}$$

The assumptions for the two- and three-stage free cash flow models are simply the assumptions we make about the projected pattern of growth in free cash flow. We'd use a two-stage model for a firm with two stages of growth: a short-term supernormal growth phase and a long-term stable growth phase. We'd use a three-stage model for a firm that we expect to have three distinct stages of growth (e.g., a growth phase, a mature phase, and a transition phase).

### LOS 34.k

Sensitivity analysis shows how sensitive an analyst's valuation results are to changes in each of a model's inputs. Some variables have a greater impact on valuation results than others. The importance of various forecasting errors can be assessed through comprehensive sensitivity analysis.

### LOS 34.l

There are two basic approaches for calculating terminal value: using a single-stage model or a multiple approach. The multiple approach uses valuation multiples (like P/E ratios) to estimate terminal value.

### LOS 34.m

If a stock's model price is lower than (higher than, equal to) the market price, the stock is considered overvalued (undervalued, fairly valued) by the market.

# CONCEPT CHECKERS

1.  The Gray Furniture Co. earned £3.50 per share last year. Investment in fixed capital was £2.00 per share, depreciation was £1.60, and the investment in working capital was £0.50 per share. Gray is currently operating at its target debt-to-asset ratio of 40%. Thus, 40% of annual investments in working capital and fixed capital will be financed with new borrowings. Shareholders require a return of 14% on their investment, and the expected growth rate is 4%. The value of Gray's stock is *closest* to:
    A.  £27.04.
    B.  £29.90.
    C.  £30.78.

2.  The Anderson Door Co. earned C$30 million before interest and taxes on revenues of C$80 million last year. Capital expenditures were C$20 million, and depreciation was C$15 million. The additions to working capital were C$6 million. The firm's weighted average cost of capital is 12.45%, the marginal tax rate is 40%, and the expected cash flow growth is 5%. The market value of debt is C$25 million. The value of the firm's equity is *closest* to:
    A.  C$73.70.
    B.  C$93.96.
    C.  C$98.70.

**Use the following information to answer Questions 3 through 5.**

The Sanford Software Co. earned $20 million before interest and taxes on revenues of $60 million last year. Investment in fixed capital was $12 million, and depreciation was $8 million. Working capital investment was $3 million. Sanford expects earnings before interest and taxes (EBIT), investment in fixed and working capital, depreciation, and sales to grow at 12% per year for the next five years. After five years, the growth in sales, EBIT, and working capital investment will decline to a stable 4% per year, and investments in fixed capital and depreciation will offset each other. Sanford's tax rate is 40%. Assume the weighted average cost of capital (WACC) is 11% during the high growth stage and 8% during the stable stage. The calculation of FCFF in years 1 through 5 is shown in the following table:

| Year | 0 | 1 | 2 | 3 | 4 | 5 |
|------|-------|-------|-------|-------|-------|--------|
| Sales | 60.00 | 67.20 | 75.26 | 84.30 | 94.41 | 105.74 |
| EBIT | 20.00 | 22.40 | 25.09 | 28.10 | 31.47 | 35.25 |
| EBIT(1 − T) | 12.00 | 13.44 | 15.05 | 16.86 | 18.88 | 21.15 |
| Dep | 8.00 | 8.96 | 10.04 | 11.24 | 12.59 | 14.10 |
| FCInv | 12.00 | 13.44 | 15.05 | 16.86 | 18.88 | 21.15 |
| WCInv | 3.00 | 3.36 | 3.76 | 4.21 | 4.72 | 5.29 |
| FCFF | 5.00 | 5.60 | 6.28 | 7.03 | 7.87 | 8.81 |

3.      Free cash flow to the firm (FCFF) in Year 6 is *closest* to:
        A.  $14.14.
        B.  $16.49.
        C.  $18.26.

4.      The terminal value in Year 5 is *closest* to:
        A.  $206.12.
        B.  $220.25.
        C.  $412.25.

5.      The value of the firm using a FCFF model is *closest* to:
        A.  $149.04.
        B.  $265.17.
        C.  $270.35.

**Use the following information to answer Questions 6 through 10.**

An analyst following Barlow Energy has compiled the following information in preparation for additional analysis she has to include in a report she has been asked to produce (data is in hundreds of millions of $):

| Security Type | Market Value | Before-Tax Required Return |
|---|---|---|
| Preferred stock | $200 | 7.0% |
| Bonds | $600 | 7.5% |
| Common stock | $700 | 14.0% |
| Total | $1,500 | |

- Bonds are trading at par.
- Preferred share dividends:        $14
- Net income available to common:   $125
- Investment in working capital:    $30
- Investment in fixed capital:      $100
- Net new borrowing:                $40
- Depreciation:                     $50
- Tax rate:                         40%
- Long-term growth rate of FCFF:    4%
- Long-term growth rate of FCFE:    4%
- WACC:                             9.27%

6.      The current FCFF for Barlow Energy is *closest* to:
        A.  $36.
        B.  $62.
        C.  $86.

7.  The total value of Barlow Energy using a single-stage FCFF model is *closest* to:
    A. $894.40.
    B. $1,631.88.
    C. $1,697.15.

8.  The value of Barlow Energy's equity using a single-stage FCFF model is *closest* to:
    A. $897.15.
    B. $1,097.15.
    C. $1,497.15.

9.  The current FCFE using the information for Barlow Energy is *closest* to:
    A. $45.
    B. $85.
    C. $99.

10. The value of Barlow Energy's equity using a single-stage model and the current FCFE is *closest* to:
    A. $468.
    B. $850.
    C. $884.

11. Which of the following is the *best* estimate of the cash flows available to the firm's investors before any financing decisions?
    A. EBITDA × (1 – tax rate).
    B. EBITDA × (1 – tax rate) + (Dep × tax rate) – FCInv – WCInv.
    C. EBITDA × (1 – tax rate) + (Dep × tax rate) – FCInv – WCInv + Int × (1 – tax rate).

12. The adjustments to cash flow from operations necessary to obtain free cash flow to the firm (FCFF) are:
    A. add noncash charges, subtract fixed capital investment, and subtract working capital investment.
    B. add after-tax interest expense and subtract fixed capital investment.
    C. add net borrowing and subtract fixed capital investment.

**Use the following information to answer Questions 13 and 14.**

Rachel Keimmel, CFA, is researching the MWC Corporation, a U.S.-based automobile parts manufacturing firm. MWC has recently entered into a long-term agreement with a German automobile company to be the sole supplier of an innovative suspension system that will be used with a newly designed, moderately priced sports car. Keimmel believes that this new agreement will favorably impact MWC's stock price. To support her belief, Keimmel reviewed MWC's financial statements and sales forecasts and reached the following conclusions:

- MWC's earnings and FCFE growth will be 15% per year for two years, then stabilize at 8% per year.
- MWC will maintain its current dividend payout ratio.
- MWC has a beta of 1.2.
- Government bonds yield 6.4%, and the market equity risk premium is 5.5%.
- The most recent dividend paid to MWC shareholders was $2.30.

Keimmel also has MWC's current cash flow statement, which follows.

**MWC Incorporated**
**Statement of Cash Flows, December 31, 2007**
**($ Thousands)**

| | | |
|---|---:|---:|
| **Cash Flow from Operating Activities** | | |
| Net income | | 29,960 |
| Depreciation | | 8,400 |
| **Changes in Working Capital** | | |
| (Increase) Decrease in receivables | (4,000) | |
| (Increase) Decrease in inventories | (6,400) | |
| Increase (Decrease) in payables | 4,800 | |
| Increase (Decrease) in other current liabilities | 1,200 | |
| Net change in working capital | | (4,400) |
| Net cash from operating activities | | 33,960 |
| | | |
| **Cash Flow from Investing Activities** | | |
| | | |
| Purchase of fixed assets (PP&E) | (12,000) | |
| Net cash from investing activities | | (12,000) |
| | | |
| **Cash Flow from Financing Activities** | | |
| Change in debt outstanding | 3,200 | |
| Payment of cash dividends | (23,920) | |
| Net cash from financing activities | | (20,720) |
| Net change in cash and cash equivalents | | 1,240 |
| Beginning-of-period cash | | 8,760 |
| End-of-period cash | | 10,000 |

13. The value of MWC's common stock using the two-stage dividend discount model is *closest* to:
    A. $56.33.
    B. $61.55.
    C. $65.88.

14. The value of MWC's common stock using the two-stage FCFE approach is *closest* to:
    A. $55.09.
    B. $59.10.
    C. $68.24.

15. The Hoffman Card Co. earned £1.50 per share last year. Investment in fixed capital was £0.80 per share, and depreciation was £0.30. Investment in working capital was £0.20 per share. Hoffman expects earnings to grow at 15% per year for the next five years and that investment in fixed capital, depreciation, and investment in working capital will grow at the same rate. After five years, the growth in earnings and working capital requirements will decline to a stable 5% per year, and investment in fixed capital and depreciation will offset each other (i.e., they will be equal). Hoffman's target debt ratio is 30%. The shareholders require a return of 17% on their investment during the high-growth stage and a return of 10% on their investment during the stable stage. The FCFE in Year 6 and the value per share of Hoffman's common stock are *closest* to:

| | FCFE in Year 6 | Share value |
|---|---|---|
| A. | £2.03 | £31.08 |
| B. | £2.88 | £31.08 |
| C. | £2.88 | £57.60 |

## CHALLENGE PROBLEMS

16. Suppose an analyst estimates equity value by discounting free cash flow to equity (FCFE) at the weighted average cost of capital (WACC) in the FCFE model and estimates firm and equity value by discounting free cash flow to the firm (FCFF) at the required return on equity in the FCFF model. The analyst would *most likely*:
    A. overestimate equity value with the FCFE model and underestimate firm value and equity value with the FCFF model.
    B. underestimate equity value with the FCFE model and overestimate firm value and equity value with the FCFF model.
    C. underestimate equity value with the FCFE model and underestimate firm value and equity value with the FCFF model.

**Use the following information to answer Questions 17 through 19.**

Meyer Henderson, CFA, is analyzing the financials of Roth Department Stores. He intends to use a free cash flow to the firm (FCFF) model to value Roth's common stock. In the 2007 financial statements and footnotes he has identified the following items:

- Item #1: Roth reported depreciation and software amortization of $23 million in 2007.
- Item #2: The deferred tax liability increased by $17 million in 2007.
- Item #3: Roth reported income of $6 million in 2007 from the reversal of previous restructuring charges related to store closings in 2006.
- Item #4: Net income totaled $173 million in 2007.
- Item #5: The net increase in noncash net working capital accounts was $47 million in 2007.
- Item #6: Net capital spending totaled $86 million in 2007.
- Item #7: Roth reported interest expense of $19 million.

Henderson estimated Roth's marginal tax rate to be 35%. He also expects Roth to be profitable for the foreseeable future, so he does not expect the deferred tax liability to reverse. As the base-year projection for his FCFF valuation, Henderson calculates FCFF for 2007 as:

$$\text{FCFF}_{2007} = \$173 + \$23 + \$6 + \$17 + [\$19(1 - 0.35)] - \$86 - \$47 = \$98.35 \text{ million}$$

17. In implementing the FCFF model to value Roth, did Henderson correctly treat Items #1 and #2?
    A. Both items treated correctly.
    B. One correctly, one incorrectly.
    C. Neither item treated correctly.

18. In implementing the FCFF model to value Roth, did Henderson correctly treat Items #3 and #4?
    A. Both items treated correctly.
    B. One correctly, one incorrectly.
    C. Neither item treated correctly.

19. In implementing the FCFF model to value Roth, did Henderson correctly treat Items #5 and #7?
    A. Both items treated correctly.
    B. One correctly, one incorrectly.
    C. Neither item treated correctly.

**Use the following information to answer Questions 20 and 21.**

At the end of 2007, Meyer Henderson, CFA, also prepared a 10-year forecast of free cash flow to equity (FCFE) and free cash flow to the firm (FCFF) from 2008 to 2017 for Trammel Medical Supplies. In early 2008, Trammel unexpectedly announced a new 15-year issue of senior debt. The proceeds are expected to be used to repurchase common stock in the open market during 2008.

20. As a result of the unexpected debt issue, Henderson should *most likely*:
    A. increase his FCFE forecast for 2008 and decrease his FCFE forecast for 2009 through 2017.
    B. decrease his FCFE forecast for 2008 and increase his FCFE forecast for 2009 through 2017.
    C. increase his FCFE forecast for 2008 and not change his FCFE forecast for 2009 through 2017.

21. As a result of the unexpected debt issue, Henderson should *most likely*:
    A. increase his FCFF forecast for 2008 and decrease his FCFF forecast for 2009 through 2017.
    B. decrease his FCFF forecast for 2008 and increase his FCFF forecast for 2009 through 2017.
    C. not change his FCFF forecast for 2008 and also not change his FCFF forecast for 2009 through 2017.

22. Given the following information, calculate free cash flow to equity:
    - Net income = $50.
    - Working capital investment = $4.
    - Beginning gross fixed assets = $90; ending gross fixed assets = $136.
    - Beginning accumulated depreciation = $30; ending accumulated depreciation = $40.
    - Depreciation expense = $27.
    - Capital expenditures = $65.
    - Net borrowing = $0.

    In addition, a piece of equipment with an original book value of $19 was sold for $10. The equipment had a book value at the time of the sale of $2. The gain was classified as unusual. Free cash flow to equity is *closest* to:
    A. $6.
    B. $10.
    C. $18.

23. Chamber Group is analyzing the potential takeover of Outmenu, Inc. Chamber has gathered the following data on Outmenu. All figures are in millions of dollars.

| | 2008 | 2007 | 2006 | 2005 |
|---|---|---|---|---|
| Net income | –$26 | $34 | $18 | $26 |
| FCFE | –$1 | –$23 | $14 | –$15 |
| FCFF | $3 | $4 | $6 | $8 |
| Dividends | $5 | $5 | $4 | $4 |
| Debt-to-equity | 93% | 91% | 78% | 84% |

    The *most appropriate* model for valuing Outmenu is the:
    A. free cash flow to equity model.
    B. dividend discount H-model.
    C. free cash flow to the firm model.

24. Suppose an analyst uses the statement of cash flows to calculate free cash flow to the firm (FCFF) as cash flow from operations less fixed capital investment, and free cash flow to equity (FCFE) as FCFF plus net borrowing. The firm has short- and long-term debt on its balance sheet. Has the analyst correctly stated, overstated, or understated FCFF and FCFE?

|    | FCFF | FCFE |
|----|------|------|
| A. | Overstated | Correct |
| B. | Understated | Understated |
| C. | Understated | Correct |

25. An analyst calculates firm value using a single-stage model on December 31, 2007 as:

$$\text{value of the firm} = \frac{\text{FCFE}_{2008}}{r - g} + \text{MVD}$$

where:

$\text{FCFE}_{2008}$ = free cash flow to equity forecast for 2008
$r$ = required return on equity
$g$ = growth rate in FCFE
$\text{MVD}$ = market value of debt on 12/31/2007

Assuming there are no nonoperating assets on the balance sheet, the analyst has *most likely*:

A. correctly calculated firm value.

B. incorrectly calculated firm value. The weighted average cost of capital should be substituted for the required return on equity.

C. incorrectly calculated firm value. The weighted average cost of capital should be substituted for the required return on equity, and $\text{FCFE}_{2007}(1 + g)$ should be substituted for $\text{FCFE}_{2008}$.

## ANSWERS – CONCEPT CHECKERS

1. **C** $FCFE = NI - (1-DR)(FCInv - Dep) - (1-DR)(WCInv) =$
   $£3.50 - [(1-0.4)(£2.00 - £1.60)] - [(1-0.4)(£0.50)] = £2.96$

   equity value per share $= \dfrac{£2.96 \times 1.04}{0.14 - 0.04} = £30.78$

2. **A** $FCFF_0 = [EBIT \times (1 - \text{tax rate})] + Dep - FCInv - WCInv$

   $FCFF_0 \text{ (in millions)} = [C\$30 \times (1 - 0.40)] + C\$15 - C\$20 - C\$6 = C\$7.0$

   value of firm (in millions) $= \dfrac{C\$7.0 \times 1.05}{0.1245 - 0.05} = C\$98.7$

   value of equity (in millions) $= C\$98.7 - C\$25.0 = C\$73.7$

3. **B** The following table shows FCFF for years 0 through 6 (in $):

   | Year | 0 | 1 | 2 | 3 | 4 | 5 | 6 |
   |---|---|---|---|---|---|---|---|
   | Sales | 60.00 | 67.20 | 75.26 | 84.30 | 94.41 | 105.74 | 109.97 |
   | EBIT | 20.00 | 22.40 | 25.09 | 28.10 | 31.47 | 35.25 | 36.66 |
   | EBIT(1 – T) | 12.00 | 13.44 | 15.05 | 16.86 | 18.88 | 21.15 | 21.99 |
   | Dep | 8.00 | 8.96 | 10.04 | 11.24 | 12.59 | 14.10 | — |
   | FCInv | 12.00 | 13.44 | 15.05 | 16.86 | 18.88 | 21.15 | — |
   | WCInv | 3.00 | 3.36 | 3.76 | 4.21 | 4.72 | 5.29 | 5.50 |
   | FCFF | 5.00 | 5.60 | 6.28 | 7.03 | 7.87 | 8.81 | 16.49 |

   $FCFF = [EBIT \times (1 - \text{tax rate})] + Dep - FCInv - WCInv$

   $FCFF_6 = 21.99 + 0 + 0 - 5.50 = 16.49$

4. **C** The terminal value (as of Year 5) is found by using the FCFF in Year 6 and WACC of 8% and growth rate of 4% in the stable growth stage:

   terminal value$_5 = \dfrac{\$16.49}{0.08 - 0.04} = \$412.25$

5. **C**   The value of the firm today is the present value of the forecasted cash flows, discounted at the WACC during the high-growth stage of 11%:

$$\text{value of firm} = \frac{\$5.60}{1.11} + \frac{\$6.28}{1.11^2} + \frac{\$7.03}{1.11^3} + \frac{\$7.87}{1.11^4} + \frac{\$8.81 + \$412.25}{1.11^5} = \$270.35$$

Using the calculator, enter $CF_0 = 0.00$; C01 = 5.60; C02 = 6.28; C03 = 7.03; C04 = 7.87; C05 = 8.81 + 412.25 = 421.06; I = 11; CPT $\rightarrow$ NPV = 270.35

6. **C**   With the bonds trading at par, the interest expense is based on the before-tax yield:

interest = $600 × 0.075 = $45

Add back preferred dividends to net income available to common to get FCFF:

$$\text{FCFF} = \text{NI}(\text{available to common}) + \text{NCC} + \big[\text{Int} \times (1 - \text{tax rate})\big] + \text{preferred dividends} - \text{FCInv} - \text{WCInv}$$
$$\text{FCFF} = 125 + 50 + \big[45 \times (1 - 0.40)\big] + 14 - 100 - 30 = \$86$$

7. **C**   The value of the firm is the present value of the constantly growing FCFF. Using single-stage FCFF model we get:

$$\text{value of firm} = \frac{\text{FCFF}_0 \times (1 + g)}{\text{WACC} - g} = \frac{\$86 \times 1.04}{0.0927 - 0.04} = \$1,697.15$$

8. **A**   The value of the equity is equal to firm value less the market value of debt and preferred stock:

value of equity = $1,697.15 – $600 – $200 = $897.15

9. **B**   FCFF = 86 (computed earlier).

$$\text{FCFE} = \text{FCFF} - \big[\text{Int} \times (1 - \text{tax rate})\big] - \text{preferred dividends} + \text{net borrowing}$$
$$= 86 - \big[45 \times (1 - 0.4)\big] - 14 + 40 = \$85$$

10. **C**   $$\text{value of equity} = \frac{\$85 \times 1.04}{0.14 - 0.04} = \$884$$

11. **B**   Free cash flow to the firm (FCFF) is the estimate of the cash flows available to the firm's investors after the firm buys and sells products, provides services, pays its cash operating expenses, and makes short- and long-term investment decisions, but before the firm makes any financing decisions. EBITDA is a poor proxy for free cash flow. FCFF is calculated as:

FCFF = [EBITDA × (1 – tax rate)] + (Dep × tax rate) – FCInv – WCInv

12. **B**   Free cash flow to the firm is equal to cash flow from operations plus after-tax interest expense [interest(1 – tax rate)] minus fixed capital investment.

13. **A** Based on the CAPM, the required return on MWC's common equity can be computed as follows:

$$r = 6.4\% + (1.2 \times 5.5\%) = 13\%$$

The current value of MWC common stock can be estimated using the two-stage DDM approach as follows:

$g = 15\%$
$D_{2007} = \$2.30$
$D_{2008} = \$2.30 \times 1.15 = \$2.65$
$D_{2009} = \$2.65 \times 1.15 = \$3.05$

$$\text{terminal value} = \frac{\$3.05 \times 1.08}{(0.13 - 0.08)} = \$65.88$$

$$\text{equity value} = \frac{\$2.65}{1.13} + \frac{\$3.05 + \$65.88}{1.13^2} = \$56.33$$

14. **B** The current value of MWC common stock can be estimated using the two-stage FCFE approach as follows:

$$\text{FCFE}_{2007} = \text{CFO} - \text{FCInv} + \text{net borrowing} = 33,960 - 12,000 + 3,200 = \$25,160$$

$$\text{shares outstanding} = \text{dividends paid / dividends per share} = \frac{\$23,920}{\$2.30} = 10,400$$

$$\text{FCFE}_{2007} \text{ per share} = \frac{\text{FCFE}_{2007}}{10,400} = \frac{\$25,160}{10,400} = \$2.42$$

$g \qquad\qquad = 15\%$
$\text{FCFE}_{2007} \quad = \$2.42$
$\text{FCFE}_{2008} \quad = \$2.42 \times 1.15 = \$2.78$
$\text{FCFE}_{2009} \quad = \$2.78 \times 1.15 = \$3.20$

$$\text{terminal value} = \frac{\$3.20 \times 1.08}{(0.13 - 0.08)} = \$69.12$$

$$\text{equity value} = \frac{\$2.78}{1.13} + \frac{\$3.20 + \$69.12}{1.13^2} = \$59.10$$

15. **B**    The following table shows FCFE for years 0 through 6 (in £).

$$FCFE = NI - [(1 - DR) \times (FCInv - Dep)] - [(1 - DR) \times WCInv]$$

|  | Year 0 | Year 1 | Year 2 | Year 3 | Year 4 | Year 5 | Year 6 |
|---|---|---|---|---|---|---|---|
| NI | 1.50 | 1.73 | 1.98 | 2.28 | 2.62 | 3.02 | 3.17 |
| (–) [(1 – DR) (FCInv – Dep)] | 0.35 | 0.40 | 0.46 | 0.53 | 0.61 | 0.70 | 0 |
| (–) [(1 – DR) (WCInv)] | 0.14 | 0.16 | 0.19 | 0.21 | 0.24 | 0.28 | 0.29 |
| (=) FCFE | 1.01 | 1.17 | 1.33 | 1.53 | 1.76 | 2.03 | 2.88 |

Example of FCFE calculation (Year 1):

$$\begin{aligned} FCFE &= NI - [(1 - DR) \times (FCInv - Dep)] - [(1 - DR) \times WCInv] \\ &= 1.73 - [(1 - 0.3) \times (0.92 - 0.35)] - [(1 - 0.3) \times 0.23] \\ &= 1.17 \end{aligned}$$

Calculate terminal value in year five using FCFE estimate for Year 6, discounted at required return of 10% in the stable growth period.

$$\text{terminal value}_5 = \frac{£2.88}{0.10 - 0.05} = £57.60$$

Use the short-term discount rate of 17% to discount the cash flows back to the present:

$$\text{equity value per share} = \frac{1.17}{1.17^1} + \frac{1.33}{1.17^2} + \frac{1.53}{1.17^3} + \frac{1.76}{1.17^4} + \frac{2.03 + 57.60}{1.17^5} = £31.08$$

Using the calculator, enter the following: $CF_0 = 0.00$; $C01 = 1.17$; $C02 = 1.34$; $C03 = 1.54$; $C04 = 1.76$; $C05 = 2.03 + 57.60 = 59.63$; $I = 17$; CPT → NPV = 31.08

## ANSWERS – CHALLENGE PROBLEMS

16. **A**    WACC is less than required return on equity. Incorrectly using the WACC (which is too low) in the FCFE model will overestimate equity value. Incorrectly using required return on equity (which is too high) in the FCFF model will underestimate firm value and equity value.

**For Questions 17 through 19,** items #1, 2, 4, 5, 6, and 7 were applied correctly. Only item #3 related to the reversal of restructuring charges was applied incorrectly: income from restructuring charge reversals is a noncash gain that should be subtracted from net income to calculate FCFF. Depreciation and software amortization should be added back to net income, after-tax interest should be added back, and the increase in deferred taxes should be added back (because it is not expected to reverse in the foreseeable future). Net working capital and fixed capital investments should be subtracted from net income to arrive at FCFF. The correct calculation of FCFF is:

$$\text{FCFF}_{2007} = \$173 + \$23 - \$6 + \$17 + [\$19(1 - 0.35)] - \$86 - \$47 = \$86.35 \text{ million}$$

17. **A**   See answer explanation above for Questions 17 through 19.

18. **B**   See answer explanation above for Questions 17 through 19.

19. **A**   See answer explanation above for Questions 17 through 19.

20. **A**   The increased net borrowing for 2008 will cause the forecasted free cash flow to *equity* (FCFE) to increase in 2008. However, in future years, the higher interest expense associated with the debt issue will cause the FCFE forecast to decrease.

21. **C**   Free cash flow to the *firm* (FCFF) represents cash flow available to all investors before any financing cash flows, including interest payments. Changes in leverage are uses of cash (i.e., financing decisions) that do not affect FCFF.

22. **B**   Recognize that the firm generated $10 in cash and a noncash $8 gain on the sale of the equipment. Then calculate FCFE as NI plus depreciation minus the noncash gain minus FCInv minus WCInv + net borrowing:

$$\text{FCFE} = \$50 + \$27 - \$8 - (\$65 - \$10) - \$4 + \$0 = \$10$$

23. **C**   Dividend discount models like the Gordon growth model and the dividend discount H-model are not appropriate in this case for two reasons: (1) dividends are not related to the firm's earnings stream, and (2) this is a takeover situation in which a free cash flow model is more appropriate.

   The FCFF model is preferred to the FCFE model because (1) FCFE is negative and volatile and (2) leverage is relatively high.

24. **C**   The firm must have interest expense on its income statement because of the debt on its balance sheet. By ignoring the after-tax interest cash flow, the analyst has understated FCFF, which is actually equal to CFO plus after-tax interest cash flow less fixed capital investment. He has, however, calculated FCFE correctly because FCFE is equal to CFO less fixed capital investment (his incorrect FCFF calculation) plus net borrowing.

25. **A**   Although the calculation is a bit unusual (we usually calculate firm value as the present value of FCFF discounted at the weighted average cost of capital), the analyst has correctly calculated firm value. The first term is equal to the market value of equity on 12/31/2007; firm value is equal to the market value of equity plus the market value of debt.

# MARKET-BASED VALUATION: PRICE AND ENTERPRISE VALUE MULTIPLES

Study Session 12

## EXAM FOCUS

This topic review covers the estimation of P/E, P/B, PEG, P/S, P/CF, and enterprise value/EBITDA ratios. The justified price multiple models draw heavily on the previous two topic reviews on dividend discount models and free cash flow models. You should be able to estimate justified price multiples for individual firms and to apply the method of comparables to estimate their (relative) values.

## WARM-UP: MULTIPLES

**Price multiples** are among the most widely used tools for valuation of equities. Comparing stocks' price multiples can help an investor judge whether a particular stock is overvalued, undervalued, or properly valued in terms of measures such as earnings, sales, cash flow, or book value per share. **Enterprise value multiples** relate the total value of a company, as reflected in the market value of its capital from all sources, to a measure of operating earnings generated, such as earnings before interest, taxes, depreciation, and amortization. **Momentum indicators** compare a stock's price or a company's earnings to their values in earlier periods.

---

LOS 35.a: Distinguish between the method of comparables and the method based on forecasted fundamentals as approaches to using price multiples in valuation, and explain economic rationales for each approach.

---

*CFA® Program Curriculum, Volume 4, page 267*

The **method of comparables** values a stock based on the average price multiple of the stock of similar companies. The economic rationale for the method of comparables is the Law of One Price, which asserts that two similar assets should sell at comparable price multiples (e.g., price-to-earnings). This is a relative valuation method, so we can only assert that a stock is over- or undervalued *relative* to benchmark value.

The **method of forecasted fundamentals** values a stock based on the ratio of its value from a discounted cash flow (DCF) model to some fundamental variable (e.g., earnings per share). The economic rationale for the method of forecasted fundamentals is that the value used in the numerator of the justified price multiple is derived from a DCF model: value is equal to the present value of expected future cash flows discounted at the appropriate risk-adjusted rate of return.

### Example: Method of comparables

MK Technologies shares are selling for $50. Earnings for the last 12 months were $2 per share. The average trailing P/E ratio for firms in MK's industry is 32 times. Determine whether MK is over- or undervalued using the method of comparables.

**Answer:**

MK's trailing P/E is:

$$\frac{\$50}{\$2} = 25 \text{ times}$$

MK is relatively undervalued because its observed trailing P/E ratio (25 times) is less than the industry average trailing P/E ratio (32 times).

### Example: Method of forecasted fundamentals

Shares of Comtronics, Inc. are selling for $30. The mean analyst earnings per share forecast for next year is $4.00, and the long-run growth rate is 5%. Comtronics has a dividend payout ratio of 60%. The required return is 14%. Calculate the fundamental value of Comtronics using the Gordon growth model and determine whether Comtronics shares are over- or undervalued using the method of forecasted fundamentals.

**Answer:**

The fundamental value according to the Gordon growth model is:

$$V_0 = \frac{D_1}{r-g} = \frac{(0.6 \times \$4.00)}{0.14 - 0.05} = \$26.67$$

The fair value P/E ratio based on forecasted fundamentals is:

$$\frac{\$26.67}{\$4.00} = 6.67 \text{ times}$$

The observed leading P/E ratio based on the current market price is:

$$\frac{\$30.00}{\$4.00} = 7.50 \text{ times}$$

Comtronics is overvalued because the observed P/E multiple of 7.5 is greater than the fair value P/E ratio of 6.67. Notice that we would have come to the same conclusion by comparing market price ($30.00) to intrinsic value ($26.67).

Study Session 12

LOS 35.b: Calculate and interpret a justified price multiple.

LOS 35.c: Describe rationales for and possible drawbacks to using alternative price multiples and dividend yield in valuation.

LOS 35.d: Calculate and interpret alternative price multiples and dividend yield.

*CFA® Program Curriculum, Volume 4, page 269*

Price multiples are ratios of a common stock's market price to some fundamental variable. The most common example is the price-to-earnings (P/E) ratio. A **justified price multiple** is what the multiple *should be* if the stock is fairly valued. If the actual multiple is greater than the justified price multiple, the stock is overvalued; if the actual multiple is less than the justified multiple, the stock is undervalued (all else equal).

## P/E Ratio

There are a number of rationales for using price-to-earnings (P/E) ratio in valuation:

- Earnings power, as measured by earnings per share (EPS), is the primary determinant of investment value.
- The P/E ratio is popular in the investment community.
- Empirical research shows that P/E differences are significantly related to long-run average stock returns.

On the other hand, P/E ratios have a number of shortcomings:

- Earnings can be *negative*, which produces a meaningless P/E ratio.
- The volatile, transitory portion of earnings makes the interpretation of P/Es difficult for analysts.
- Management discretion within allowed accounting practices can distort reported earnings, and thereby lessen the comparability of P/Es across firms.

We can define two versions of the P/E ratio: trailing and leading P/E. The difference between the two is how earnings (the denominator) are calculated. *Trailing P/E* uses earnings over the *most recent* 12 months in the denominator. *Leading P/E ratio* (a.k.a. forward or prospective P/E) uses next year's expected earnings, which is defined as either expected earnings per share (EPS) for the next four quarters, or expected EPS for the next fiscal year.

$$\text{trailing P/E} = \frac{\text{market price per share}}{\text{EPS over previous 12 months}}$$

$$\text{leading P/E} = \frac{\text{market price per share}}{\text{forecasted EPS over next 12 months}}$$

Trailing P/E is not useful for forecasting and valuation if the firm's business has changed (e.g., as a result of an acquisition). Leading P/E may not be relevant if earnings are sufficiently volatile so that next year's earnings are not forecastable with any degree of accuracy.

---

**Example: Calculating P/E ratio**

Byron Investments, Inc., reported €32 million in earnings during fiscal year 2007. An analyst forecasts an EPS over the next 12 months of €1.00. Byron has 40 million shares outstanding at a market price of €18.00 per share. Calculate Byron's trailing and leading P/E ratios.

**Answer:**

$$2007 \text{ EPS} = \frac{€32,000,000}{40,000,000} = €0.80$$

$$\text{trailing P/E} = \frac{€18.00}{€0.80} = 22.5$$

$$\text{leading P/E} = \frac{€18.00}{€1.00} = 18.0$$

---

## P/B Ratio

*Advantages* of using the price-to-book (P/B) ratio include:

- Book value is a cumulative amount that is usually positive, even when the firm reports a loss and EPS is negative. Thus, a P/B can typically be used when P/E cannot.
- Book value is more stable than EPS, so it may be more useful than P/E when EPS is particularly high, low, or volatile.
- Book value is an appropriate measure of net asset value for firms that primarily hold liquid assets. Examples include finance, investment, insurance, and banking firms.
- P/B can be useful in valuing companies that are expected to go out of business.
- Empirical research shows that P/Bs help explain differences in long-run average stock returns.

*Disadvantages* of using P/B include:

- P/Bs do not reflect the value of intangible economic assets, such as human capital.
- P/Bs can be misleading when there are significant differences in the asset size of the firms under consideration because in some cases the firm's business model dictates the size of its asset base. A firm that outsources its production will have fewer assets, lower book value, and a higher P/B ratio than an otherwise similar firm in the same industry that doesn't outsource.
- Different accounting conventions can obscure the true investment in the firm made by shareholders, which reduces the comparability of P/Bs across firms and countries. For example, research and development costs (R&D) are expensed in the United States, which can understate investment.

- Inflation and technological change can cause the book and market values of assets to differ significantly, so book value is not an accurate measure of the value of shareholders' investment. This makes it more difficult to compare P/Bs across firms.

The price-to-book ratio is defined as:

$$\text{P/B ratio} = \frac{\text{market value of equity}}{\text{book value of equity}} = \frac{\text{market price per share}}{\text{book value per share}}$$

where:

book value of equity = common shareholders' equity

= (total assets − total liabilities) − preferred stock

We often make adjustments to book value to create more useful comparisons of P/B ratios across different stocks. A common adjustment is to use tangible book value, which is equal to book value of equity less intangible assets. Examples of intangible assets include goodwill from acquisitions (which makes sense because it is not really an asset) and patents (which is more questionable since the asset and patent are separable). Furthermore, balance sheets should be adjusted for significant off-balance-sheet assets and liabilities and for differences between the fair and recorded value of assets and liabilities. Finally, book values often need to be adjusted to ensure comparability. For example, companies using first in, first out (FIFO) for inventory valuation cannot be accurately compared with peers using last in, first out (LIFO). Thus, book values should be restated on a consistent basis.

 *Professor's Note: See Study Session 7 for more details on the typical adjustments that analysts make to the balance sheet.*

---

**Example: Calculating P/B ratio**

Based on the information in the following figure, calculate the current P/B for Crisco Systems, Inc. and Soothsayer Corp.

**Data for Crisco Systems, Inc. and Soothsayer Corp.**

| Company | Book Value of Equity 2008 (millions of $) | Sales 2008 (millions of $) | Shares Outstanding 2008 (millions) | Price FYE 2008 ($) |
|---|---|---|---|---|
| Crisco Systems, Inc. | $28,039 | $18,878 | 7,001 | $17.83 |
| Soothsayer Corp. | $6,320 | $9,475 | 5,233 | $12.15 |

**Answer:**

Crisco Systems, Inc.:

$$\text{book value per share} = \frac{\text{book value of equity}}{\text{number of shares outstanding}} = \frac{\$28{,}039}{7{,}001} = \$4.01$$

$$\text{P/B} = \frac{\text{market price per share}}{\text{book value per share}} = \frac{\$17.83}{\$4.01} = 4.45 \text{ times}$$

Soothsayer Corp.:

$$\text{book value per share} = \frac{\text{book value of equity}}{\text{number of shares outstanding}} = \frac{\$6{,}320}{5{,}233} = \$1.21$$

$$\text{P/B} = \frac{\text{market price per share}}{\text{book value per share}} = \frac{\$12.15}{\$1.21} = 10.04 \text{ times}$$

## P/S Ratio

The *advantages* of using the price-to-sales (P/S) ratio include:

- P/S is meaningful even for distressed firms, since sales revenue is always positive. This is not the case for P/E and P/B ratios, which can be negative.
- Sales revenue is not as easy to manipulate or distort as EPS and book value, which are significantly affected by accounting conventions.
- P/S ratios are not as volatile as P/E multiples. This may make P/S ratios more reliable in valuation analysis when earnings for a particular year are very high or very low relative to the long-run average.
- P/S ratios are particularly appropriate for valuing stocks in mature or cyclical industries and start-up companies with no record of earnings. It is also often used to value investment management companies and partnerships.
- Like P/E and P/B ratios, empirical research finds that differences in P/S are significantly related to differences in long-run average stock returns.

The *disadvantages* of using P/S ratios include:

- High growth in sales does not necessarily indicate high operating profits as measured by earnings and cash flow.
- P/S ratios do not capture differences in cost structures across companies.
- While less subject to distortion, revenue recognition practices can still distort sales forecasts. For example, analysts should look for company practices that speed up revenue recognition. An example is sales on a bill-and-hold basis, which involves selling products and delivering them at a later date. This practice accelerates sales into an earlier reporting period and distorts the P/S ratio.

P/S multiples are computed by dividing a stock's price per share by sales or revenue per share, or by dividing the market value of the firm's equity by its total sales:

$$\text{P/S ratio} = \frac{\text{market value of equity}}{\text{total sales}} = \frac{\text{market price per share}}{\text{sales per share}}$$

**Example: Calculating P/S ratio**

Based on the information in the following figure, calculate the current P/S for Crisco Systems, Inc. and Soothsayer Corp.

**Data for Crisco Systems, Inc. and Soothsayer Corp.**

| Company | Book Value of Equity 2008 (millions of $) | Sales 2008 (millions of $) | Shares Outstanding 2008 (millions) | Price FYE 2008 ($) |
|---|---|---|---|---|
| Crisco Systems, Inc. | $28,039 | $18,878 | 7,001 | $17.83 |
| Soothsayer Corp. | $6,320 | $9,475 | 5,233 | $12.15 |

**Answer:**

Crisco Systems, Inc.:

$$\text{sales per share} = \frac{\text{sales}}{\text{number of shares outstanding}} = \frac{\$18,878 \text{ million}}{7,001 \text{ million}} = \$2.70$$

$$\text{P/S} = \frac{\text{market price per share}}{\text{sales per share}} = \frac{\$17.83}{\$2.70} = 6.60 \text{ times}$$

Soothsayer Corp.:

$$\text{sales per share} = \frac{\text{sales}}{\text{number of shares outstanding}} = \frac{\$9,475 \text{ million}}{5,233 \text{ million}} = \$1.81$$

$$\text{P/S} = \frac{\text{market price per share}}{\text{sales per share}} = \frac{\$12.15}{\$1.81} = 6.71 \text{ times}$$

## P/CF Ratio

*Advantages* of using the price-to-cash flow (P/CF) ratio include:

- Cash flow is harder for managers to manipulate than earnings.
- Price to cash flow is more stable than price to earnings.
- Reliance on cash flow rather than earnings handles the problem of differences in the quality of reported earnings, which is a problem for P/E.
- Empirical evidence indicates that differences in price to cash flow are significantly related to differences in long-run average stock returns.

There are two drawbacks to the price-to-cash flow ratio, both of which are related to the definition of cash flow. We discuss the specific cash flow definitions next.

- Items affecting actual cash flow from operations are ignored when the EPS plus noncash charges estimate is used. For example, noncash revenue and net changes in working capital are ignored.
- From a theoretical perspective, free cash flow to equity (FCFE) is preferable to operating cash flow. However, FCFE is more volatile than operating cash flow, so it is not necessarily more informative.

## Dividend Yield

The dividend yield (D/P) is the ratio of the common dividend to the market price. It is most often used for valuing indexes. *Advantages* of the dividend yield approach include:

- Dividend yield contributes to total investment return.
- Dividends are not as risky as the capital appreciation component of total return.

*Disadvantages* of the dividend yield approach include:

- The focus on dividend yield is incomplete because it ignores capital appreciation.
- The dividend displacement of earnings concept argues that dividends paid now displace future earnings, which implies a trade-off between current and future cash flows.

Total return on an investment has two components: dividend yield and capital appreciation. *Dividend yield* (D/P) is the ratio of trailing or leading dividend divided by current market price per share:

$$\text{trailing D/P} = \frac{4 \times \text{most recent quarterly dividend}}{\text{market price per share}}$$

$$\text{leading D/P} = \frac{\text{forecasted dividends over next four quarters}}{\text{market price per share}}$$

The supposed lower risk of dividends relative to capital appreciation assumes that the market is biased in its risk assessment of the components of return.

**Example: Calculating dividend yield**

OnePrice Inc. just paid a dividend of $0.50 per share. The consensus forecasted dividends for OnePrice Inc. over the next four quarters are $0.50, $0.55, $0.60, and $0.65. The current market price is $47.50. Calculate the leading and trailing dividend yield.

**Answer:**

$$\text{trailing D/P} = \frac{4 \times \$0.50}{\$47.50} = 0.042 = 4.2\%$$

$$\text{leading D/P} = \frac{\$0.50 + \$0.55 + \$0.60 + \$0.65}{\$47.50} = \frac{\$2.30}{\$47.50} = 0.048 = 4.8\%$$

---

LOS 35.e: Calculate and interpret underlying earnings, explain methods of normalizing earnings per share (EPS), and calculate normalized EPS.

*CFA® Program Curriculum, Volume 4, page 276*

**Underlying Earnings**

Calculating the P/E ratio is easy, and estimating the market price is usually straightforward. However, estimating the appropriate earnings measure is crucial to successfully using the P/E ratio in market-based valuation. The key focus of an analyst is estimating **underlying earnings** (a.k.a. persistent, continuing, or core earnings), which are earnings that exclude nonrecurring components, such as gains and losses from asset sales, asset write-downs, provisions for future losses, and changes in accounting estimates.

*Professor's Note: There is an important link here to financial statement analysis. The basic inputs to most valuation models (like earnings) are found in the financial statements. However, management has significant discretion in determining reported earnings by classifying specific items as nonrecurring. The analyst's job is to identify the recurring components of earnings that reflect the firm's true earning power.*

**Example: Calculating underlying earnings**

Using the data in the following figure, calculate the trailing P/E for Magnolia Enterprises as of September 2008 using underlying earnings.

**Data for Magnolia Enterprises [amounts in Canadian dollars (C$)]**

| Quarter Ending | Stock Price (C$) | Reported EPS (C$) | Nonrecurring Items Gain on Asset Sales (C$) | Nonrecurring Items Extraordinary Expense (C$) |
|---|---|---|---|---|
| December 2007 | 38.50 | 1.45 | | |
| March 2008 | 46.25 | 1.30 | 0.30 | |
| June 2008 | 48.50 | 1.40 | | 0.55 |
| September 2008 | 44.85 | 1.35 | | |

**Answer:**

12-month EPS $= 1.45 + 1.30 + 1.40 + 1.35 = C\$5.50$

underlying earnings $= 5.50 - 0.30 + 0.55 = C\$5.75$

trailing P/E $= \dfrac{C\$44.85}{C\$5.75} = 7.80$ times

Earnings contain a transitory portion that is due to cyclicality. While viewed as currently transitory, business cycles are expected to repeat over the long term. The countercyclical tendency to have high P/Es due to lower EPS at the bottom of the cycle and low P/Es due to high EPS at the top of the cycle is known as the *Molodovsky effect*.

### Normalized Earnings

Analysts adjust P/Es for cyclicality by estimating **normalized (or normal) earnings per share**, which is an estimate of EPS in the middle of the business cycle. The following two methods are used to normalize earnings:

1. Under **the method of historical average EPS,** the normalized EPS is estimated as the average EPS over some recent period, usually the most recent business cycle.

2. Under **the method of average return on equity,** normalized EPS is estimated as the average return on equity (ROE) multiplied by the current book value per share (BVPS). Once again, average ROE is often measured over the most recent business cycle. The reliance on BVPS reflects the effect of firm size changes more accurately than does the method of historical average EPS.

The method of historical average EPS ignores size effects, so the method of average ROE is preferred.

**Example: Calculating normalized earnings**

Using the data in the following figure, calculate normalized earnings using the method of historical average EPS and the method of average return on equity for Magnolia Enterprises.

**Data for Magnolia Enterprises [amounts in Canadian dollars (C$)]**

| Year | 2006 | 2007 | 2008 | 2009 |
|------|------|------|------|------|
| EPS | C$4.20 | C$3.75 | C$4.75 | C$4.30 |
| BVPS | C$26.02 | C$27.78 | C$29.25 | C$32.29 |
| ROE | 14.0% | 12.0% | 16.0% | 14.0% |

**Answer:**

$$\text{normalized earnings (average EPS approach)} = \frac{4.20 + 3.75 + 4.75 + 4.30}{4} = C\$4.25$$

$$\text{average ROE} = \frac{0.14 + 0.12 + 0.16 + 0.14}{4} = 0.14 = 14.00\%$$

$$\begin{aligned} \text{normalized earnings (average ROE approach)} &= \text{average ROE} \times \text{BVPS}_{2009} \\ &= 0.14 \times C\$32.29 \\ &= C\$4.52 \end{aligned}$$

Normalized earnings are C$4.25 based on the method of historical average EPS and C$4.52 based on the method of average return on equity.

---

## LOS 35.f: Explain and justify the use of earnings yield (E/P).

*CFA® Program Curriculum, Volume 4, page 278*

Negative earnings render P/E ratios meaningless. In such cases, it is common to use normalized EPS and/or restate the ratio as the **earnings yield (E/P)** because price is never negative. A high E/P suggests a *cheap* security, and a low E/P suggests an *expensive* security, so securities can be ranked from cheap to expensive based on E/P ratios.

LOS 35.g: Describe fundamental factors that influence alternative price multiples and dividend yield.

LOS 35.h: Calculate and interpret the justified price-to-earnings ratio (P/E), price-to-book ratio (P/B), and price-to-sales ratio (P/S) for a stock, based on forecasted fundamentals.

*CFA® Program Curriculum, Volume 4, page 283*

*Professor's Note: We organized the material related to these two LOS by ratio. We start with the formula for the justified price multiple. If you know the formula, you know the fundamental factors. Notice that the LOS say "discuss" all of the justified price multiples and dividend yield, but only ask us to calculate three: P/E, P/B, and P/S.*

### Justified P/E Multiple

As we said earlier, the justified P/E price multiple is a P/E ratio with the "P" in the numerator equal to the fundamental value derived from a valuation model. The best way to analyze the fundamental factors that affect the P/E ratio is to use the single-stage Gordon growth model:

$$V_0 = \frac{D_0 \times (1+g)}{(r-g)} = \frac{D_1}{(r-g)}$$

where:
$V_0$ = fundamental value
$D_0$ = dividend just paid
$D_1$ = dividends expected to be received at end of Year 1
$r$ = required return on equity
$g$ = dividend growth rate

If we express $D_0$ as the product of current earnings per share ($E_0$) and the payout ratio ($D_0 / E_0$) and express the retention rate as $b$, the previous formula becomes trailing P/E:

$$\text{justified trailing P/E} = \frac{P_0}{E_0} = \frac{D_0 \times (1+g) \big/ E_0}{r-g} = \frac{(1-b) \times (1+g)}{r-g}$$

Recognizing that $E_1 = E_0(1+g)$ and $D_1 = D_0(1+g)$, the leading P/E is calculated as:

$$\text{justified leading P/E} = \frac{P_0}{E_1} = \frac{D_1 \big/ E_1}{r-g} = \frac{1-b}{r-g}$$

*Professor's Note: Remember that if earnings are expected to grow, $E_1$ will be greater than $E_0$, and the justified leading P/E $(P_0/E_1)$ will be smaller than the justified trailing P/E $(P_0/E_0)$ because you're dividing by a larger number when you are calculating leading P/E. In fact, trailing P/E will be larger than leading P/E by a factor of $(1 + g)$: justified trailing P/E = justified leading P/E × $(1 + g)$.*

By examining the formulas for justified (leading and trailing) P/E, we can conclude that the fundamental factors that affect P/E are expected growth rate and required return (which is related to risk). The justified P/E ratio is:

- Positively related to the growth rate of expected cash flows, whether defined as dividends or free cash flows, all else equal.
- Inversely related to the stock's required rate of return, all else equal.

---

**Example: Calculating justified P/E ratio for Comtronics again**

Shares of Comtronics are selling for $30. The mean analyst earnings per share forecast for next year is $4, and the long-run growth rate is 5%. Comtronics has a dividend payout ratio of 60% and a required return of 14%. Calculate the justified leading P/E ratio.

**Answer:**

$$\text{justified leading P/E} = \frac{0.60}{0.14 - 0.05} = 6.67 \text{ times}$$

This is the same answer we got when we calculated Comtronics' P/E the "long way" in the example at the beginning of this topic review.

---

**Example: Calculating justified P/E ratio**

A stock has a payout ratio of 40%. The shareholders require a return of 11% on their investment, and the expected growth rate in dividends is 5%. Calculate the trailing and leading P/E multiple based on these forecasted fundamentals.

**Answer:**

$$\text{justified trailing P/E} = \frac{P_0}{E_0} = \frac{0.40 \times 1.05}{0.11 - 0.05} = 7.00$$

$$\text{justified leading P/E} = \frac{P_0}{E_1} = \frac{0.40}{0.11 - 0.05} = 6.67$$

or

$$\text{justified trailing P/E} = 6.67 \times (1.05) = 7.00$$

---

## Justified P/B Multiple

Using the sustainable growth relation of $g = ROE \times b$ and observing that $E_1 = B_0 \times ROE$, we can also derive the justified P/B from the Gordon growth model as:

$$\text{justified P/B ratio} = \frac{ROE - g}{r - g}$$

where:
ROE = return on equity
r = required return on equity
g = expected growth rate in dividends and earnings

We can draw two useful conclusions from this formula concerning the fundamentals that influence the P/B ratio:

- P/B increases as ROE increases, all else equal.
- The larger the spread between ROE and *r*, all else equal, the higher the P/B ratio. This makes sense if you remember that ROE is the return on the firm's investment projects and *r* is the required return. The larger the spread, all else equal, the more value the firm is creating through its investment activities and the higher its market value as represented by $V_0$.

We can then use fundamental forecasts of ROE, *r*, and *g* to find a value for this ratio.

---

**Example: Calculating justified P/B ratio**

A firm's ROE is 14%, its required rate of return is 8%, and its expected growth rate is 4%. Calculate the firm's justified P/B based on these fundamentals.

**Answer:**

$$\text{justified P/B ratio} = \frac{ROE - g}{r - g} = \frac{0.14 - 0.04}{0.08 - 0.04} = 2.5$$

---

## Justified P/S Multiple

Since net profit margin ($PM_0$) is equal to $E_0/S_0$, we can also restate the Gordon growth model as:

$$\text{justified } \frac{P_0}{S_0} = \frac{(E_0/S_0) \times (1-b) \times (1+g)}{r - g}$$

Net profit margin ($E_0/S_0$) thus influences P/S directly as well as indirectly through its effect on the sustainable growth rate, *g*:

$$g = \text{retention ratio} \times \text{net profit margin} \times \left(\frac{\text{sales}}{\text{assets}}\right) \times \left(\frac{\text{assets}}{\text{shareholders' equity}}\right)$$

This means that the P/S ratio will increase, all else equal, if:

- Profit margin increases.
- Earnings growth rate increases.

We can also do a little algebra and solve for P/S as a function of trailing P/E, which might be an easier formula to remember:

$$\text{justified } \frac{P_0}{S_0} = \left(E_0/S_0\right) \times \left[\frac{(1-b)\times(1+g)}{r-g}\right] = \text{net profit margin} \times \text{justified trailing P/E}$$

---

**Example: Calculating justified P/S ratio**

A stock has a dividend payout ratio of 40%, a return on equity (ROE) of 8.3%, an EPS of $4.25, sales per share of $218.75, and an expected growth rate in dividends and earnings of 5%. Shareholders require a return of 10% on their investment. Calculate the justified P/S multiple based on these fundamentals.

**Answer:**

The ratio $E_0/S_0$ is the profit margin. In this example, the profit margin is ($4.25 / $218.75) = 0.0194. Therefore, we get:

$$\frac{P_0}{S_0} = \frac{0.0194 \times 0.4 \times 1.05}{0.10 - 0.05} = 0.163 \text{ times}$$

---

## Justified P/CF Multiple

The *justified price to cash flow* based on fundamentals can be calculated by finding the value of the stock using a DCF model and dividing the result by the chosen measure of cash flow. For example, equity value using the single-stage FCFE model is:

$$V_0 = \frac{FCFE_0 \times (1+g)}{r-g}$$

P/CF will increase, all else equal, if:

- Required return decreases.
- Growth rate increases.

### Justified EV/EBITDA Multiple

The justified EV/EBITDA based on fundamentals is simply the enterprise value based on a forecast of fundamentals divided by EBITDA forecast based on fundamentals. The ratio is:

- Positively related to the growth rate in FCFF and EBITDA.
- Negatively related to the firm's overall risk level and weighted average cost of capital (WACC).

### Justified Dividend Yield

The dividend yield relative to fundamentals may be expressed in terms of the Gordon growth model as:

$$\frac{D_0}{P_0} = \frac{r - g}{1 + g}$$

Dividend yield is:

- Positively related to the required rate of return.
- Negatively related to the forecasted growth rate in dividends. This implies that choosing high dividend yield stocks reflects a value rather than a growth investment strategy.

---

**LOS 35.i: Calculate and interpret a predicted P/E, given a cross-sectional regression on fundamentals, and explain limitations to the cross-sectional regression methodology.**

---

*CFA® Program Curriculum, Volume 4, page 284*

A **predicted P/E** can be estimated from linear regression of historical P/Es on its fundamental variables, including expected growth and risk. While such empirical analysis can provide an analyst with useful insight, there are three *main limitations:*

- The predictive power of the estimated P/E regression for a different time period and/or sample of stocks is uncertain.
- The relationships between P/E and the fundamental variables examined may change over time.
- Multicollinearity is often a problem in these time series regressions, which makes it difficult to interpret individual regression coefficients.

 *Professor's Note: Remember from Study Session 3 that multicollinearity refers to the condition in which a high correlation exists between or among two or more of the independent variables in a multiple regression.*

**Example: Calculating predicted P/E**

An analyst is valuing a public utility with a dividend payout ratio of 0.50, a beta of 0.95, and an expected earnings growth rate of 0.06. A regression on other public utilities produces the following regression equation:

predicted P/E = 6.75 + (4.00 × dividend payout) + (12.35 × growth) – (0.5 × beta)

The firm's P/E ratio is 12.0. Calculate the predicted P/E on the basis of the values of the explanatory variables for the company, and determine whether the stock is over- or underpriced.

**Answer:**

predicted P/E = 6.75 + (4.00 × 0.50) + (12.35 × 0.06) – (0.5 × 0.95) = 9.02

Actual P/E is greater than predicted P/E, so the firm is overpriced.

 *Professor's Note: This is an example of predicting the value of a dependent variable from an estimated regression equation from Study Session 3. A P/E prediction model like this could form the basis for a quant question on the exam.*

## WARM-UP: BENCHMARKS

 *Professor's Note: The phrase "benchmark value of a multiple" is another name for the justified price multiple using the method of comparables. We use the term "benchmark" in the discussion that follows to be consistent with the wording of the LOS.*

The method of comparables approach to valuation compares a stock's price multiple to a benchmark of the multiple using the following steps:

*Step 1:* Select and calculate the multiple that will be used.
*Step 2:* Select the benchmark and calculate the mean or median of its multiple over the group of comparable stocks.
*Step 3:* Compare the stock's multiple to the benchmark.
*Step 4:* Examine whether any observed difference between the multiples of the stock and the benchmark are explained by the underlying determinants of the multiple, and make appropriate valuation adjustments.

Frequently encountered P/E benchmarks include:

- P/E of another company's stock in a similar industry with similar operating characteristics.
- Average or median P/E of peer group within the company's industry.
- Average or median P/E for the industry.
- P/E of an equity index.
- Average historical P/E for the stock.

LOS 35.j: Evaluate a stock by the method of comparables, and explain the importance of fundamentals in using the method of comparables.

LOS 35.r: Evaluate whether a stock is overvalued, fairly valued, or undervalued based on comparisons of multiples.

*CFA® Program Curriculum, Volume 4, page 286*

The basic idea of the method of comparables is to compare a stock's price multiple to that of a benchmark portfolio. *Firms with multiples below the benchmark are undervalued, and firms with multiples above the benchmark are overvalued.* However, the fundamentals of the stock should be similar to the fundamentals of the benchmark before we can make direct comparisons and draw any conclusions about whether the stock is overvalued or undervalued. In other words, we have to ensure that we're comparing apples to apples. That's why the fundamental variables (i.e., the fundamentals) that affect each multiple are important in applying the method of comparables.

Let's use the P/E ratio as an example. Remember that justified P/E is positively related to growth rates and negatively related to required rate of return and risk. Suppose we determine that the P/E of our stock is less than the benchmark. There are (at least) three possible explanations for this:

- The stock is undervalued.
- The stock is properly valued, but the stock has a lower expected growth rate than the benchmark, which leads to a lower P/E.
- The stock is properly valued, but it has a higher required rate of return (higher risk) than the benchmark, which leads to a lower P/E.

In order to conclude that the stock is truly undervalued, we have to make sure that the stock is comparable to the benchmark; it should have similar expected growth and similar risk.

**Example: Evaluating P/E ratios with the method of comparables**

An analyst has gathered P/E information on two stocks, Allbright Interiors and Basic Designs.

**Market Data on Allbright Interiors and Basic Designs**

|  | *Trailing P/E* | *Leading P/E* | *5-Year Growth Rate* | *Beta* |
|---|---|---|---|---|
| Allbright | 10.0 | 8.7 | 11.0% | 1.3 |
| Basic Designs | 14.0 | 12.7 | 9.0% | 1.4 |
| Peer median | 13.3 | 12.1 | 11.0% | 1.3 |

Evaluate the value and P/E of each stock based on the method of comparables.

**Answer:**

Allbright has a lower P/E than the peer median, despite the fact that it has a comparable growth rate and beta. This indicates Allbright is undervalued. Basic Designs, on the other hand, has a higher P/E, despite lower expected growth and a higher beta, which suggests it's overvalued relative to the benchmark.

The same steps used in valuing stocks with P/Es apply when using P/Bs. The *major difference* between the approaches is that book value forecasts are not widely disseminated like they are for EPS. Thus, most analysts use *trailing book values* in calculating P/Bs. Relative P/B valuation must consider differences in ROE, risk, and expected growth in making comparisons among stocks.

P/S valuation using the method of comparables follows the same steps as for P/E and P/B. However, P/S ratios are usually calculated based on *trailing sales*. Analysts need to control for profit margin, expected growth, risk, and the quality of accounting data in making comparisons.

**Example: Evaluating P/B and P/S ratios with the method of comparables**

Crisco Systems belongs to the Networking Products industry group, and Soothsayer belongs to the Enterprise Software/Services industry group. Recall that the P/B ratios for Crisco and Soothsayer were 4.45 and 10.04, respectively, and the P/S ratios were 6.60 and 6.71. Determine whether the two stocks are overvalued or undervalued compared to their peer group means and medians.

**Basic Data From the Computer Industry**

| *Peer Group* | *Mean P/B* | *Median P/B* | *Mean P/S (sales in millions of $)* | *Median P/S (sales in millions of $)* |
|---|---|---|---|---|
| Networking Products | 2.065 | 1.170 | 3.733 | 0.900 |
| Enterprise Software/ Services | 7.866 | 2.770 | 3.341 | 1.920 |

**Answer:**

The P/B ratio for Crisco Systems exceeds the mean P/B ratio for the peer group (2.065) as well as the median P/B ratio (1.170) for the peer group; therefore, by this measure the stock would appear to be overvalued. The P/S ratio also exceeds both the mean P/S (3.733) and the median P/S (0.900) for the peer group, which also indicates that the stock is overvalued.

The P/B ratio for Soothsayer exceeds the peer group mean P/B (7.866) as well as the peer group median P/B (2.770) and suggests that the stock is overvalued. Similarly, the P/S ratio for Soothsayer exceeds the peer group mean P/S (3.341) as well as the peer group median P/S (1.920) and indicates that Soothsayer stock is overvalued as well.

Note the significant disparity between the mean and median values for each peer group. This is a clear indication of the presence of outliers in the data.

In line with other valuations by comparables discussed earlier (P/E, P/B, and P/S), a lower EV/EBITDA relative to peer firms indicates relative undervaluation, everything else being equal, and a higher ratio indicates overvaluation.

The process for dividend yield is similar to that for other multiples. An analyst compares the target company's dividend yield with that of peers to assess whether it is attractively priced. This assumes that the peers have been identified on the basis of comparable risk. Particular emphasis should be placed on determining whether any difference in dividend yield is due to expected growth differences. High dividend yield relative to the benchmark indicates undervaluation, all else equal.

---

LOS 35.k: Calculate and interpret the P/E-to-growth ratio (PEG), and explain its use in relative valuation.

---

*CFA® Program Curriculum, Volume 4, page 290*

The relationship between earnings growth and P/E is captured by the **P/E-to-growth (PEG) ratio**:

$$\text{PEG ratio} = \frac{\text{P/E ratio}}{g}$$

The PEG is interpreted as P/E per unit of expected growth. Remember that the growth rate is one of the fundamental factors that affect P/E (P/E is directly related to the growth rate). The PEG ratio, in effect, "standardizes" the P/E ratio for stocks with different expected growth rates. The implied valuation rule is that stocks with lower PEGs are more attractive than stocks with higher PEGs, assuming that risk is similar.

**Example: Calculating and using the PEG ratio**

Med-Ready, Inc. has a leading P/E of 28.75 and a 5-year consensus growth rate forecast of 14.5%. The median PEG for a group of companies comparable in risk to Med-Ready is 2.34. Calculate the firm's PEG and explain whether the stock appears to be correctly valued, overvalued, or undervalued.

**Answer:**

The firm's PEG is 28.75 / 14.5 = 1.98. Given the comparable group median PEG of 2.34, it appears that Med-Ready may be undervalued. However, it is important for the analyst to determine whether the peer group PEG is also based on leading P/Es and whether the comparable firms are similar in risk.

There are a number of drawbacks to using the PEG ratio:

- The relationship between P/E and $g$ is not linear, which makes comparisons difficult.
- The PEG ratio still doesn't account for risk.
- The PEG ratio doesn't reflect the duration of the high-growth period for a multistage valuation model, especially if the analyst uses a short-term high-growth forecast.

---

**LOS 35.l: Calculate and explain the use of price multiples in determining terminal value in a multistage discounted cash flow (DCF) model.**

---

*CFA® Program Curriculum, Volume 4, page 299*

A terminal value that is projected as of the end of the investment horizon should reflect the earnings growth that a firm can sustain over the long run, beyond that point in time. Analysts often use terminal price multiples like P/E, P/B, P/S, and P/CF to estimate terminal value. No matter which ratio is used, terminal value is calculated as the product of the price multiple (e.g., P/E ratio) and the fundamental variable (e.g., EPS).

There are two methods of estimating the price multiple: based on fundamentals and based on comparables. The terminal price multiple based on fundamentals is the product of the justified price multiple and an estimate of the fundamental value. For example, the terminal value based on a justified P/E ratio is:

terminal value in year n = (justified leading P/E ratio) × (forecasted earnings in year n + 1)

terminal value in year n = (justified trailing P/E ratio) × (forecasted earnings in year n)

The terminal price multiple based on comparables is calculated as the benchmark price multiple and an estimate of the fundamental value. For example, the terminal value based on a benchmark P/E is:

terminal value in year n = (benchmark leading P/E ratio) ×
(forecasted earnings in year n + 1)

terminal value in year n = (benchmark trailing P/E ratio) ×
(forecasted earnings in year n)

The strength of the comparables approach is that it uses market data exclusively. In contrast, the fundamentals approach requires estimates of the growth rate, required rate of return, and payout ratio. One weakness of the comparables approach is that a benchmark marred by mispricing will transfer that error to the estimated terminal value.

---

**Example: Calculating terminal value with price multiples**

An analyst estimates the EPS of Polar Technology in five years to be C$2.10, the EPS in six years to be C$2.32, and the median trailing industry P/E to be 35. Calculate the terminal value in Year 5.

**Answer:**

terminal value in Year 5 = (benchmark trailing P/E ratio) × (forecasted earnings in Year 5)
= 35 × C$2.10 = C$73.50

---

LOS 35.m: Explain alternative definitions of cash flow used in price and enterprise value (EV) multiples, and describe limitations of each definition.

*CFA® Program Curriculum, Volume 4, page 318*

There are at least four definitions of cash flow available for use in calculating the P/CF ratio: (1) earnings-plus-noncash-charges (CF); (2) adjusted cash flow (adjusted CFO); (3) free cash flow to equity (FCFE); and (4) earnings before interest, taxes, depreciation, and amortization (EBITDA). Expect to see any one of them on the exam.

One commonly used proxy for cash flow is **earnings-plus-noncash-charges** (CF):

CF = net income + depreciation + amortization

The limitation of this definition, as we mentioned previously, is that it ignores some items that affect cash flow, such as noncash revenue and changes in net working capital.

Another proxy for cash flow is cash flow from operations (CFO) from the cash flow statement. CFO is often adjusted for non-recurring cash flows. Also, IFRS allows interest expense to be classified as operating cash flow or financing cash flow. U.S. GAAP requires interest expense to be classified as operating cash flow. Therefore, analysts often adjust CFO by adding back the after-tax interest cost and call it **adjusted CFO**:

$$\text{adjusted CFO} = \text{CFO} + [\text{net cash interest outflow} \times (1 - \text{tax rate})]$$

Analysts also often use **free cash flow to equity** (FCFE) and **earnings before interest, taxes, depreciation, and amortization** (EBITDA) as proxies for cash flow. As we mentioned previously, theory suggests that FCFE is the preferred way to define cash flow, but it is more volatile than straight cash flow.

$$\text{FCFE} = \text{CFO} - \text{FCInv} + \text{net borrowing}$$

where:
FCInv = fixed capital investment
net borrowing = (long- and short-term debt issues) – (long- and short-term debt repayments)

EBITDA is a pretax, pre-interest measure that represents a flow to both equity and debt. Thus, it is better suited as an indicator of total company value than just equity value. More on this point is provided in our discussion of the enterprise value-to-EBITDA ratio.

Analysts typically use *trailing* price to cash flow ratio, which relies on the most recent four quarters of cash flow per share. Given one of the four definitions of cash flow, the P/CF ratio is calculated as:

$$\text{P / CF ratio} = \frac{\text{market value of equity}}{\text{cash flow}} = \frac{\text{market price per share}}{\text{cash flow per share}}$$

where:
cash flow = CF, adjusted CFO, FCFE, or EBITDA

### Example: Calculating P/CF

Data Management Systems, Inc., (DMS) reported net income of $32 million, depreciation and amortization of $41 million, net interest expense of $12 million, and cash flow from operations of $44 million. The tax rate is 30%. Calculate the P/CF ratio using CF and adjusted CFO as proxies for cash flow. DMS has 25 million shares of common stock outstanding, trading at $47 per share.

**Answer:**

CF $= \$32$ million $+ \$41$ million $= \$73$ million

adjusted CFO $= \$44$ million $+ [\$12$ million $\times (1 - 0.30)] = \$52.4$ million

market value of equity $= 25$ million shares $\times \$47$ per share $= \$1,175$ million

P/CF $= \dfrac{\$1,175 \text{ million}}{\$73 \text{ million}} = 16.1$ times

P/adjusted CFO $= \dfrac{\$1,175 \text{ million}}{\$52.4 \text{ million}} = 22.4$ times

LOS 35.n: Calculate and interpret EV multiples, and evaluate the use of EV/ EBITDA.

*CFA® Program Curriculum, Volume 4, page 324*

Because EBITDA is a flow to both equity and debt, it should be related to a numerator that measures total company value. **Enterprise value** (EV) is total company value:

EV = market value of common stock + market value of preferred equity
+ market value of debt + minority interest – cash and investments

The rationale for subtracting cash and investments is that an acquirer's net price paid for an acquisition target would be lowered by the amount of the target's liquid assets. Thus, EV/EBITDA indicates the value of the overall company, not equity.

 *Professor's Note: For our discussion going forward, we will assume minority interest and preferred equity is zero (which is typical). If, on the exam, you are given values for preferred stock and/or minority interest, do include them.*

EV/EBITDA is the ratio of enterprise value to EBITDA:

$$\text{EV/EBITDA ratio} = \frac{\text{enterprise value}}{\text{EBITDA}}$$

where:
enterprise value = market value of common stock +
        market value of debt – cash and investments
EBITDA = recurring earnings from continuing operations +
        interest + taxes + depreciation + amortization

or for forecasting

= EBIT + depreciation + amortization

EV/EBITDA is useful in a number of situations:

- The ratio may be more useful than P/E when comparing firms with different degrees of financial leverage.
- EBITDA is useful for valuing capital-intensive businesses with high levels of depreciation and amortization.
- EBITDA is usually positive even when EPS is not.

EV/EBITDA has a number of drawbacks, however:

- If working capital is growing, EBITDA will overstate CFO. Further, the measure ignores how different revenue recognition policies affect CFO.
- Because FCFF captures the amount of capital expenditures, it is more strongly linked with valuation theory than EBITDA. EBITDA will be an adequate measure if capital expenses equal depreciation expenses.

---

**Example: Calculating EV/EBITDA**

An analyst gathered the following data for Boulevard Industries [all amounts in Swiss francs (Sf)]:

- Recent share price                    Sf 22.50
- Shares outstanding                    40 million
- Market value of debt                  Sf 137 million
- Cash and marketable securities        Sf 62.3 million
- Investments                           Sf 327 million
- Net income                            Sf 137.5 million
- Interest expense                      Sf 6.9 million
- Depreciation and amortization         Sf 10.4 million
- Taxes                                 Sf 95.9 million

Based on this information, calculate the EV/EBITDA ratio for Boulevard Industries.

**Answer:**

$$\text{EBITDA} = 137.5 + 6.9 + 95.9 + 10.4 = \text{Sf } 250.7 \text{ million}$$

$$\text{EV} = (22.50 \times 40) + 137 - 62.3 - 327 = \text{Sf } 647.7 \text{ million}$$

$$\text{EV/EBITDA} = \frac{\text{Sf } 647.7 \text{ million}}{\text{Sf } 250.7 \text{ million}} = 2.6 \text{ times}$$

---

An alternative measure of a company's overall value is **total invested capital** (TIC), sometimes referred to as **market value of invested capital**. Total invested capital is the market value of the company's equity and debt. Unlike enterprise value, TIC includes cash and short-term investments.

In addition to EV/EBITDA and TIC/EBITDA, analysts employ enterprise value ratios with EBIT, FCFF, or other items in the denominator. For example, the *enterprise value to sales* (EV/S) ratio can be used as an alternative to the P/S ratio. The EV/S ratio is appropriate for comparing companies with significantly different capital structures.

## LOS 35.o: Explain sources of differences in cross-border valuation comparisons.

*CFA® Program Curriculum, Volume 4, page 333*

Using relative valuation methods that require the use of comparable firms is challenging in an international context due to **differences in accounting methods, cultures, risk, and growth opportunities.** Further, benchmarking is difficult because P/Es for individual firms in the same industry vary widely internationally and country market P/Es can vary significantly. Common differences in international accounting treatment fall into several categories: goodwill, deferred income taxes, foreign exchange adjustments, R&D, pension expense, and tangible asset revaluations.

The usefulness of all price multiples is affected to some degree by differences in international accounting standards. The least affected are P/adjusted CFO and P/FCFE, while P/B, P/E, P/EBITDA, and EV/EBITDA will be more seriously affected because they are more influenced by management's choice of accounting methods and estimates.

## LOS 35.p: Describe momentum indicators and their use in valuation.

*CFA® Program Curriculum, Volume 4, page 335*

**Momentum indicators** relate either the market price or a fundamental variable like EPS to the time series of historical or expected value. Common momentum indicators include earnings surprise, standardized unexpected earnings, and relative strength.

**Unexpected earnings or earnings surprise** is the difference between reported earnings and expected earnings:

$$\text{earnings surprise} = \text{reported EPS} - \text{expected EPS}$$

This is usually scaled by a measure that expresses the variability of analysts' EPS forecasts. The economic rationale for examining earnings surprises is that positive surprises may lead to persistent positive abnormal returns.

Similarly, the **standardized unexpected earnings** (SUE) measure is defined as:

$$\text{standardized unexpected earnings}\,(\text{SUE}) = \frac{\text{earnings surprise}}{\text{standard deviation of earnings surprise}}$$

A given size forecast error is more meaningful the smaller the size of the historical forecast errors.

Relative strength indicators compare a stock's price or return performance during a given time period with its own historical performance or with some group of peer stocks. The economic rationale is that patterns of persistence or reversal may exist in stock returns. These are thought to possibly depend on the length of an investor's time horizon.

**LOS 35.q: Explain the use of the arithmetic mean, the harmonic mean, the weighted harmonic mean, and the median to describe the central tendency of a group of multiples.**

*CFA® Program Curriculum, Volume 4, page 340*

The price-to-earnings multiple for a stock index is not equal to the mean or weighted mean of the P/Es of the portfolio stocks. Consider two stocks: one priced at $10 with earnings of $1 per share (P/E = 10) and one priced at $16 with earnings of $2 (P/E = 8). For a portfolio with one share of each stock, earnings per share are 1 + 2 = 3 and the "price" of a portfolio share is 10 + 16 = 26. The portfolio price-to-earnings is 26 / 3 = 8.67.

We will demonstrate that the portfolio or index P/E (as well as other relative value ratios based on price) is best calculated as the **weighted harmonic mean** P/E. With the P/Es denoted by $X$ and the weights as $w$, we have:

$$\text{weighted harmonic mean} = \frac{1}{\sum\limits_{i=1}^{n} \dfrac{w_i}{X_i}}$$

Consider the following alternative measures of the mean P/E for the portfolio:

arithmetic mean = (8 + 10) / 2 = 9

weighted mean = (10 / 26) × 10 + (16 / 26) × 8 = 8.76

$$\text{harmonic mean} = \frac{2}{\left(\dfrac{1}{10}\right) + \left(\dfrac{1}{8}\right)} = 8.88$$

$$\text{weighted harmonic mean} = \frac{1}{\left(\dfrac{10}{26}\right)\left(\dfrac{1}{10}\right) + \left(\dfrac{16}{26}\right)\left(\dfrac{1}{8}\right)} = 8.67$$

An analyst must be aware of how portfolio P/Es are calculated to understand them. Note that when there are extreme (high or low) outliers, the arithmetic mean will be the most affected. Analysts should be aware that the harmonic mean puts more weight on smaller values. In this case, the median or weighted harmonic mean with the outliers excluded may be the most appropriate measures of the P/E for a portfolio or index. For an equal weighted portfolio or index, the harmonic mean and weighted harmonic mean will be equal.

## KEY CONCEPTS

### LOS 35.a

The method of comparables uses a price multiple for a similar firm or the average price multiple for a portfolio of stocks or an index as a benchmark value. The underlying economic argument for this method is that the value of a dollar of earnings or a dollar of book value, for example, should be the same across similar stocks or stocks in the same industry. Valuation based on the method of comparables is relative, based on the current market values of other stocks.

Rather than using current price multiples for other stocks, the method of forecasted fundamentals uses price multiples based on forecasted values for fundamental characteristics such as growth, dividend payout, or ROE. Under this method, we are assuming that a particular valuation model gives the stock's intrinsic value. As an example, consider the relation P/E = payout ratio / (required return – growth rate). This is the P/E for the stock if its price is equal to its value calculated using the constant growth model, an estimate of the absolute value of the stock.

### LOS 35.b

A justified price multiple can be "justified" by either the method of comparables or by the method of forecasted fundamentals. As an example, consider the P/E justified by the constant growth (Gordon growth) model value. Stocks with P/Es less than their justified P/Es, based on forecasts of the fundamental variables involved, are judged to be undervalued. A similar argument can be made for stocks with P/Es less than that for a similar stock or benchmark P/E determined by the method of comparables.

### LOS 35.c

Rationales for using price-to-earnings (P/E) ratio in valuation:
- Earnings power, as measured by earnings per share (EPS), is the primary determinant of investment value.
- The P/E ratio is popular in the investment community.
- Empirical research shows that P/E differences are significantly related to long-run average stock returns.

Disadvantages of using the price-to-earnings ratio include:
- Earnings can be negative.
- The volatile, transitory portion of earnings makes interpretation difficult.
- Management discretion distorts reported earnings.

Rationales for using price-to-book (P/B) ratio in valuation:
- Book value is a cumulative amount that is usually positive, even when the firm reports a loss and EPS is negative. Thus, a P/B can typically be used when P/E cannot.
- Book value is more stable than EPS, so it may be more useful than P/E when EPS is particularly high, low, or volatile.
- Book value is an appropriate measure of net asset value for firms that primarily hold liquid assets. Examples include finance, investment, insurance, and banking firms.

- P/B can be useful in valuing companies that are expected to go out of business.
- Empirical research shows that P/Bs help explain differences in long-run average stock returns.

Disadvantages of using the price-to-book ratio include:
- P/Bs do not recognize the value of nonphysical assets.
- P/Bs can mislead when there are significant size differences.
- Different accounting conventions can obscure the true investment in the firm made by shareholders.
- Inflation and technological change can cause the book and market value of assets to differ significantly.

Rationales for using price-to-sales (P/S) ratio in valuation:
- P/S is meaningful even for distressed firms.
- Sales revenue is not as easy to manipulate or distort as EPS and book value.
- P/S ratios are not as volatile as P/E multiples.
- P/S ratios are particularly appropriate for valuing stocks in mature or cyclical industries and start-up companies with no record of earnings.
- Empirical research finds that differences in P/S are significantly related to differences in long-run average stock returns.

Disadvantages of using the price-to-sales ratio include:
- Higher sales do not necessarily indicate higher operating profits.
- P/S ratios do not capture differences in cost structures across companies.
- While less subject to distortion than earnings, revenue recognition practices can distort sales forecasts.

Rationales for using price-to-cash flow (P/CF) ratio in valuation:
- Cash flow is harder for managers to manipulate than earnings.
- Price to cash flow is more stable than price to earnings.
- Reliance on cash flow rather than earnings handles the problem of differences in the quality of reported earnings, which is a problem for P/E.
- Empirical evidence indicates that differences in price to cash flow are significantly related to differences in long-run average stock returns.

Disadvantages of using the price to cash flow include:
- The EPS plus noncash charges estimate ignores items affecting actual cash flow from operations.
- FCFE is preferred but is more volatile than operating cash flow.

Rationales for using dividend yield in valuation:
- Dividend yield contributes to total investment return.
- Dividends are not as risky as the capital appreciation component of total return.

Disadvantages of using dividend yield include:
- Dividend yield is only one component of the return on a stock.
- All else equal, higher dividends will lead to slower growth, which drives the other component of returns, price appreciation.

## LOS 35.d

- The trailing P/E ratio is market price per share divided by earnings per share over the last four reported quarters.
- The leading P/E ratio is market price per share divided by estimated earnings per share for the next four quarters.
- The price/sales ratio is the market price per share divided by sales per share.
- The price/book ratio is the market price per share divided by the book value (shareholders' equity) per share.
- The price/cash flow ratio is the market price per share divided by cash flow per share, which can be calculated in various ways.
- For all of these price ratios, a higher value indicates a greater relative stock value.
- The (expected) dividend yield is the expected dividend over the next four quarters divided by the current market price per share.

## LOS 35.e

Underlying earnings are earnings that exclude nonrecurring components. Normalized earnings are earnings adjusted for the business cycle using either the method of historical EPS or the method of average ROE. The method of average ROE is preferred.

## LOS 35.f

A high earnings yield (E/P) suggests a cheap security, and a low E/P suggests an expensive security, so securities can be ranked from cheap to expensive based on E/P ratios.

## LOS 35.g

All else equal:

- The price-to-earnings ratio will be higher the greater the growth rate of earnings and the lower the required rate of return.
- The price-to-sales ratio will be higher the greater the net profit margin and the lower the required rate of return.
- The price-to-cash flow ratio will be higher the greater the growth rate of free cash flow to equity and the lower the required rate of return.
- The price-to-book ratio will be higher the greater the spread between ROE and the required rate of return.
- The dividend yield will be higher the greater the required rate of return and the lower the growth rate of earnings.

## LOS 35.h

Based on discounted cash flow valuation:

- The justified leading price-to-earnings ratio based on forecasted fundamentals can be calculated as:

$$P/E = \frac{P_0}{E_1} = \frac{\text{payout ratio}}{r - g}$$

- The justified price-to-book value ratio based on forecasted fundamentals can be calculated as:

$$\frac{P_0}{B_0} = \frac{ROE - g}{r - g}$$

- The justified price-to-sales ratio based on forecasted fundamentals can be calculated as:

$$\frac{P_0}{S_0} = \frac{(E_0 \,/\, S_0) \times (1-b) \times (1+g)}{r-g}$$

## LOS 35.i
Predicted P/E can be estimated from linear regression of historical P/Es on its fundamental variables.

## LOS 35.j,r
The basic idea of the method of comparables is to compare a stock's price multiple to the benchmark. Firms with multiples below the benchmark are undervalued, and firms with multiples above the benchmark are overvalued.

When using the method of comparables to identify attractively priced stocks, the analyst must account for differences in the stocks' fundamentals. A stock with a high P/E ratio may still be attractive because of its rapid growth, while a stock with a high dividend yield (low price-to-dividend) may be unattractive because earnings do not support the dividend and no growth is anticipated.

## LOS 35.k
The price earnings-to-growth (PEG) ratio is calculated as $\text{PEG ratio} = \dfrac{\text{P/E ratio}}{g}$. Lower PEGs are more attractive than stocks with higher PEGs, all else equal.

## LOS 35.l
Analysts often use price multiples such as P/E, P/B, P/S, and P/CF to estimate terminal value. No matter which ratio we use, terminal value is calculated as the product of the expected price multiple (e.g., P/E ratio) and the terminal value of the fundamental variable (e.g., EPS).

## LOS 35.m
There are four measures of cash flow commonly used for cash flow multiples and enterprise value multiples:

1. Earnings plus noncash charges: EPS plus per-share depreciation, amortization, and depletion.

2. Cash flow from operations (CFO): Often adjusted by subtracting nonrecurring cash flows, and for different classifications of cash flows under differing accounting standards. This measure is more technically correct than earnings plus noncash charges.

3. Free cash flow to equity (FCFE): CFO minus capital expenditures, minus (plus) principal payments to (from) debtholders. Most closely linked to value theory but more volatile than other measures. Consider using average FCFE.

4.  Earnings before interest, taxes, depreciation, and amortization (EBITDA): Depreciation and amortization are added to EBIT (for forecasting), or interest, taxes, depreciation, and amortization can be added to recurring earnings from continuing operations (for historical values). As a pre-interest earnings measure, EBITDA is a measure of cash flow to the firm, to both debt and equity holders.

### LOS 35.n

Enterprise value (EV) is measured as the market value of debt, common equity, and any preferred equity, minus the value of cash and investments. EV/EBITDA is a commonly used measure of relative company value.

Advantages of EV/EBITDA:
*   It is useful for comparing firms with different degrees of financial leverage.
*   EBITDA is useful for valuing capital-intensive businesses with high depreciation.
*   EBITDA is usually positive even when EPS is not.

Disadvantages of EV/EBITDA:
*   If working capital is growing, EBITDA will overstate CFO.
*   FCFF is more strongly linked with valuation theory than EBITDA.

### LOS 35.o

Using relative valuation methods that require the use of comparable firms is challenging in an international context due to differences in accounting methods, cultures, risk, and growth opportunities.

### LOS 35.p

Momentum indicators relate either the market price or a fundamental variable-like EPS to the time series of historical or expected value. Common momentum indicators include earnings surprise, standardized unexpected earnings, and relative strength.

### LOS 35.q

When calculating the P/E or other price multiple for an index or portfolio, the arithmetic mean may be misleading. The most appropriate measure is the weighted harmonic mean of the individual asset P/Es using the portfolio or index weights.

$$\text{weighted harmonic mean} = \frac{1}{\displaystyle\sum_{i=1}^{n}\frac{w_i}{X_i}}$$

## CONCEPT CHECKERS

1.  The stock of Western Graphics Co. paid a dividend of $0.40 per share *last* year on earnings of $1.00 per share. The firm's earnings and dividends are expected to grow at 5% per year forever. Shareholders require a return of 12% on their investment. The justified trailing and leading P/E multiples are *closest* to:

    | Trailing P/E | Leading P/E |
    |---|---|
    | A.  6.0 | 5.7 |
    | B.  6.0 | 6.3 |
    | C.  5.7 | 6.3 |

2.  An analyst is valuing an electric utility with a dividend payout ratio of 0.65, a beta of 0.56, and an expected earnings growth rate of 0.032. A regression on other electric utilities produces the following equation:

    predicted P/E = 8.57 + (5.38 × dividend payout) + (15.53 × growth) – (0.61 × beta)

    The predicted P/E on the basis of the values of the explanatory variables for the company is *closest* to:
    A.  12.2.
    B.  15.4.
    C.  20.8.

3.  Party Favors, Inc. has a leading P/E of 18.75 and a 5-year consensus growth rate forecast of 15.32%. The median PEG, based on leading P/E, for a group of companies comparable in risk to Party Favors, Inc. is 0.92. The stock appears to be:
    A.  overvalued because its PEG ratio is 0.82.
    B.  overvalued because its PEG ratio is 1.22.
    C.  undervalued because its PEG ratio is 0.82.

4.  Consumer Products, Inc. has a trailing P/E of 27.52, while the median peer group P/E is 33.25. Assuming that there are no differences in the fundamentals among the peer firms and Consumer Products, the firm is:
    A.  correctly valued.
    B.  overvalued.
    C.  undervalued.

5.  Creative Toys recently paid a dividend of $1.35 a share. It has a payout ratio of 67%, a ROE of 23%, and an expected growth rate in earnings and dividends for the foreseeable future of 7.6%. Shareholders require a return of 14% on their investment. The justified price to book value multiple is *closest* to:
    A.  1.22.
    B.  1.19.
    C.  2.41.

6. An analyst researching Blue Ridge Camping has determined that the firm has:
   - A payout ratio of 75%.
   - A return on equity (ROE) of 18%.
   - An earnings per share (EPS) of $5.35.
   - Sales per share of $342.
   - Expected earnings/dividends/sales growth of 4.5%.
   - Shareholders required return of 15%.

   The firm's justified price to sales ratio (P/S) multiple based on the above fundamentals is *closest* to:
   A. 0.0780.
   B. 0.1114.
   C. 0.1164.

7. Sabrina Valentine, CFA, has gathered the following data for Carolina Steel, Inc. (CSI):

   | | |
   |---|---|
   | Recent share price | $31.25 |
   | Shares outstanding | 30 million |
   | Market value of debt | $115 million |
   | Cash and marketable securities | $47.6 million |
   | Investments | $247 million |
   | Net income | $119.4 million |
   | Interest expense | $5.8 million |
   | Depreciation | $6.9 million |
   | Amortization | $2.3 million |
   | Taxes | $85.9 million |

   The EV/EBITDA ratio for CSI is *closest* to:
   A. 3.44.
   B. 4.26.
   C. 4.78.

8. Which of the following investment strategies is *most consistent* with choosing high dividend yield stocks?
   A. Blended.
   B. Momentum.
   C. Value.

Study Session 12

**Cross-Reference to CFA Institute Assigned Reading #35 – Market-Based Valuation: Price and Enterprise Value Multiples**

**Use the following information to answer Questions 9 through 11.**

| Company | Book Value of Equity 2007 (millions of $) | Sales 2007 (millions of $) | Shares Outstanding 2007 (millions) | Price ($) |
|---------|---------|---------|---------|---------|
| Pfeiffer, Inc. | 19,950 | 32,373 | 6,162 | 31.37 |
| Mapps, Inc. | 61,020 | 32,187 | 10,771 | 25.63 |

| Peer Group | Mean P/B | Median P/B | Mean P/S (sales in millions of $) | Median P/S (sales in millions of $) |
|---------|---------|---------|---------|---------|
| Medical-Drugs | 5.622 | 4.250 | 8.708 | 4.530 |
| Applications Software | 4.100 | 2.140 | 3.420 | 1.440 |

Pfeiffer belongs to the Medical-Drugs group and Mapps belongs to the Applications Software group.

9.  The current price-to-book and price-to-sales ratios for Pfeiffer are *closest* to:
    | | P/B | P/S |
    |---|---|---|
    | A. | 3.238 | 5.254 |
    | B. | 3.238 | 5.971 |
    | C. | 9.688 | 5.971 |

10. The current price-to-book and price-to-sales ratios for Mapps are *closest* to:
    | | P/B | P/S |
    |---|---|---|
    | A. | 4.524 | 8.578 |
    | B. | 5.665 | 2.988 |
    | C. | 4.524 | 2.988 |

11. Which of the following statements is *most accurate*, given the financial data on Pfeiffer, Mapps, and the two industries?
    A.  Both stocks are relatively overvalued.
    B.  Both stocks are relatively undervalued.
    C.  One stock is relatively overvalued and the other is relatively undervalued.

12. Jeremiah Claxton, CFA, is a junior portfolio manager for a large university endowment fund. Claxton's supervisor, Joanne LeMonte, has asked him to compare the valuation of Home Decor, Inc. and Lester's Companies, Inc. and make a recommendation for an addition to the fund's retail portfolio. LeMonte has specifically asked Claxton to consider the price-to-cash flow valuation metric when making his recommendation. Claxton has gathered the following information.

### Comparison Between Lester's and Home Decor (per share amounts)

| | Recent Price | Trailing CF per Share | P/CF | Trailing FCFE per Share | P/FCFE | Consensus 5-Year Growth Forecast | Beta |
|---|---|---|---|---|---|---|---|
| Lester's | $47.8 | $2.00 | 23.90 | $0.36 | 132.78 | 17.5% | 1.22 |
| Home | $28.4 | $1.36 | 20.88 | $0.99 | 28.69 | 22.2% | 1.36 |

Claxton has also determined that the CAPM betas of the two firms are not significantly different at the 1% level. Based on the information in the table, which of the following statements is *most accurate*?

A. Only one of the stocks is relatively overvalued.
B. Both stocks are relatively undervalued.
C. Both stocks are relatively overvalued.

13. The 12-month trailing EPS for Sample Fabrication Company as of December 31, 2007, is $1.29. Sample stock trades at $42.50 per share as of 12/31/07. In the first two quarters of 2007, Sample reported an extraordinary loss of $0.22 per share. In the third quarter, the company reported a loss from the write-down of inventory of $0.04 per share. In the fourth quarter, Sample reported a gain of $0.08 per share from a change in accounting estimate when it increased the estimate of useful life of certain manufacturing equipment. Sample's trailing P/E ratio based on underlying earnings is *closest* to:
A. 24.6.
B. 28.9.
C. 32.9.

14. The average ROE for Lever, Inc. over the last business cycle was 32%. Lever's earnings per share for 2008 is expected to be $5. The dividend payout ratio is 30%, and the current book value per share is $14. Shares are trading in the market at $54. Lever's normalized earnings per share are *closest* to:
A. $4.48.
B. $5.00.
C. $5.26.

15. A firm has a justified price-to-sales ratio of 2.0 times, a net profit margin of 5%, and a long-term growth rate of 4%. The justified leading P/E (based on the Gordon growth model) is *closest* to:
A. 34.8.
B. 38.5.
C. 40.0.

## CHALLENGE PROBLEMS

16.    At the end of 2007, an analyst estimates the value of Copyright, Inc. common stock to be $84 per share using a two-stage, dividend discount H-model and forecasts earnings for 2008 to be $4.20 per share. Copyright is *most likely*:
A.  underpriced if its actual leading P/E is 15.0 times.
B.  underpriced if its actual leading P/E is 23.0 times.
C.  overpriced if its actual leading P/E is 16.6 times.

**Use the following information to answer Questions 17 through 20.**

Lois Fischer, CFA, is a senior analyst with Merlin Equity Investors. Fischer believes that the retail industry will perform well over the next several quarters and is interested in selecting a retail stock on the basis of its price-to-book multiple. Fischer's research has resulted in a list of five stocks from which she will make her final selection: Wally's, Home Decor, Redrug, Lester's, and Harmon's (all reporting under U.S. GAAP). The following table contains the information upon which Fischer will base her decision.

**P/B Comparables for Retail Firms**

|  | Price-to-Book Value | | | | | | |
| --- | --- | --- | --- | --- | --- | --- | --- |
|  | 2005 | 2006 | 2007 | 3-Year Average | Current | 2-Year ROE Forecast | Beta |
| Wally's* | 9.85 | 8.01 | 6.93 | 8.26 | 6.53 | 20.00% | 0.98 |
| Harmon's* | 6.35 | 4.60 | 4.16 | 5.04 | 3.29 | 19.95% | 1.02 |
| Redrug** | 14.93 | 11.08 | 13.32 | 13.11 | 5.78 | 18.20% | 0.58 |
| Home Decor*** | 9.75 | 7.24 | 8.88 | 8.62 | 3.31 | 19.29% | 1.36 |
| Lester's*** | 7.65 | 6.25 | 6.66 | 6.85 | 4.32 | 18.90% | 1.22 |
| *Retail industry (department & discount) | | | | | 5.75 | 19.98% | |
| **Retail industry (drugs) | | | | | 4.69 | 15.27% | |
| ***Retail industry (home improvement) | | | | | 3.62 | 19.29% | |

Annabelle Clementi, CFA, is Fischer's supervisor and has more than 15 years of experience analyzing firms in the retail industry. Clementi typically uses the P/B ratio when comparing retail stocks with the industry and among peers. However, Clementi has concluded that firms in the home improvement segment of the retail industry utilize their assets so efficiently that P/B valuation is not appropriate. Since these firms are typically characterized as having relatively strong cash flows, Clementi has decided to assess them using valuation measures that are based on cash flows and cash flow-related concepts. With this in mind, Clementi has obtained the following financial statements for Lester's, Inc., a major player in the home improvement segment of the retail industry. Other

Study Session 12

**Cross-Reference to CFA Institute Assigned Reading #35 – Market-Based Valuation: Price and Enterprise Value Multiples**

relevant information that will assist her with the valuation of Lester's includes the following:

- Lester's financial statements are prepared using U.S. GAAP.
- Actual interest paid for the year was $240 million. The reported cash flow from operating activities includes this effect, net of tax savings.
- Assume the marginal tax rate is 37%.
- Lester's is currently trading at $42.10 per share.

**Lester's, Inc. Income Statement**

*Period Ending December 31, 2007*

| | |
|---|---:|
| Total Revenue | 22,111,108,000 |
| Cost of Revenue | (15,743,267,000) |
| **Gross Profit** | $ 6,367,841,000 |
| | |
| **Operating Expenses** | |
| Depreciation | 534,102,000 |
| Selling General and Administrative Expenses | 3,379,253,000 |
| Nonrecurring | 139,870,000 |
| Other Operating Expenses | 516,828,000 |
| **Total Operating Expenses** | $ 4,570,053,000 |
| | |
| Operating Income | 1,797,788,000 |
| Total Other Income and Expenses, Net | 58,431,000 |
| **Earnings Before Interest and Taxes** | 1,856,219,000 |
| Interest Expense | (231,968,000) |
| **Income Before Tax** | $ 1,624,251,000 |
| | |
| Income Tax Expense | 600,989,000 |
| Equity Earnings or Loss Unconsolidated Subsidiary | N/A |
| Minority Interest | N/A |
| **Net Income From Continuing Operations** | $ 1,023,262,000 |
| | |
| **Nonrecurring Events** | |
| Discontinued Operations | N/A |
| Extraordinary Items | N/A |
| Effect of Accounting Changes | N/A |
| Other Items | N/A |
| | |
| **Net Income** | 1,023,262,000 |
| Preferred Stock and Other Adjustments | N/A |
| **Net Income Applicable to Common Shares** | $ 1,023,262,000 |
| | |
| **Earnings per Common Share** | |
| Basic | $ 1.62 |
| | |
| **Weighted Average Shares Outstanding** | |
| Basic | 631,643,000 |

**Lester's, Inc. Statement of Cash Flows**

*Period Ending December 31, 2007*

| | |
|---|---:|
| Net Income | $ 1,023,262,000 |
| | |
| **Cash Flow Operating Activities** | |
| Depreciation | 534,102,000 |
| | |
| **Changes in Operating Activities** | |
| Changes in Accounts Receivables | (4,593,000) |
| Changes in Liabilities | 306,869,000 |
| Changes in Inventories | (325,406,000) |
| Changes in Other Operating Activities | (36,792,000) |
| **Cash Flow From Operating Activities** | $ 1,497,442,000 |
| | |
| **Cash Flow Investing Activities** | |
| Capital Expenditures | (2,199,334,000) |
| **Cash Flows From Investing Activities** | $ (2,199,334,000) |
| | |
| **Cash Flow Financing Activities** | |
| Dividends Paid | (59,884,000) |
| Sale (Purchase) of Stock | 115,870,000 |
| Net Borrowings | 873,480,000 |
| Other Cash Flows From Financing Activities | N/A |
| **Cash Flows From Financing Activities** | $ 929,466,000 |
| | |
| Effect of Exchange Rate | N/A |
| Change in Cash and Cash Equivalents | 227,574,000 |
| Cash and Cash Equivalents at Beginning of Period | 455,658,000 |
| **Cash and Cash Equivalents at End of Period** | $ 683,232,000 |

17. Based on the information in the first figure, which of the following statements *least likely* supports Fischer's recommendation of Home Decor over Lester's?
    A. Home Decor's P/B ratio relative to the industry.
    B. Home Decor's P/B ratio relative to Lester's P/B ratio.
    C. Home Decor's historical P/B ratios.

18. Which of the following statements is *least likely* a justification of Fischer's selection of Harmon's over Wally's on the basis of the information in the first figure?
    A. Harmon's level of systematic risk relative to Wally's.
    B. Harmon's P/B ratio relative to the industry.
    C. Wally's P/B ratio relative to the industry.

Study Session 12

**Cross-Reference to CFA Institute Assigned Reading #35 – Market-Based Valuation: Price and Enterprise Value Multiples**

19. Clementi requests that Fischer calculate several ratios using the previous information. The P/CF for Lester's using earnings-plus-noncash-charges for cash flow is *closest* to:
    A. 15.89.
    B. 17.08.
    C. 25.99.

20. Clementi requests that Fischer calculate the P/CFO for Lester's, using adjusted cash flow from operations for cash flow for comparison with other companies. The adjusted P/CFO for Lester's is *closest* to:
    A. 15.
    B. 17.
    C. 19.

# ANSWERS – CONCEPT CHECKERS

1. **A**  trailing P/E = $\dfrac{P_0}{E_0} = \dfrac{(1-b)\times(1+g)}{r-g} = \dfrac{\left(\dfrac{\$0.40}{\$1.00}\right)\times 1.05}{0.12-0.05} = 6.0$

   leading P/E = $\dfrac{P_0}{E_1} = \dfrac{1-b}{r-g} = \dfrac{0.40}{0.12-0.05} = 5.7$

2. **A**  Predicted P/E = 8.57 + (5.38 × 0.65) + (15.53 × 0.032) − (0.61 × 0.56) = 12.2

3. **B**  The firm's PEG is 18.75 / 15.32 = 1.22. Given the comparable group median PEG of 0.92, it appears that Party Favors, Inc. may be overvalued.

4. **C**  Consumer Products appears to be undervalued with a trailing P/E of 27.52 compared with the benchmark of 33.25.

5. **C**  Based on the fundamentals: $\dfrac{P_0}{B_0} = \dfrac{0.23-0.076}{0.14-0.076} = 2.41$

6. **C**  Profit margin is measured as E/S. In this example, the profit margin is $5.35 / $342 = 0.0156. Thus:

   $$\dfrac{P_0}{S_0} = \dfrac{0.0156\times 0.75\times 1.045}{0.150-0.045} = 0.1164 \text{ times}$$

7. **A**  $EBITDA = 119.4 + 5.8 + 85.9 + 6.9 + 2.3 = \$220.3$ million

   $EV = (31.25\times 30) + 115 - 47.6 - 247 = \$757.9$ million

   EV/EBITDA = $\dfrac{\$757.9}{\$220.3} = 3.44$

8. **C**  Dividend yield is positively related to the required rate of return and negatively related to the forecasted growth rate in dividends. Thus, choosing high dividend yield stocks reflects a value- rather than a growth-style orientation.

9. **C**  book value / share = $\dfrac{\text{book value of equity}}{\text{number of shares outstanding}} = \dfrac{\$19,950}{6,162} = \$3.238$

   P/B = $\dfrac{\text{market price per share}}{\text{book value per share}} = \dfrac{\$31.37}{\$3.238} = 9.688$

   sales/share = $\dfrac{\text{sales}}{\text{number of shares outstanding}} = \dfrac{\$32,373}{6,162} = \$5.254$

   P/S = $\dfrac{\text{market price per share}}{\text{sales per share}} = \dfrac{\$31.37}{\$5.254} = 5.971$

10. **A** book value/share = $\dfrac{\text{book value of equity}}{\text{number of shares outstanding}} = \dfrac{\$61,020}{10,771} = \$5.665$

$P/B = \dfrac{\text{market price per share}}{\text{book value per share}} = \dfrac{\$25.63}{\$5.665} = 4.524$

sales/share = $\dfrac{\text{sales}}{\text{number of shares outstanding}} = \dfrac{\$32,187}{10,771} = \$2.988$

$P/S = \dfrac{\text{market price per share}}{\text{sales per share}} = \dfrac{\$25.63}{\$2.988} = 8.578$

11. **A** Both stocks are relatively overvalued. The P/B and P/S ratios for Pfeiffer are 9.688 and 5.971. The P/B ratio for Pfeiffer exceeds the mean P/B ratio for the peer group (5.622) as well as the median P/B ratio (4.250) for the peer group, and therefore, by this measure, the stock would appear to be overvalued. The P/S ratio also exceeds the median P/S (4.530) for the peer group, which further suggests that the stock is relatively overvalued.

    The P/B and P/S ratios for Mapps are 4.524 and 8.578. The P/B ratio for Mapps is greater than the mean P/B ratio for the peer group (4.100), and Mapps's median P/B ratio exceeds the median ratio (2.140) for the peer group, and therefore, by this measure, Mapps is overvalued. Mapps's P/S ratio exceeds both the mean P/S (3.420) and the median P/S (1.440) for the peer group. The P/S ratio also indicates that Mapps is relatively overvalued.

12. **A** Home Decor appears to be undervalued relative to Lester's. This conclusion is based on the fact that (1) Home Decor is selling at a P/CF of 20.88, which is 87.4% of the P/CF for Lester's (23.90), and (2) the P/FCFE for Home Decor (28.69) is 21.6% of the P/FCFE for Lester's (132.78). We would expect that Home Decor would have a higher P/CF because of its higher expected growth. However, because P/CF is actually lower, this is an indication that Home Decor is undervalued relative to Lester's.

13. **B** Underlying earnings = $1.29 + $0.22 + $0.04 − $0.08 = $1.47

    P/E ratio $= \dfrac{\$42.50}{\$1.47} = 28.9$

14. **A** Only the average ROE and the book value per share are relevant for calculating normalized earnings:

    normalized earnings = average ROE × BVPS = 0.32 × $14 = $4.48 per share

15. **B** trailing P/E $= \dfrac{P/S}{\text{net profit margin}} = \dfrac{2.0}{0.05} = 40$

    leading P/E $= \dfrac{\text{trailing P/E}}{1+g} = \dfrac{40}{1.04} = 38.5$

## ANSWERS – CHALLENGE PROBLEMS

16. **A**  Copyright's justified leading P/E multiple using the valuation from the H-model is $84 / $4.20 = 20 times. The firm is underpriced if its actual P/E is less than 20; it is overpriced if its actual P/E is greater than 20.

17. **C**  In the home improvement segment of the retail industry, Home Decor appears to be a more attractive investment than Lester's for the following reasons:
    - Home Decor is trading at a P/B that is 91% of the average P/B for the home improvement segment of the retail industry, with a forecasted ROE that is the same as that of the industry. This indicates that Home Decor is undervalued relative to its industry.
    - Home Decor is currently trading at a P/B that is 76.6% of the P/B for Lester's, with an estimated ROE that is slightly greater than the forecasted ROE for Lester's. This indicates that Home Decor is undervalued relative to Lester's.
    - Lester's is trading at a P/B that is 119% of the industry average P/B, with a forecasted ROE that is slightly below the industry's forecasted ROE. This indicates that Lester's is overvalued relative to its industry.
    - It should be noted that Home Decor's higher beta may account for Home Decor's low P/B and high forecast ROE relative to Lester's.

18. **A**  In the department and discount segment of the retail industry, Harmon's appears to be a more attractive investment than Wally's for the following reasons:
    - Harmon's is trading at a P/B that is 57% of the average P/B for the department and discount store segment of the retail industry with a forecasted ROE that is very close to that of the industry. This indicates that Harmon's is undervalued relative to the industry.
    - Harmon's is currently trading at a P/B that is 50% of the current P/B for Wally's, with an estimated ROE that is just slightly less than the forecasted ROE for Wally's. This indicates that Harmon's is undervalued relative to Wally's. It should be noted that the beta values for Harmon's and Wally's are only slightly different, indicating similar risk.
    - Wally's is trading at a P/B that is 114% of the industry average P/B, with a forecasted ROE that is only slightly above the ROE forecast for the industry. This indicates that Wally's is overvalued relative to its industry.

19. **B**  P = $42.10/share

    CF = net income + depreciation = $1,023,262,000 + $534,102,000 = $1,557,364,000

    number of basic shares outstanding = 631,643,000

    CF/share = $1,557,364,000 / 631,643,000 = $2.4656

    P/CF = $42.10 / $2.4656 = 17.08 times

20. **B** It is appropriate to make one adjustment to CFO in this problem to reflect nonrecurring items:

- The nonrecurring expense of $139,870,000 that appears on the income statement should be added back after adjusting for taxes.

CFO (reflecting nonrecurring items) = $1,497,442,000 + $139,870,000(1 – 0.37) = $1,585,560,100

No adjustment is necessary for interest expense as it is classified as an operating activity under U.S. GAAP (and all comparables are reporting under the same reporting regime—i.e., U.S. GAAP).

adjusted CFO per share = $1,585,560,100 / 631,643,000 = $2.51

adjusted P/CFO = $42.10 / $2.51 = 16.77 or closest to 17

# RESIDUAL INCOME VALUATION

Study Session 12

## EXAM FOCUS

This topic review introduces the fourth type of valuation model found in the CFA curriculum: Residual income models. You should understand the differences between these models and the dividend discount, free cash flow, and market multiple models. The successful application of residual income models depends on making the appropriate adjustments to the financial statements, so you also should be able to use the techniques you learned in the financial statement analysis material from Study Session 7 in applying these models. The concept of continuing residual income is also related to the material on competitive strategy and industry structure in Study Session 11. With all these links to other concepts in the Level II curriculum, this material is highly testable.

LOS 36.a: Calculate and interpret residual income, economic value added, and market value added.

*CFA® Program Curriculum, Volume 4, page 368*

**Residual income** (RI), or economic profit, is the net income of a firm less a charge that measures stockholders' opportunity cost of capital. The rationale for the residual income approach is that it recognizes the cost of equity capital in the measurement of income. This concept of economic income is not reflected in traditional accounting income, whereby a firm can report positive net income but not meet the return requirements of its equity investors. Accounting net income includes a cost of debt (i.e., interest expense), but does not reflect dividends or other equity capital-related funding costs. This means that accounting income may overstate returns from the perspective of equity investors. Conversely, residual income explicitly *deducts all capital costs*.

**Example: Calculating residual income**

Madeira Fruit Suppliers, Inc. (MFS) distributes fruit to grocery stores in large U.S. cities. The book value of its assets is $1.4 billion, which is financed with $800 million in equity and $600 million in debt. Its before-tax cost of debt is 3.33%, and its marginal tax rate is 34%. MFS has a cost of equity of 12.3%. MFS's abbreviated income statement is shown in the following figure.

**Partial Income Statement for MFS**

| | |
|---|---|
| EBIT | $142,000,000 |
| Less: Interest expense | (20,000,000) |
| Pretax income | 122,000,000 |
| Less: Income tax expense | (41,480,000) |
| Net income | $80,520,000 |

Determine whether MFS is profitable by calculating residual income and explaining its relationship to reported accounting income.

**Answer:**

While the accounting net income of $80,520,000 indicates that MFS is profitable, it remains to be seen whether the firm is profitable after deducting a charge for equity. The dollar-based equity charge is:

equity charge = equity capital × cost of equity = $800 million × 0.123
= $98,400,000

RI is calculated as:

| | |
|---|---|
| Net income | $80,520,000 |
| − Equity charge | 98,400,000 |
| Residual income | −$17,880,000 |

Even though MFS is profitable in the traditional accounting sense, it is economically unprofitable after taking into account the necessary charge to meet stockholders' opportunity cost of supplying capital to the company.

## EVA and MVA

**Economic value added** (EVA®) measures the value added for shareholders by management during a given year. EVA is calculated as:

$$\text{EVA} = \text{NOPAT} - (\text{WACC} \times \text{invested capital})$$
$$= [\text{EBIT} \times (1 - t)] - \$\text{WACC}$$

where:

NOPAT = net operating profit after tax

WACC = after-tax weighted average cost of capital in decimal terms (e.g., 0.05)

$t$ = marginal tax rate

$WACC = dollar cost of capital

invested capital = net working capital + net fixed assets
= book value of long-term debt + book value of equity

*Professor's Note: Notice the difference in calculation between residual income and EVA. Residual income is net income (after subtracting interest expense) minus a charge for equity capital based on the cost of equity. EVA is NOPAT (before subtracting interest expense minus a charge for debt and equity capital based on the WACC). Conceptually, however, they are both measuring economic income.*

The analyst should make the following adjustments (if applicable) to the financial statements before calculating NOPAT and invested capital:

- Capitalize and amortize research and development charges (rather than expense them), and add them back to earnings to calculate NOPAT.
- Add back charges on strategic investments that will generate returns in the future.
- Capitalize (but do not amortize) goodwill, add amortization expense back to earnings to get NOPAT, and add accumulated amortization back to invested capital. These adjustments are important if the financial statements are prepared using IAS. Under the new rules for U.S. GAAP, goodwill is not amortized; instead, it's subject to an annual impairment test.
- Eliminate deferred taxes and consider only cash taxes as an expense.
- Treat operating leases as capital leases and adjust nonrecurring items.
- Add LIFO reserve to invested capital and add back change in LIFO reserve to NOPAT.

**Market value added** (MVA) is the difference between the market value of a firm's long-term debt and equity and the book value of invested capital supplied by investors. It measures the value created by management's decisions since the firm's inception. MVA is calculated as:

MVA = market value – invested capital

---

**Example: Calculating EVA and MVA**

VBM, Inc., reports NOPAT of $2,100, a WACC of 14.2%, and invested capital of $18,000. The market price of the firm's stock is $25 per share, and VBM has 800 shares outstanding. The market value of the firm's long-term debt is $4,000. Calculate VBM's EVA and MVA.

**Answer:**

First calculate EVA:

$WACC = 0.142 \times \$18,000 = \$2,556$
EVA = $\$2,100 – \$2,556 = –\$456$

The market value of the company is the market value of the equity plus the market value of the debt:

MV of company = ($25 × 800) + $4,000 = $24,000

The firm's MVA is:

MVA = $24,000 – $18,000 = $6,000

---

## LOS 36.b: Describe the uses of residual income models.

*CFA® Program Curriculum, Volume 4, page 370*

There are several commercially available residual income-based valuation models. It is interesting to note that these models, like EVA and MVA, usually apply the concept of residual income to the measurement of managerial effectiveness and executive compensation. However, for the exam we're most interested in the equity valuation applications of residual income models. Residual income models have also been proposed as a method to measure goodwill impairment.

## LOS 36.c: Calculate the intrinsic value of a common stock using the residual income model, and compare value recognition in residual income and other present value models.

*CFA® Program Curriculum, Volume 4, page 373*

We can forecast residual income given some basic accounting information and an estimate of future earnings growth using the following formula:

$$RI_t = E_t - (r \times B_{t-1}) = (ROE - r) \times B_{t-1}$$

where:
$RI_t$ = residual income in year t
$E_t$ = expected EPS for year t
r = required return on equity
$B_{t-1}$ = book value of equity in year t – 1
ROE = expected return on new investments (expected return on equity)

---

**Example: Forecasting residual income**

Laura Kraft, CFA, was assigned the task of forecasting the residual income for Delilah Cosmetics, Inc. over the next two years. To accomplish this task, Kraft assembled the information provided in the following figure. Kraft assumed a required rate of return of 11%. Forecast Delilah's residual income for 2009 and 2010.

**Delilah Data Forecast**

| | |
|---|---|
| Current market price | €24.00 |
| Current book value per share | €18.00 |
| Consensus annual EPS estimates | |
| January 2009 | €2.05 |
| January 2010 | €2.22 |
| Dividend payout ratio 2009 and 2010 | 65% |

**Answer:**

**Delilah Residual Income Forecast**

|  | FY 2009 | FY 2010 |
| --- | --- | --- |
| Beginning book value ($B_{t-1}$) | €18.00 | €18.72 |
| Earnings per share forecast ($E_t$) | 2.05 | 2.22 |
| Dividend forecast ($D_t = E_t \times$ payout ratio) | 1.33 | 1.44 |
| Forecast book value per share ($B_{t-1} + E_t - D_t$) | 18.72 | 19.50 |
| Equity charge per share ($r \times B_{t-1}$) | 1.98 | 2.06 |
| Per share $RI_t$ [$E_t - (r \times B_{t-1})$] | €0.07 | €0.16 |

The residual income valuation model breaks the intrinsic value of a stock into two elements: (1) current book value of equity and (2) present value of expected *future* residual income:

$$V_0 = B_0 + \left\{ \frac{RI_1}{(1+r)^1} + \frac{RI_2}{(1+r)^2} + \frac{RI_3}{(1+r)^3} + \ldots \right\}$$

where:
$B_0$ = current book value of equity
$RI_t$ = $E_t - (r \times B_{t-1}) = (ROE - r) \times B_{t-1}$
$r$ = required return on equity
$ROE$ = expected return on new investments (expected return on equity)

*Don't let this formula intimidate you!* All the above expression really says is that a stock's intrinsic value, $V_0$, is equal to its current book value per share, $B_0$, plus the present value of all its expected future residual income, which is the difference between end-of-period earnings and equity charges based on beginning-of-period book value.

The difficulty in implementing this model is that we have to make some assumptions about the pattern of residual income growth in the future because it's difficult to take the present value of an infinite stream of residual incomes without more restrictive assumptions. In the following example, we make it easy by assuming the company ceases operations at the end of three years, so we only have three residual income forecasts to discount back.

**Example: Computing intrinsic value with a residual income model**

Consolidated Pipe Products has a required rate of return of 14%. The current book value is C$6.50. Earnings forecasts for 2009, 2010, and 2011 are C$1.10, C$1.00, and C$0.95, respectively. Dividends in 2009 and 2010 are forecasted to be C$0.50 and C$0.60, respectively. The dividend in 2011 is a liquidating dividend, which means that Consolidated will pay out its entire book value in dividends and cease doing business at the end of 2011. Calculate the value of Consolidated's stock using the residual income model.

**Answer:**

The residual income forecast is shown in the following table, with calculated values in blue.

**Consolidated Pipe Residual Income Forecast**

|  | 2009 | 2010 | 2011 |
|---|---|---|---|
| Beginning book value per share ($B_{t-1}$) | C$6.50 | C$7.10 | C$7.50 |
| Earnings per share forecast ($E_t$) | 1.10 | 1.00 | 0.95 |
| Dividends per share forecast ($D_t$) | 0.50 | 0.60 | 8.45 |
| Forecast book value per share ($B_{t-1} + E_t - D_t$) | 7.10 | 7.50 | 0.00 |
| Equity charge per share ($r \times B_{t-1}$) | 0.91 | 0.99 | 1.05 |
| Per share RI $[E_t - (r \times B_{t-1})]$ | C$0.19 | C$0.01 | –C$0.10 |

The intrinsic value of Consolidated Pipe Products is its current book value plus the present value of the future residual income forecasts:

$$V_0 = C\$6.50 + \frac{C\$0.19}{1.14^1} + \frac{C\$0.01}{1.14^2} - \frac{C\$0.10}{1.14^3} = C\$6.61$$

We can also use the cash flow function on our calculators to solve this problem and save ourselves a little time. Here are the keystrokes:

$CF_0$ = 6.50; C01 = 0.19; C02 = 0.01; C03 = –0.10; I = 14; CPT → NPV = 6.61

Value tends to be recognized earlier in the RI approach than in other present value-based approaches. To see this, recall that with a dividend discount model (DDM) or free cash flow to equity (FCFE) model, a large portion of the estimated intrinsic value comes from the present value of the expected terminal value. Yet the uncertainty of the expected terminal value is usually greater than any of the other forecasted cash flows because it occurs several years in the future. Valuation with residual income models, however, is relatively less sensitive to terminal value estimates, which reduces forecast error. This is because intrinsic values estimated with residual income models include the firm's current book value (which is known and doesn't need to be forecasted), and the current book value usually represents a substantial percentage of the estimated intrinsic value.

---

## LOS 36.d: Explain fundamental determinants of residual income.

---

*CFA® Program Curriculum, Volume 4, page 380*

The general residual income models make no assumptions regarding the long-term future earnings or dividend growth. However, if we make the simplifying assumption of a constant dividend and earnings growth rate, we can develop a residual income model that highlights the fundamental drivers of residual income. Assuming the stock is correctly priced (i.e., $P_0 = V_0$), value can be expressed in terms of book value:

$$V_0 = B_0 + \left[ \frac{(ROE - r) \times B_0}{r - g} \right]$$

This model is actually just another version of the Gordon growth model, so if you can use the same inputs, both models will give you the same value estimates.

This version of the residual income model is referred to as the **single-stage residual income valuation model**. In this formulation (assuming constant earnings and dividend growth) the first term is the current book value, the value of the company's assets net of liabilities. The second term in brackets is the present value of the expected future residual income. We can use this relationship to identify the **fundamental drivers** of residual income:

- If return on equity (ROE) is equal to the required return on equity, the justified market value of a share of stock is equal to its book value. When ROE is higher than the required return on equity, the firm will have positive residual income and will be valued at more than book value.
- $\left[ \frac{(ROE - r) \times B_0}{r - g} \right]$ is the additional value generated by the firm's ability to produce returns in excess of the cost of equity and, consequently, is the present value of a firm's expected economic profits (i.e., residual income).

Tobin's Q is a related concept:

$$Q = \frac{\text{market value of debt} + \text{market value of equity}}{\text{replacement cost of total assets}}$$

 *Professor's Note: The single-stage model assumes constant ROE and constant earnings growth, which implies that residual income will persist indefinitely. Residual income is likely to approach zero over time, however, as competitive forces drive industry profit margins to normal levels. Thus, in practice, the single-stage model is modified to handle declining RI by forecasting continuing residual income.*

LOS 36.e: Explain the relation between residual income valuation and the justified price-to-book ratio based on forecasted fundamentals.

*CFA® Program Curriculum, Volume 4, page 380*

As with the DDM and FCFE models, residual income models can be used to estimate justified price multiples. Among the various market multiples, residual income models are most closely related to the price-to-book value (P/B) ratio because the justified P/B is directly linked to expected future residual income. This can be seen by observing the single-stage model. If ROE is greater than the required return on equity, the second term (the present value of residual income) will be positive, the market value will be greater than book value, and the justified P/B ratio will be greater than one.

LOS 36.f: Calculate and interpret the intrinsic value of a common stock using single-stage (constant-growth) and multistage residual income models.

*CFA® Program Curriculum, Volume 4, page 381*

**Example: Calculating value with a single-stage residual income model**

Western Atlantic Railroad has a book value of $23.00 per share. The company's return on new investments (ROE) is 14%, and its required return on equity is 12%. The dividend payout ratio is 60%. Calculate the value of the shares using a single-stage residual income model and the present value of expected economic profits.

**Answer:**

First, calculate the growth rate:

$g$ = retention ratio × ROE = $(1 - 0.6) \times 0.14 = 0.056 = 5.6\%$

Then, calculate intrinsic value using the single-stage model:

$$V_0 = \$23.00 + \left[\frac{(0.14 - 0.12) \times \$23.00}{0.12 - 0.056}\right] = \$23.00 + \$7.19 = \$30.19$$

The present value of the firm's expected economic profits is $7.19.

**Example: Western Atlantic Railroad valuation with Gordon growth model**

Use the information in the previous example to calculate the value of Western Atlantic common stock using the Gordon growth model.

**Answer:**

Earnings in Year 1 ($E_1$) is equal to beginning book value multiplied by ROE: $E_1$ = $23.00 × 0.14 = $3.22. With a dividend payout ratio of 60%, $D_1$ = $3.22 (0.6) = $1.932. Then, using the Gordon growth model:

$$V_0 = \frac{\$1.932}{0.12 - 0.056} = \$30.19$$

Notice that this is the same estimate as in the previous example where we used the single-stage residual income model.

 *Professor's Note: Multistage residual income models will be discussed in LOS 42.h.*

LOS 36.g: Calculate the implied growth rate in residual income, given the market price-to-book ratio and an estimate of the required rate of return on equity.

*CFA® Program Curriculum, Volume 4, page 381*

We can rearrange the single-stage residual income valuation model and solve for the growth rate in terms of the other variables:

$$g = r - \left[ \frac{B_0 \times (ROE - r)}{V_0 - B_0} \right]$$

This expression can now be used to directly compute the market's expectations of residual income growth implied by the current market price under the assumption that intrinsic value is equal to market price.

**Example: Calculating implied growth rate**

You are considering the purchase of Tellis Telecommunications, Inc., which has a P/B ratio of 2.50. ROE is expected to be 13%, current book value per share is €8.00, and the cost of equity is 11%. Calculate the growth rate implied by the current P/B ratio.

**Answer:**

The P/B ratio of 2.50 and the current book value per share of €8.00 imply a current market price of €20.00(8 × 2.50). This implies a growth rate of:

$$g = 0.11 - \left[ \frac{€8.00 \times (0.13 - 0.11)}{€20.00 - €8.00} \right] = 0.0967 = 9.67\%$$

---

LOS 36.h: Explain continuing residual income, and justify an estimate of continuing residual income at the forecast horizon, given company and industry prospects.

---

*CFA® Program Curriculum, Volume 4, page 382*

Previously, we mentioned the problem of forecasting residual income indefinitely into the future, which makes it difficult to calculate the present value of residual income and implement the residual income model. However, we can simplify the model by using the same multistage approach we used for DDM and free cash flow models. We'll forecast residual income over a short-term horizon (e.g., five years) and then make some simplifying assumptions about the pattern of residual income growth over the long term after five years. **Continuing residual income** is the residual income that is expected over the long term.

Residual income will continue beyond a specified earnings horizon depending on the fortunes of the industry, as well as on the sustainability of a specific firm's competitive prospects over the longer term. The projected rate at which residual income is expected to fade over the life cycle of the firm is captured by a **persistence factor**, ω, which is between zero and one.

To simplify the model, we typically make one of the following assumptions about continuing residual income at the end of the short-term period:

- Residual income is expected to persist at its current level forever.
- Residual income is expected to drop immediately to zero.
- Residual income is expected to decline to a long-run average level consistent with a mature industry.
- Residual income is expected to decline over time as ROE falls to the cost of equity (in which case residual income is eventually zero).

An analysis of the firm's position in its industry and the structure of the industry will be necessary to justify one of these assumptions. The third scenario is the most realistic if we assume that over time, industry competition reduces economic profits to the point at which firms begin to leave the industry and ROE stabilizes at a long-run normal level. The strength of the persistence factor will depend partly on the sustainability of the firm's competitive advantage and the structure of the industry. The more sustainable the competitive advantage and the better the industry prospects, the higher the persistence factor.

Higher persistence factors will be associated with the following:

- Low dividend payouts.
- Historically high residual income persistence in the industry.

Lower persistence factors will be associated with the following:

- High return on equity.
- Significant levels of nonrecurring items.
- High accounting accruals.

 *Professor's Note: Be prepared for an exam question that links this material with the material in the topic review of competitive strategy in Study Session 11.*

Think of the continuing residual income model as a multistage model similar to the multistage DDM and FCF models from Study Session 11. In the residual income model, intrinsic value is the sum of three components:

$$V_0 = B_0 + \text{(PV of interim high-growth RI)} + \text{(PV of continuing residual income)}$$

*Step 1:* Calculate the current book value per share.

*Step 2:* Calculate residual income in each year 1 to T − 1 during the interim high-growth period and discount them back to today at the required return on equity.

*Step 3:* Calculate continuing residual income that begins at the end of the high-growth period starting in year T, and then calculate the present value of continuing residual income as of the end of year T − 1 using the following formula:

$$\text{PV of continuing residual income in year } T-1 = \frac{RI_T}{1+r-\omega}$$

where:
$\omega$ = persistence factor, $0 \leq \omega \leq 1$

**Assumption #1: Residual Income Persists at the Current Level Forever**

If $\omega = 1$, residual income is expected to persist at the current level forever after year T − 1, so residual income in every year after T equals residual income in year T. The present value of continuing residual income at the end of year T − 1 is the present value of a perpetuity:

$$\text{PV of continuing residual income in year } T-1 = \frac{RI_T}{1+r-\omega} = \frac{RI_T}{1+r-1} = \frac{RI_T}{r}$$

### Assumption #2: Residual Income Drops Immediately to Zero

If $\omega = 0$, residual income is expected to drop immediately to zero beginning in year $T + 1$, and the present value of continuing residual income in year $T - 1$ is:

$$\text{PV of continuing residual income in year } T-1 = \frac{RI_T}{1+r-\omega} = \frac{RI_T}{1+r-0} = \frac{RI_T}{1+r}$$

### Assumption #3: Residual Income Declines Over Time to Zero

If residual income is expected to decline over time after year $T$ as ROE falls to the cost of equity capital, then the persistence factor, $\omega$, is between zero and one, and the present value of continuing residual income in year $T - 1$ is equal to:

$$\text{PV of continuing residual income in year } T-1 = \frac{RI_T}{1+r-\omega}$$

### Assumption #4: Residual Income Declines to Long-Run Level in Mature Industry

There is another, simpler approach to calculating the PV of continuing residual income that does not rely on the formula or $\omega$, the persistence factor, if residual income is expected to decline to a normal long-run level consistent with a mature industry after year $T$.

First, recall from the single-stage residual income model that market value equals book value plus the present value of residual income. Therefore, at any point in time ($T$), the present value of future residual income is the difference between market value ($P_T$) and book value ($B_T$):

$$\text{PV of continuing residual income in year } T = P_T - B_T$$

How do we estimate $P_T$?

Given a forecasted price-to-book ratio and book value at the end of the year $T$, the value of the stock is:

$$P_T = B_T \times (\text{forecasted price-to-book ratio})$$

To make this approach consistent with the first three that use the persistence factor equation, we can also calculate the present value of continuing residual income at time $T - 1$:

$$\text{PV of continuing residual income in year } T-1 = \frac{(P_T - B_T) + RI_T}{1+r}$$

**Example: Calculating value with a multistage residual income model (part 1)**

Java Metals is expecting an ROE of 15% over each of the next five years. Its current book value is $5.00 per share, it pays no dividends, and all earnings are reinvested. The required return on equity is 10%. Forecasted earnings in years 1 through 5 are equal to ROE times beginning book value. Calculate the intrinsic value of the company using a residual income model, assuming that after five years, continuing residual income falls to zero.

**Answer:**

The following table provides an estimate of the present value of residual income.

**Java Metals Residual Income Forecast**

| Year | $E_t$ | Ending Book Value $(B_{t-1})$ | ROE | Equity Charge $(r \times B_{t-1})$ | Residual Income $[E - (r \times B_{t-1})]$ |
|------|-------|-------------------------------|-----|-------------------------------------|---------------------------------------------|
| 0 | | $5.00 | | | |
| 1 | $0.75 | 5.75 | 0.15 | $0.50 | $0.25 |
| 2 | 0.86 | 6.61 | 0.15 | 0.57 | 0.29 |
| 3 | 0.99 | 7.60 | 0.15 | 0.66 | 0.33 |
| 4 | 1.14 | 8.74 | 0.15 | 0.76 | 0.38 |
| 5 | 1.31 | 10.05 | 0.15 | 0.87 | 0.44 |

Under the assumption that residual income after five years is zero (i.e., $\omega = 0$), the terminal value (the present value of continuing residual income) at the end of Year 4 is $0.44/1.10 = $0.40. Intrinsic value today is:

$$V_0 = \$5.00 + \left[ \frac{\$0.25}{1.10} + \frac{\$0.29}{1.10^2} + \frac{\$0.33}{1.10^3} + \frac{\$0.38 + \$0.40}{1.10^4} \right] = \$6.25$$

Remember, you can also use your calculator to solve for the answer: CF0 = 5, C01 = 0.25, C02 = 0.29, C03 = 0.33, C04 = 0.38 + 0.40 = 0.78, I = 10, CPT → NPV = $6.25.

**Example: Calculating value with a multistage residual income model (part 2)**

Suppose we change our assumption regarding Java's residual income after five years to assume instead that it remains constant at $0.44 forever. Calculate the new intrinsic value of Java.

**Answer:**

The intrinsic value of Java is higher than the first case because we assume the residual income persists at the same level forever, so $RI_5 = RI_6 = \ldots = \$0.44$, and $\omega = 1$. The $0.44 perpetuity beginning in Year 5 is worth $4.40 ($0.44/0.10) in Year 4. The intrinsic value is:

$$V_0 = \$5.00 + \left[ \frac{\$0.25}{1.10} + \frac{\$0.29}{1.10^2} + \frac{\$0.33}{1.10^3} + \frac{\$0.38 + \$4.40}{1.10^4} \right] = \$8.98$$

**Example: Calculating value with a multistage residual income model (part 3)**

Now let's make the more realistic assumption that after Year 5, Java's residual income will decay over time to zero with a persistence factor of 0.4. Calculate the new intrinsic value of Java.

**Answer:**

Residual income begins to decline after Year 5, so the terminal value in Year 4 includes the present value of Year 5 residual income.

$$\text{terminal value in year } 4 = \frac{\$0.44}{1 + 0.10 - 0.40} = \$0.63$$

The intrinsic value today is book value plus the present value of years 1 through 4 residual income plus the present value of the terminal value in Year 4.

$$V_0 = \$5.00 + \left[ \frac{\$0.25}{1.10} + \frac{\$0.29}{1.10^2} + \frac{\$0.33}{1.10^3} + \frac{\$0.38 + \$0.63}{1.10^4} \right] = \$6.40$$

Notice that the more conservative assumption of a lower persistence factor reduces the intrinsic value of the stock because the firm's competitive advantage and economic profits eventually disappear.

Study Session 12

**Example: Calculating value with a multistage residual income model (part 4)**

Suppose instead that at the end of Year 5 we assume that Java's ROE falls to a long-run average level and the price-to-book ratio falls to 1.2. Calculate Java's intrinsic value.

**Answer:**

The book value per share at the end of Year 5 is $10.05, which means the market price is expected to be $10.05 × 1.2 = $12.06. The present value of continuing residual income is:

$$\text{PV of continuing residual income in year 4} = \frac{(\$12.06 - \$10.05) + \$0.44}{1.10}$$

$$= \frac{\$2.45}{1.10} = \$2.23$$

Then intrinsic value is:

$$V_0 = \$5.00 + \left[ \frac{\$0.25}{1.10} + \frac{\$0.29}{1.10^2} + \frac{\$0.33}{1.10^3} + \frac{\$0.38 + \$2.23}{1.10^4} \right] = \$7.50$$

---

**LOS 36.i: Compare residual income models to dividend discount and free cash flow models.**

---

*CFA® Program Curriculum, Volume 4, page 386*

DDM and FCFE models measure value by discounting a stream of expected cash flows. The residual income model starts with a book value and adds to this the present value of the expected stream of residual income. Theoretically, the intrinsic value derived using expected dividends, expected free cash flow to equity, or book value plus expected residual income should be identical if the underlying assumptions used to make the necessary forecasts are the same. In reality, however, it is rarely possible to forecast all of the common inputs with the same degree of accuracy, and the different models yield different results. It may be helpful though, to use a residual income model alongside a DDM or FCFE model to assess the consistency of results. If the different models provide dramatically different estimates, the inconsistencies may result from the models' underlying assumptions.

LOS 36.j: Explain strengths and weaknesses of residual income models, and justify the selection of a residual income model to value a company's common stock.

*CFA® Program Curriculum, Volume 4, page 388*

**Strengths** of residual income models include the following:

- Terminal value does *not* dominate the intrinsic value estimate, as is the case with dividend discount and free cash flow valuation models.
- Residual income models use accounting data, which is usually easy to find.
- The models are applicable to firms that do *not* pay dividends or that do not have positive expected free cash flows in the short run.
- The models are applicable even when cash flows are volatile.
- The models focus on economic profitability rather than just on accounting profitability.

**Weaknesses** of residual income models include the following:

- The models rely on accounting data that can be manipulated by management.
- Reliance on accounting data requires numerous and significant adjustments.
- The models assume that the clean surplus relation holds or that its failure to hold has been properly taken into account.

*Professor's Note: The clean surplus relation can be expressed as $B_t = B_{t-1} + E_t - D_t$, which means that ending book value of equity equals the beginning book value plus earnings less dividends, excluding ownership transactions. This is the relationship that we used in the preceding examples to forecast end-of-period book value. Any accounting charges that are taken directly to the equity accounts (such as currency translation gains and losses) will cause the clean surplus relation not to hold.*

Residual income models are *appropriate* under the following circumstances:

- A firm does not pay dividends, or the stream of payments is too volatile to be sufficiently predictable.
- Expected free cash flows are negative for the foreseeable future.
- The terminal value forecast is highly uncertain, which makes dividend discount or free cash flow models less useful.

Residual income models are *not appropriate* under the following circumstances:

- The clean surplus accounting relation is violated significantly.
- There is significant uncertainty concerning the estimates of book value and return on equity.

## LOS 36.k: Describe accounting issues in applying residual income models.

*CFA® Program Curriculum, Volume 4, page 390*

 *Professor's Note: This section is really just a brief summary of all the financial statement analysis material in Study Sessions 5, 6, and 7. As an analyst, your job is to take financial statements prepared according to GAAP, convert them to something that better reflects economic reality, and use these updated statements to estimate value. Here we discuss the typical adjustments necessary to implement residual income models, but most of these adjustments were also addressed in more detail in the financial statement analysis material.*

Conceptually, the residual income model is very straightforward; we just forecast residual income using some easily available accounting numbers and estimate the value of the equity. Unfortunately, in practice it's not quite so simple because we have to make a lot of adjustments to reported net income to arrive at a true measure of comprehensive income, which is an income measure that includes all the firm's valuation changes. Following is a discussion of some common accounting issues that come up when we try to apply residual income models.

### Clean Surplus Violations

The clean surplus relationship (i.e., ending book value = beginning book value + net income – dividends) may not hold when items are charged directly to shareholders' equity and do not go through the income statement. Therefore, we have to adjust net income to account for these items if they are not expected to reverse in the future. Items that can bypass the income statement include:

- Foreign currency translation gains and losses that flow directly to retained earnings under the all-current method.
- The minimum liability adjustment in pension accounting.
- Changes in the market value of debt and equity securities classified as available-for-sale.

The effect of violations of the clean surplus relationship is that net income is not correct, but book value is still correct. The risk in applying the residual income model when the clean surplus relation doesn't hold is that the ROE forecast will not be accurate if the clean surplus violations are not expected to offset in future years. For example, suppose the analyst determines that the clean surplus relation is violated because of the cumulative translation adjustment (CTA), resulting from the application of the all-current method of currency translation. (See Study Session 6 if the all-current method doesn't sound familiar!) If the CTA tends to reverse over time and is not consistently positive or negative, the ROE can be forecasted without taking into account the CTA.

## Variations from Fair Value

The accrual method of accounting causes many balance sheet items to be reported at book values that are significantly different than their market values. Common adjustments to the balance sheet necessary to reflect fair value include the following:

- *Operating leases* should be capitalized by increasing assets and liabilities by the present value of the expected future operating lease payments.
- *Special purpose entities* (SPEs) whose assets and liabilities are not reflected in the financial statements of the parent company should be consolidated.
- *Reserves and allowances* should be adjusted. For example, the allowance for bad debts, which is an offset to accounts receivable, should reflect the expected loss experience.
- *Inventory* for companies that use LIFO (last in, first out) should be adjusted to FIFO (first in, first out) by adding the LIFO reserve to inventory and equity, assuming no deferred tax impact.
- The *pension asset or liability* should be adjusted to reflect the funded status of the plan, which is equal to the difference between the fair value of the plan assets and the projected benefit obligation (PBO).
- *Deferred tax liabilities* should be eliminated and reported as equity if the liability is not expected to reverse (e.g., if the deferred tax liability results from different depreciation methods for tax and financial statement reporting purposes, and if the company is growing).

## Intangible Asset Effects on Book Value

Two intangible assets require special attention: (1) goodwill and (2) R&D expenditures.

**Goodwill** that results from an acquisition in which the buyer paid fair value should be included on the balance sheet for purposes of calculating book value of equity. In addition, the effect of any amortization of goodwill should be excluded from the estimate of ROE.

*Professor's Note: The recommendation to not adjust the balance sheet by removing goodwill contradicts the material in Study Session 7. These discrepancies in the CFA curriculum appear occasionally. Here's my advice: If the question relates to a residual income model, don't remove goodwill from the balance sheet; if the question is part of a financial statement analysis item set, do make the adjustment and remove goodwill.*

*Amortization of goodwill is no longer allowed under U.S. GAAP or IFRS, but you may see a question on the exam about a company that does amortize goodwill because the company's financial statements are not prepared according to U.S. GAAP or IFRS.*

The suggested analytical treatment of **R&D expenditures** is less definitive, but we can make the general statement that the ROE estimate for a mature company should reflect the long-term productivity of the company's R&D expenditures: Productive R&D

expenditures increase ROE and residual income, and unproductive expenditures reduce ROE and residual income.

## Nonrecurring Items and Other Aggressive Accounting Practices

Nonrecurring items should not be included in residual income forecasts because they represent items that are not expected to continue in the future. Items that may need adjustment in measuring recurring earnings include discontinued operations, accounting changes, unusual items, extraordinary items, and restructuring charges.

Firms may adopt other types of aggressive accounting practices that overstate the book value of assets and earnings by, for example, accelerating revenues to the current period or deferring expenses to a later period.

## International Accounting Differences

Residual income models, which are based on accrual accounting information, may not be as useful in valuing foreign firms because of differences in national accounting standards. Some things to consider in applying residual income models in global valuation settings include the following:

- How reliable are earnings forecasts?
- Are there systematic violations of the clean surplus relation?
- Do poor quality accounting rules result in financial statements that bear no resemblance to the economic reality of the business?

---

LOS 36.l: Evaluate whether a stock is overvalued, fairly valued, or undervalued based on a residual income model.

---

*CFA® Program Curriculum, Volume 4, page 381*

If a stock is trading at a price (market price) higher than the price implied by the residual income model (model price), the stock is considered to be **overvalued**. Similarly, if the market price is lower than the model price, the stock is considered to be **undervalued**, and if the model price is equal to the market price, the stock is considered to be **fairly valued**.

## KEY CONCEPTS

### LOS 36.a

Residual income is net income less a charge for common stockholders' opportunity cost of capital.

EVA and MVA are alternatives to residual income as measures of economic profit. These models are typically used in the measurement of managerial effectiveness and executive compensation. However, they are gaining acceptance as appropriate models for equity valuation.

$$EVA = NOPAT - (WACC \times invested\ capital) = EBIT \times (1 - t) - \$WACC$$

$$MVA = market\ value - invested\ capital$$

### LOS 36.b

Residual income and related models are used for equity valuation, tests for goodwill impairment, measurement of managerial effectiveness, and calculation of executive compensation.

### LOS 36.c

Residual income is calculated from accounting data as:

$$RI_t = E_t - (r \times B_{t-1})$$

where:
$E_t$ = expected EPS for year t
$r$ = required return on equity
$B_{t-1}$ = book value in year t − 1

The residual income model breaks the intrinsic value of a stock into two elements: (1) current book value of equity and (2) present value of expected future residual income:

$$V_0 = B_0 + \left\{ \frac{RI_1}{(1+r)^1} + \frac{RI_2}{(1+r)^2} + \frac{RI_3}{(1+r)^3} \ldots \right\}$$

where:
$B_0$ = current book value
$r$ = required return on equity

Valuation with residual income models is relatively less sensitive to terminal value estimates than dividend discount and free cash flow models. This is because intrinsic values estimated with residual income models include the firm's current book value, which usually represents a substantial percentage of the estimated intrinsic value.

### LOS 36.d

The fundamental drivers of residual income are ROE in excess of the cost of equity and the earnings growth rate.

LOS 36.e
If ROE is equal to the required return on equity, the justified market value of a share of stock is equal to its book value. When ROE is higher than the required return on equity, the firm will have positive residual income and will be valued at more than book value. In that case, the P/B ratio will be greater than one.

LOS 36.f
The single-stage residual income model is:

$$V_0 = B_0 + \left[ \frac{(ROE - r) \times B_0}{r - g} \right]$$

LOS 36.g
The growth rate implied by the market price in a single-stage residual income model is:

$$g = r - \left[ \frac{B_0 \times (ROE - r)}{V_0 - B_0} \right]$$

LOS 36.h
For multistage residual income models, first forecast residual income over a short-term horizon, and then make some simplifying assumptions about the pattern of residual income growth over the long term. Continuing residual income is the residual income that is expected over the long term. The present value of continuing residual income in year $T - 1$ is equal to:

$$\frac{RI_T}{(1 + r - \omega)}$$

- If residual income is expected to persist at the current level forever, $\omega = 1$.
- If residual income is expected to drop immediately to zero, $\omega = 0$.
- If residual income is expected to decline over time after year T as ROE falls to the cost of equity capital, then the persistence factor, $\omega$, is between zero and one.

Another way to estimate continuing residual income without using the persistence factor is to assume residual income is expected to decline to a normal long-run level consistent with a mature industry. Then the premium over book value $(P_T - B_T)$ is equal to the present value of continuing residual income in year T, and the present value of continuing residual income in year $T - 1$ is:

$$\frac{(P_T - B_T) + RI_T}{1 + r}$$

In the residual income model, intrinsic value is the sum of three components:

$$V_0 = B_0 + (\text{PV of interim high-growth RI}) + (\text{PV of continuing residual income})$$

## LOS 36.i

DDM and FCFE models estimate value as the discounted present value of expected future cash flows. The residual income model estimates value as book value plus the present value of the expected stream of annual residual income.

Residual income models may be used to assess the consistency of other valuation models.

## LOS 36.j

The following are strengths of residual income models:

- Terminal value does not dominate the intrinsic estimate.
- Residual income models use accounting data, which is usually easy to find.
- The models are applicable to firms that do not pay dividends or that do not have positive expected free cash flows in the short run.
- The models are applicable even when cash flows are volatile.
- The models focus on economic rather than just on accounting profitability.

The following are weaknesses of the residual income models:

- The models rely on accounting data that can be manipulated by management.
- Reliance on accounting data requires numerous and significant adjustments.
- The models assume that the clean surplus relation holds or that its failure to hold has been properly taken into account.

Residual income models are appropriate under the following circumstances:

- A firm does not pay dividends, or the stream of payments is too volatile to be sufficiently predictable.
- Expected free cash flows are negative for the foreseeable future.
- The terminal value forecast is highly uncertain, which makes dividend discount or free cash flow models less useful.

Residual income models are not appropriate under the following circumstances:

- The clean surplus accounting relation is violated significantly.
- There is significant uncertainty concerning the forecast of book value and return on equity.

## LOS 36.k

In applying the residual income valuation approach, analysts often must take into account the following:

- Violations of the clean surplus relationship.
- Balance sheet adjustments for fair value.
- Intangible assets.
- Nonrecurring items.
- Other aggressive accounting practices.
- International accounting differences.

## LOS 36.l

If model price is lower than (higher than, equal to) the market price, the stock is considered overvalued (undervalued, fairly valued).

## CONCEPT CHECKERS

1.  The present value of Sporting Shoes (SS) projected residual income for the next five years plus beginning book value is C$75.00 per share. Beyond that time horizon, the firm will sustain a residual income of C$11.25 per share, which is the residual income for Year 6. The cost of equity is 10%. The justified value of SS's common stock is *closest* to:
    A.  C$69.85.
    B.  C$112.50.
    C.  C$144.85.

2.  Meyer Henderson, CFA, estimates the value of Trammel Medical Supplies to be $68 per share using a residual income model. In his estimate of continuing residual income, he assumes that, after Year 6, residual income will persist at the same level forever. How many of the following assumptions concerning residual income would *most likely* cause his value estimate to fall below $68?

    Assumption #1: Return on equity is expected to fall immediately to Trammel's cost of equity capital.
    Assumption #2: Return on equity is expected to fall over time to Trammel's cost of equity capital with a persistence factor of 0.2.
    Assumption #3: Return on equity is expected to fall over time to the long-run industry average.

    A.  One.
    B.  Two.
    C.  Three.

**Use the following information to answer Questions 3 and 4.**

Josef Robien, CFA, is valuing the common stock of British Cornucopia Bank (BCB). In this effort, Robien has made the following assumptions:

*   Earnings per share (EPS) will be 20% of the beginning book value per share for each of the next three years.
*   Book value per share is estimated at £10.62 on December 31, 2007.
*   BCB will pay cash dividends equal to 40% of EPS.
*   At the end of three years, BCB's common stock will trade at four times its book value.
*   Beta for BCB is 0.7, the risk-free rate is 4.5%, and the equity risk premium is 5.0%.

3.  The residual income per share in 2010 and the present value of continuing residual income as of the end of 2009 are *closest* to:

    | | 2010 residual income | Continuing residual income |
    |---|---|---|
    | A. | £1.43 | £42.89 |
    | B. | £1.59 | £42.89 |
    | C. | £1.59 | £59.64 |

4.  The value per share of BCB stock using the residual income model is *closest* to:
    A.  £39.17.
    B.  £49.80.
    C.  £53.20.

5.  An investor is considering the purchase of Capital City Investments, Inc., which has a price-to-book value (P/B ratio) of 5.00. Return on equity (ROE) is expected to be 18%, the market price per share is $25.00, and the growth rate is expected to be 8%. Assume the shares are currently priced at their fair value. The cost of equity implied by the current P/B ratio is *closest* to:
    A.  6%.
    B.  8%.
    C.  10%.

**Use the following information to answer Questions 6 through 8.**

Aaron Mechanic, CFA, is responsible for valuing the shares of Duotronics Research Laboratories (DRL). The stock is currently trading at €8.75, and Mechanic gathers the following financial information about the company:

*   Expected return on equity (ROE) = 16% annually for each of the next four years.
*   Current book value (BV) of equity = €435,000,000.
*   Shares outstanding: 60 million.
*   Required rate of return on equity = 12%.
*   No dividends paid.
*   All earnings are reinvested.
*   Continuing residual income = 0 after four years.

6.  Based on the residual income model, the intrinsic value and the *most likely* recommendation Mechanic would issue for the stock of DRL are:

    | Intrinsic value | Recommendation |
    | --- | --- |
    | A.  €1.10 | Sell |
    | B.  €8.34 | Buy |
    | C.  €8.34 | Sell |

7.  Mechanic is considering revising his expectation of the continuing residual income after the 4-year horizon period and believes that it will remain constant at the Year 4 forecast level of residual income for the foreseeable future. Based on the residual income model, the intrinsic value and the *most likely* recommendation Mechanic would issue for the stock of DRL are:

    | Intrinsic value | Recommendation |
    | --- | --- |
    | A.  €8.75 | Buy |
    | B.  €10.73 | Buy |
    | C.  €10.73 | Sell |

8.  George Karanopoulos, CFA, is Mechanic's immediate supervisor. He believes that Mechanic's assumption of constant residual income after the initial forecast period is unrealistic. He has suggested that Mechanic re-estimate the value of DRL based on a persistence factor of ω = 0.3 after Year 4. Based on the residual income model, the intrinsic value and the *most likely* recommendation Mechanic would issue for the stock of DRL are:

    | Intrinsic value | Recommendation |
    |---|---|
    | A. €8.95 | Sell |
    | B. €8.45 | Buy |
    | C. €8.45 | Sell |

9.  Karuba Manufacturing has a book value of $15 per share and is expected to earn $3.00 per share indefinitely. The company does not reinvest any of its earnings. Karuba's beta is 0.75, the risk-free rate is 4%, and the expected market risk premium is 8%. The value of Karuba stock according to the dividend discount model and the residual income model are *closest* to:

    | Dividend discount model | Residual income model |
    |---|---|
    | A. $42.86 | $15.00 |
    | B. $42.86 | $30.00 |
    | C. $30.00 | $30.00 |

10. Century Scales has a required return on equity of 12% and is expected to grow indefinitely at a rate of 5%. The expected return on equity (ROE) that would justify a price-to-book multiple of 2.14 is *closest* to:
    A. 10%.
    B. 15%.
    C. 20%.

## CHALLENGE PROBLEMS

11. Marg Myers, CFA, has determined that Rocky Romano Ice Cream Company can be valued using a single-stage residual income model. Myers estimates Rocky's return on equity (ROE) is greater than the cost of equity capital, which is greater than the sustainable growth rate. Book value per share is greater than zero. What can Myers conclude about Rocky's present value (PV) of future expected residual income (RI) and Rocky's justified price-to-book ratio?

    | PV of expected RI | Justified price-to-book ratio |
    |---|---|
    | A. Greater than zero | Greater than one |
    | B. Less than zero | Greater than one |
    | C. Greater than zero | Less than one |

12. Krackel, Inc., has a book value per share as of FYE 2006 of $4.50. The required return on equity is 10%. Earnings per share in 2007 are forecast to be $0.45. Assume Krackel can be valued using a single-stage residual income model. The justified price-to-book ratio and the present value of expected residual income are *closest* to:

    | Justified price-to-book ratio | PV of expected RI |
    |---|---|
    | A. 1.0 | $0.00 |
    | B. 1.45 | $0.00 |
    | C. 1.45 | $4.05 |

13. Kim Dae-Eun, CFA, values Olympic Productions at $78 per share with a residual income model using historical data to estimate return on equity and book value as reported on the balance sheet. Subsequently, he determines that Olympic has, for the past five years, been improperly capitalizing and amortizing expenditures that it should have expensed as they were incurred. What will be the effect on his forecasts of return on equity (ROE), book value, and intrinsic value if he revises his valuation estimate to take these "financial shenanigans" into account?

    | | ROE | Book value | Intrinsic value |
    |---|---|---|---|
    | A. | No effect | No effect | No effect |
    | B. | Decrease | No effect | Decrease |
    | C. | Decrease | Decrease | Decrease |

14. Kim Dae-Eun, CFA, values Zues Printing Company at $46 per share with a residual income model using historical data to estimate return on equity and book value as reported on the balance sheet. Subsequently, he determines that Zues uses the all-current method of foreign currency translation and has, for the past ten years, consistently reported foreign currency translation gains as part of comprehensive income. He expects these foreign currency gains will continue in the future. What will be the effect on his forecasts of return on equity (ROE), book value, and intrinsic value if he revises his valuation estimate to take this new information into account?

    | | ROE | Book value | Intrinsic value |
    |---|---|---|---|
    | A. | Increase | Increase | Increase |
    | B. | Increase | No effect | Increase |
    | C. | No effect | Increase | Increase |

15.    Jill Smart is an analyst with Allenton Partners. Jill is reviewing the valuation of three companies (P, Q, and R) using the residual income model and their corresponding current market prices.

The information below summarizes the findings:

|  | Stock | | |
|---|---|---|---|
|  | P | Q | R |
| Market price | 35 | 40 | 38 |
| Residual income model value | 40 | 35 | 38 |

Based on the above information, which statement *best* describes the market's valuation of P, Q, and R?
A.   P is overvalued, Q is undervalued, and R is fairly valued.
B.   P is undervalued, Q is fairly valued, and R is overvalued.
C.   P is undervalued, Q is overvalued, and R is fairly valued.

# ANSWERS – CONCEPT CHECKERS

1.  **C**  The stock's terminal value as of Year 5 is:

$$TV_5 = \frac{C\$11.25}{0.10} = C\$112.50$$

The present value of this Year 5 terminal value is:

$$PV = \frac{C\$112.50}{(1.10)^5} = C\$69.85$$

Thus, the justified value of SS is currently C\$75.00 + C\$69.85 = C\$144.85.

2.  **C**  All three alternative assumptions will reduce continuing residual income below the level implied by the assumption that it remains constant forever. A falling ROE will reduce residual income over time because residual income decreases as the spread between ROE and the cost of equity decreases. Therefore, the value estimate will drop below \$68 in all three cases.

3.  **B**  BCB's required rate of return, $r$, can be computed using the capital asset pricing model (CAPM) as follows:

$r = 4.5\% + (0.7 \times 5.0\%) = 8.0\%$

The calculation of RI = $\text{Earnings}_t - r \times \text{Book}_{t-1}$ for the next three years is shown in the following table.

**Expected RI Computations**

|  | 2008 | 2009 | 2010 | 2011 |
| --- | --- | --- | --- | --- |
| Beginning book value per share ($B_{t-1}$) | £10.62 | £11.89 | £13.32 | £14.91 |
| Earnings per share forecast ($E_t = 0.2 \times B_{t-1}$) | 2.12 | 2.38 | 2.66 | |
| Dividends per share forecast ($D_t = 0.4 \times E_t$) | 0.85 | 0.95 | 1.07 | |
| Forecast book value per share ($B_{t-1} + E_t - D_t$) | 11.89 | 13.32 | 14.91 | |
| Equity charge per share ($B_{t-1} \times r$) | 0.85 | 0.95 | 1.07 | |
| Per share RI [$E_t - (B_{t-1} \times r)$] | £1.27 | £1.43 | £1.59 | |

The present value in 2007 of 2008 and 2009 residual income is:

$$PV(RI_{2008, 2009}) = \frac{£1.27}{1.08} + \frac{£1.43}{1.08^2}$$
$$= 1.18 + 1.23$$
$$= £2.41$$

As indicated in the preceding table, the book value at the beginning of 2011 (end of 2010) is £14.91. The market price in 2010 for BCB is assumed to be four times $B_{2010}$, so:

$$P_{2010} = 4 \times 14.91 = £59.64$$

The present value of continuing residual income as of the end of 2009 is:

$$\frac{(P_{2010} - B_{2010}) + RI_{2010}}{1+r} = \frac{(£59.64 - £14.91) + £1.59}{1.08} = £42.89$$

4.  **B**  The present value of residual income in 2007 is:

$$\frac{£42.89}{1.08^2} = £36.77$$

Adding the present value of continuing residual income to the sum of the discounted RIs and the current book value yields a value per share of BCB stock of:

£10.62 + £2.41 + £36.77 = £49.80

5.  **C**  We know that: $V_0 = B_0 + \left(\frac{(ROE - r) \times B_0}{r - g}\right)$.

Since the shares are fairly priced, $V_0 = P = \$25.00$. It follows that:

$$B_0 = \frac{V_0}{P/B} = \frac{\$25.00}{5.00} = \$5.00$$

Substituting, we get:

$$\$25.00 = \$5.00 + \left(\frac{(0.18 - r) \times \$5.00}{r - 0.08}\right)$$

$$4.00 = \left(\frac{0.18 - r}{r - 0.08}\right) \Rightarrow 4r - 0.32 = 0.18 - r$$

$$5r = 0.50 \Rightarrow r = 0.10 = 10\%$$

6.  **C**  $B_0 = \frac{\text{book value of equity}}{\text{shares outstanding}} = \frac{€435,000,000}{60,000,000} = €7.25$ per share

| Year | $E_t$ | $B_{t-1}$ | ROE* | Equity Charge $(r \times B_{t-1})$ | Residual Income $E_t - (r \times B_{t-1})$ |
|---|---|---|---|---|---|
| 0 | | €7.25 | | | |
| 1 | €1.16 | 8.41 | 0.16 | €0.87 | €0.29 |
| 2 | 1.35 | 9.76 | 0.16 | 1.01 | 0.34 |
| 3 | 1.56 | 11.32 | 0.16 | 1.17 | 0.39 |
| 4 | 1.81 | 13.13 | 0.16 | 1.36 | 0.45 |

* Earnings per share (EPS) is equal to beginning book value multiplied by ROE.

In this case, $\omega = 0$. The present value of continuing residual income in Year 3 =

$$\frac{RI_4}{1+r-\omega} = \frac{0.45}{1+0.12-0} = \frac{0.45}{1.12} = \$0.40.$$

$$V_0 = €7.25 + \left[ \frac{€0.29}{1.12} + \frac{€0.34}{1.12^2} + \frac{€0.39+€0.40}{1.12^3} \right] = €8.34$$

Since the shares are valued at €8.34 each and the current market price per share is €8.75, the shares are overpriced, and the analyst should consider issuing a sell recommendation.

7. **B** We now modify the information in the last problem and assume that residual income remains constant at €0.45 after the initial forecast period, so $\omega = 1$. Continuing residual income in Year 3 is $\frac{0.45}{1+0.12-1} = \frac{0.45}{0.12} = €3.75$.

$$V_0 = €7.25 + \left[ \frac{€0.29}{1.12} + \frac{€0.34}{1.12^2} + \frac{€0.39+€3.75}{1.12^3} \right] = €10.73$$

In this case, the value of the shares exceeds the current price of €8.75 and the analyst should consider issuing a buy recommendation.

8. **C** Residual income begins to decline after Year 4, ($\omega = 0.3$) so the present value of continuing residual income in Year 3 is:

$$\text{present value of continuing residual income in year 3} = \frac{€0.45}{1+0.12-0.3} = €0.55$$

The intrinsic value today is book value plus the present value of years 1 through 3 residual income plus the present value of continuing residual income:

$$V_0 = €7.25 + \left[ \frac{€0.29}{1.12} + \frac{€0.34}{1.12^2} + \frac{€0.39+€0.55}{1.12^3} \right] = €8.45$$

Since the shares are valued at €8.45 and the current market price is €8.75, the shares are overpriced and the analyst should consider issuing a sell recommendation.

9. **C** Dividend discount model:

$$r = 4\% + (0.75 \times 8\%) = 10\%$$

$$\text{dividend} = \text{earnings} = \$3.00$$

$$\text{value} = \frac{\$3.00}{0.10} = \$30.00$$

Residual income model:

$$\text{residual income} = \$3.00 - (0.10 \times \$15) = \$1.50$$

$$\text{value} = \$15.00 + \frac{\$1.50}{0.10} = \$30.00$$

10. **C**   Use the single-stage residual income model to solve for the justified P/B multiple, then solve for ROE given the other variables:

$$V_0 = B_0 + \left[\frac{(\text{ROE} - r) \times B_0}{r - g}\right] \Rightarrow \frac{V_0}{B_0} = 1 + \frac{\text{ROE} - r}{r - g}$$

$$2.14 = 1 + \frac{\text{ROE} - 0.12}{0.12 - 0.05} \Rightarrow \text{ROE} = 0.20 = 20\%$$

# ANSWERS – CHALLENGE PROBLEMS

11. **A**   The single-stage residual income model is:

$$V_0 = B_0 + \left[\frac{(\text{ROE} - r) \times B_0}{r - g}\right]$$

The second term in the equation is the present value of future expected residual income. Rocky's ROE is greater than its cost of equity capital, so that second term is positive. That means intrinsic value is greater than book value, and the justified price-to-book ratio is greater than one.

12. **A**   ROE is equal to forecasted earnings per share divided by current book value per share:

$$\text{ROE} = \frac{\$0.45}{\$4.50} = 0.10 = 10\%$$

The single-stage residual income model is:

$$V_0 = B_0 + \left[\frac{(\text{ROE} - r) \times B_0}{r - g}\right]$$

The second term in the equation is the present value of future expected residual income. The ROE is equal to the cost of equity capital (both are 10%), so the second term is zero. That means intrinsic value is equal to book value and the justified price-to-book ratio is equal to one.

13. **C**   Improperly capitalizing expenditures that should have been expensed will cause return on equity and book value forecasts to be overstated. Correcting the valuation to reflect the overstatement of both of these forecasts would cause the ROE estimate to decrease, the book value per share to decrease, and the intrinsic value from the residual income model to decrease.

14. **B**     The foreign currency translation gains were recorded directly to equity as part of comprehensive income and were not reflected in income, so his ROE forecast was understated. If he expects these gains to continue, he should revise his forecast upward of ROE. Book value was not affected, however, because the gains were recorded to equity. Correcting the valuation to reflect these changes would cause his ROE estimate to increase, the book value per share to stay the same, and the intrinsic value from the residual income model to increase.

15. **C**     Stock P has model price higher than the market price and hence is undervalued. Stock Q has model price lower than the market price and hence is overvalued. Stock R has model price equal to the market price and hence is fairly valued.

# PRIVATE COMPANY VALUATION

Study Session 12

## EXAM FOCUS

For the exam, be familiar with differences between private and public companies and know the different definitions and approaches for value estimation. Be prepared to normalize earnings, determine an appropriate discount rate, and calculate private firm value using the income, market, and asset-based approaches. Know when and how discounts for control and marketability are applied.

## WARM-UP

The valuation of private companies has application in both the private equity and public equity world. Public firms frequently possess or consider buying start-up operations that can be valued using private equity valuation principles. Goodwill from acquisitions and venture capital investments can also be valued using private firm valuation principles and techniques.

LOS 37.a: Compare public and private company valuation.

*CFA® Program Curriculum, Volume 4, page 424*

Private firms encompass sole proprietorships, privately held corporations, and previously public companies that have been taken private. The characteristics that distinguish private and public companies can be delineated into company-specific and stock-specific factors.

### Company-Specific Factors

Company-specific factors include the following.

*Stage of lifecycle:* Private companies are typically less mature than public firms. Sometimes, however, private firms are mature firms or bankrupt firms near liquidation. The valuation analysis will vary with the lifecycle stage of the firm.

*Size:* Private firms typically have less capital, fewer assets, and fewer employees than public firms and, as such, can be riskier. Accordingly, private firms are often valued using greater risk premiums and greater required returns compared to public firms. A lack of access to public equity markets can constrain a private firm's growth. However, the regulatory burden associated with issuing public equity may outweigh the benefits of greater access to funds.

*Quality and depth of management:* Smaller private firms may not be able to attract as many qualified applicants as public firms. This may reduce the depth of management, slow growth, and increase risk at private firms.

*Management/shareholder overlap:* In most private firms, management has a substantial ownership position. In this case, external shareholders have less influence and the firm may be able to take a longer-term perspective.

*Short-term investors:* Although manager compensation in public firms often includes incentive compensation such as stock options, shareholders often focus on short-term measures of performance such as the level and consistency of quarterly earnings. In such cases, management may take a shorter-term view compared to private firms where managers are long-term holders of significant equity interests.

*Quality of financial and other information:* Public firms are required to make timely, in-depth financial disclosures. A potential creditor or equity investor in a private firm will have less information than is available for a public firm. This leads to greater uncertainty, higher risk, and reduces private firm valuations.

Note that in the case of fairness opinions for private firm valuations, the analyst typically has complete access to the firm's financial statements and business records.

*Taxes:* Private firms may be more concerned with taxes than public firms due to the impact of taxes on private equity owners/managers.

## Stock-Specific Factors

The stock-specific differences between private and public firms often include the following:

*Liquidity:* Private company equity typically has fewer potential owners and is less liquid than publicly traded equity. Thus, a liquidity discount is often applied in valuing privately held shares.

*Restrictions on marketability:* Private companies often have agreements that prevent shareholders from selling, reducing the marketability of shares.

*Concentration of control:* The control of private firms is usually concentrated in the hands of a few shareholders, which may lead to greater perquisites and other benefits to owners/managers at the expense of minority shareholders.

Overall, company-specific factors can have positive or negative effects on private company valuations, whereas stock-specific factors are usually a negative. Compared to public companies, private companies have greater heterogeneity so that the appropriate discount rates and methods for valuing them vary widely as well.

LOS 37.b: Describe uses of private business valuation, and explain applications of greatest concern to financial analysts.

*CFA® Program Curriculum, Volume 4, page 426*

There are three reasons for valuing the total capital and/or equity capital of private companies: transactions, compliance, and litigation.

## Transaction-Related Valuations

Transaction-related valuations are necessary when selling or financing a firm.

*Venture capital financing:* Firms in the development stage often need external financing for capital investment and receive private financing from venture capital investors. To reduce risk to the venture capital investor, the capital is often provided in rounds after the achievement of specific benchmarks known as *milestones*. Valuations are usually subject to negotiation and are somewhat informal due to the uncertainty of future cash flows.

*Initial public offering (IPO):* A public sale of the firm's equity increases its liquidity. Investment banks often perform IPO valuations using the values of similar public firms as a benchmark.

*Sale in an acquisition:* Development-stage or mature private firms are often sold to generate liquidity for the owners. Valuations are usually performed by both the firm and the buyer and are subject to negotiation.

*Bankruptcy proceedings:* For firms in bankruptcy, accurate valuation can help determine whether the firm should be liquidated or reorganized. If it is determined that the firm can continue as a going concern, accurate valuation is important in its restructuring.

*Performance-based managerial compensation:* If a firm compensates employees with stock options, grants of restricted stock, or employee stock ownership plans, accurate valuation is necessary for both accounting and tax purposes.

## Compliance-Related Valuations

Compliance-related valuations are performed for legal or regulatory reasons and primarily focus on financial reporting and tax issues.

*Financial reporting:* Valuations in this area are often related to goodwill impairment tests in which units of a public firm are valued using private company valuation methods. The reporting of stock-based compensation also requires accurate valuation.

*Tax purposes:* At the firm level, transfer pricing, property taxes, and corporate restructuring may necessitate valuations. For individual equity owners, estate and gift tax issues may necessitate valuations.

## Litigation-Related Valuations

Litigation-related valuations may be required for shareholder suits, damage claims, lost profits claims, or divorce settlements.

Because the valuation methods for transactions, compliance, and litigation are often quite different, most appraisers specialize in a single area. Transaction-related valuations are usually performed by investment bankers, compliance-related valuations by those with accounting or tax knowledge, and litigation-related valuations by those comfortable with a legal setting and specific jurisdictions.

---

**LOS 37.c: Explain various definitions of value, and demonstrate how different definitions can lead to different estimates of value.**

---

*CFA® Program Curriculum, Volume 4, page 428*

## Definitions of Value

The appropriate valuation method depends on what the valuation will be used for and whether the firm is a going concern. The following are some common definitions of value:

*Fair market value:* Most often used for tax purposes in the United States, fair market value is a cash price characterized by:

- A hypothetical willing and able seller sells the asset to a willing and able buyer.
- An arm's length transaction (neither party is compelled to act) in a free market.
- A well-informed buyer and seller.

*Fair value for financial reporting:* This is similar to fair market value and is used for financial reporting. Using International Financial Reporting Standards (IFRS) and U.S. GAAP, fair value is the current price paid to purchase an asset or to transfer a liability. It is characterized by:

- An arm's length transaction.
- A well-informed buyer and seller.

*Fair value for litigation:* This is similar to fair value but its definition depends on U.S. state statutes and legal precedent in the jurisdiction of the litigation.

*Market value:* This is frequently used for appraisals of real estate and other real assets where the purchase will be levered. The International Valuation Standards Committee defines market value as the value estimated on a particular date characterized by:

- A willing seller and buyer.
- An arm's length transaction.
- An asset that has been marketed.
- A well-informed and prudent buyer and seller.

*Investment value:* Focuses on the value to a particular buyer and is important in private company valuation. Investment value may be different for different investors, depending on:

- Estimates of future cash flows.
- Perceived firm risk.
- Appropriate discount rates.
- Individual financing costs.
- Perceived synergies with existing buyer assets.

*Intrinsic value:* This is derived from investment analysis and is described as the market value once other investors arrive at this "true" value. Intrinsic value is independent of any short-term mispricing.

## The Effect of Value Definitions on Estimated Value

The definition of value affects the estimated value of an asset. For example, suppose a buyer does not perceive any of the synergies with existing assets that the majority of potential buyers do. If the majority has determined that the asset's *investment value* is $1,000, the *fair market value* could be $1,000. For an investor that does not realize any synergies, however, the *investment value* may only be $800.

Another example comes from the definition of fair value. Under U.S. GAAP SFAS 157, fair value is the exit price (i.e., the price received by the seller), which will likely be lower than the entry price paid by the buyer in a transaction. IFRS does not specify an exit or entry price in fair value determination.

A valuation or appraisal should only be used for its intended purpose. A valuation performed on one date according to a specific definition and for a specific purpose may not be relevant for other purposes and dates.

For example, the *fair market value* of equity for a controlling interest will likely be much different than the *investment value* of a minority interest that has little influence over the firm's decisions. The valuation of a minority interest in a private company may incorporate minority and/or marketability discounts not applicable in other situations. Furthermore, valuations prepared for tax purposes will likely require adjustment before they can be used for financial reporting.

---

LOS 37.d: Explain the income, market, and asset-based approaches to private company valuation and factors relevant to the selection of each approach.

---

*CFA® Program Curriculum, Volume 4, page 430*

The three major approaches to private company valuation are the income approach, the market approach, and the asset-based approach.

1. *Income approach:* Values a firm as the present value of its expected future income. Such valuation may be based on a variety of different assumptions and variations.
2. *Market approach:* Values a firm using the price multiples based on recent sales of comparable assets.
3. *Asset-based approach:* Values a firm's assets minus its liabilities.

These methods are similar to those used to value public companies, but they have different names. In the public equity world, the income approach is known as *discounted cash flow* or *present value analysis*. The income approach and the asset-based approach are termed absolute valuation models. That is, the value generated is not relative to recent valuations of other assets, as they are with the market approach.

The selection of an appropriate valuation approach depends on the firm's operations and its lifecycle stage. Early in its life, a firm's future cash flows may be subject to so much uncertainty that an asset-based approach would be most appropriate. As the firm moves to a high growth phase, it might be appropriately valued using an income approach, including a particular form of the income approach known as a *free cash flow valuation model*. A mature firm might be more appropriately valued using the market approach.

Firm size is also a consideration in choosing a valuation methodology. Price multiples from large public firms should not be used to value a small private firm without some assurance that the risk and growth prospects of the firms are similar.

A firm's assets typically consist of both operating and nonoperating assets. Nonoperating assets, those not crucial to the firm's primary operations and focus, are typified by excess cash and investment accounts. However, nonoperating assets constitute a portion of firm value and must be included when valuing a firm.

---

LOS 37.e: Explain cash flow estimation issues related to private companies and adjustments required to estimate normalized earnings.

---

*CFA® Program Curriculum, Volume 4, page 431*

In valuing a firm, the appropriate earnings definition is **normalized earnings**: "firm earnings *if* the firm were acquired." The adjustments required to arrive at normalized earnings are discussed in the following.

 *Professor's Note: In a previous topic review, we calculated normalized earnings as the average earnings over the business cycle. Here, the calculation of normalized earnings requires adjustment for firm-specific characteristics.*

### Estimating Normalized Earnings

Normalized earnings should exclude nonrecurring and unusual items. In the case of private firms with a concentrated control, there may be discretionary or tax-motivated expenses that need to be adjusted when calculating normalized earnings. These adjustments can be quite significant when the firm is small.

When a closely controlled firm does business with its owners or other businesses controlled by its owners, firm expenses may be inflated and reported earnings, therefore, may be artificially low. Artificially low earnings may also be the result of excessively high owner compensation or of personal expenses charged to the firm. These expenses will also affect the firm's tax expense. The adjustments are potentially larger when the owners' family members have connections to the firm. Use of company-owned assets (e.g., aircraft, personal residences, company-provided life insurance, loans for managers/owners) potentially require an adjustment to earnings.

On the other hand, if a firm is performing poorly, the owners may be receiving compensation below market levels. In this case, reported earnings would overstate normalized earnings.

Any real estate owned by the firm may merit treatment separate from that of firm operations for the following reasons:

- The real estate may have different risk characteristics than firm operations.
- The real estate may have different growth prospects than firm operations.
- The cost of the real estate owned by the firm will be reported as depreciation expense. However, depreciation is most often based on historical cost and may understate the current cost in the market of the use of the assets.

To address the last issue, some analysts will remove any income and expenses from real estate on the income statement. If it is used in the firm's business, a market-estimated rental expense is used in calculating or estimating earnings. The value of real estate is therefore separated from its operations and treated as a nonoperating asset. If the real estate is leased from a related party, the lease rate should be adjusted to a market rate.

Other adjustments are common to both private and public companies (e.g., adjustments for differences in depreciation and inventory methods). Additionally, some private firm financial statements are *reviewed* rather than audited; some may be only compiled (i.e., no auditor opinion is provided). In any case, the analyst should be prepared to make further adjustments.

### Example: Normalized earnings

Tim Groh is the principal shareholder, CEO, and founder of Arbutus Generators. Arbutus reports the following:

1. Groh's compensation of $2,500,000 is included in the firm's selling, general, and administrative (SG&A) expenses.

2. Arbutus leases a warehouse for $100,000 a year from one of its largest suppliers.

3. Arbutus owns a vacant office building with reported SG&A expenses of $150,000 and $25,000 of depreciation expense.

4. Arbutus's capital structure has too little leverage.

An analyst determines that a market-based compensation figure for Groh's position is $1,000,000 and that the office building is not needed for core operations. The market lease rate of the warehouse is $130,000.

Based on 1–4 above, what adjustments should the analyst make to Arbutus's reported income to estimate normalized earnings (earnings), assuming the firm will be acquired?

**Answer:**

1. Because the market rate is $1,500,000 less, SG&A expenses should be reduced by $1,500,000 to reflect a normalized compensation expense.

2. Because the market lease rate is $30,000 higher than reported, SG&A expenses should be increased by $30,000 to reflect a normalized lease rate.

3. Because the office building is non-core, SG&A expenses should be reduced by $150,000, and depreciation expense should be reduced by $25,000.

4. Because the capital structure is non-optimal, the analyst will drop interest expense from the calculation of operating income under the assumption that the capital structure will be changed if the firm is acquired. As we will see, interest expense is added back when calculating free cash flow to the firm.

## Strategic and Nonstrategic Buyers

A transaction may be either strategic or financial (nonstrategic). In a strategic transaction, valuation of the firm is based in part on the perceived synergies with the acquirer's other assets. A financial transaction assumes no synergies, as when one firm buys another in a dissimilar industry.

When estimating normalized earnings for a strategic transaction, the analyst should incorporate any synergies as an increase in revenues or as a reduction in costs.

**Example: Incorporating synergies**

An analyst is valuing a firm for two different buyers. Buyer A is a firm, in the same industry as the target firm, which expects to reduce costs at the target firm by eliminating redundancies. Buyer B is a firm in another industry.

Calculate the normalized EBITDA for each buyer given the information below.

| | |
|---|---|
| Reported EBITDA | $4,800,000 |
| Current executive compensation | $900,000 |
| Market-based executive compensation | $600,000 |
| Current SG&A expenses | $8,000,000 |
| SG&A expenses after synergistic savings | $7,600,000 |

**Answer:**

Both strategic (Buyer A) and nonstrategic (Buyer B) buyers will attempt to reduce executive compensation to market levels. So the adjustment for both buyers to generate normalized EBITDA is $4,800,000 + ($900,000 – $600,000) = $5,100,000.

However, only Buyer A will be able to realize synergistic savings of $400,000 ($8,000,000 – $7,600,000). So normalized EBITDA for Buyer A is $5,500,000 and for Buyer B it is $5,100,000.

## Estimating Cash Flow

Calculating free cash flow to the firm or to equity holders for private firms can be particularly challenging given uncertain future cash flows and figures that are often generated using the current owners' input.

As noted previously, the valuation of equity depends on the definition of value used. Also, controlling and noncontrolling equity interests will have quite different values. These differences should be accounted for in cash flow estimates and assumptions.

When there is significant uncertainty about a private company's future operations, the analyst should examine several scenarios when estimating future cash flows. For development stage firms, scenarios could include a sale of the firm, an IPO, bankruptcy, or continued private operation. For a mature firm, scenarios might include different ranges of cash flows based on different assumed growth rates.

For each scenario, the analyst must assign a discount rate and probability based on the scenario's risk and probability of occurring. A firm value for each scenario is estimated, and a weighted average of these values is used to estimate firm value. Alternatively, a weighted average scenario cash flow may be discounted using a single discount rate to arrive at an estimate of firm value.

Cash flow estimates often are based on current management estimates or result from analyst consultation with management. The analyst should be aware of the potential bias in management estimates. For example, management may overstate the value of goodwill or understate future capital needs.

Although analysts use FCFF or FCFE depending on the purposes of the valuation, FCFF is usually more appropriate when the significant changes in the firm's capital structure are anticipated. The reasoning is that the discount rate used for FCFF valuation, the weighted average cost of capital (WACC), is less sensitive to leverage changes than the cost of equity, the discount rate used for FCFE valuation. Thus, the FCFF valuation is less sensitive to the degree of financial leverage assumed in the analysis than the FCFE valuation.

*Professor's Note: The calculations and adjustments here are similar to those in our previous coverage of the estimation of FCFF in that they start at operating income before interest expense. Noncash charges (NCC) are stated as depreciation and amortization here, and fixed capital investment is stated as capital expenditures.*

### Example: Estimation of FCFF

An analyst has normalized the earnings and expenses for a private firm under consideration as an acquisition. Because the capital structure is non-optimal, the analyst assumes that the capital structure will be changed if the firm is acquired and will use the FCFF approach to value the firm.

The following assumptions are used to create a pro forma income statement and to estimate FCFF.

| | |
|---|---|
| Current revenues | $20,000,000 |
| Revenue growth | 4% |
| Gross profit margin | 30% |
| Depreciation expense as a percent of sales | 2% |
| Working capital as a percent of sales | 10% |
| SG&A expenses | $2,200,000 |
| Tax rate | 30% |

Additionally, capital expenditures will cover depreciation plus 6% of the firm's incremental revenues.

Create a pro forma income statement and estimate FCFF.

**Answer:**

| *Pro Forma Income Statement* | |
|---|---|
| Revenues | $20,800,000 |
| Cost of goods sold | $14,560,000 |
| Gross profit | $6,240,000 |
| SG&A expenses | $2,200,000 |
| Pro forma EBITDA | $4,040,000 |
| Depreciation and amortization | $416,000 |
| Pro forma EBIT | $3,624,000 |
| Pro forma taxes on EBIT | $1,087,200 |
| Operating income after tax | $2,536,800 |
| | |
| *Adjustments to obtain FCFF* | |
| Plus: depreciation and amortization | $416,000 |
| Minus: capital expenditures | $464,000 |
| Minus: increase in working capital | $80,000 |
| FCFF | $2,408,800 |

The following provides a line by line explanation for the previous calculations.

| Pro Forma Income Statement | Explanation |
| --- | --- |
| Revenues | Current revenues times the growth rate: $20,000,000 × 1.04 |
| Cost of goods sold | Revenues times one minus the gross profit margin: $20,800,000 × (1 − 0.30) |
| Gross profit | Revenues times the gross profit margin: $20,800,000 × 0.30 |
| SG&A expenses | Given in the question |
| Pro forma EBITDA | Gross profit minus SG&A expenses: $6,240,000 − $2,200,000 |
| Depreciation and amortization | Revenues times the given depreciation expense: $20,800,000 × 0.02 |
| Pro forma EBIT | EBITDA minus depreciation and amortization: $4,040,000 − $416,000 |
| Pro forma taxes on EBIT | EBIT times tax rate: $3,624,000 × 0.30 |
| Operating income after tax | EBIT minus taxes: $3,624,000 − $1,087,200 |

| Adjustments to obtain FCFF | Explanation |
| --- | --- |
| Plus: depreciation and amortization | Add back noncash charges from above |
| Minus: capital expenditures | Expenditures cover depreciation and increase with revenues: $416,000 + [0.06 × ($20,800,000 − $20,000,000)] |
| Minus: increase in working capital | The working capital will increase as revenues increase 0.10 × ($20,800,000 − $20,000,000) |
| FCFF | Operating income net of the adjustments above |

LOS 37.f: Calculate the value of private company using free cash flow, capitalized cash flow, and/or excess earnings methods.

*CFA® Program Curriculum, Volume 4, page 434*

The income approach refers to valuation methods based on the idea that the value of an asset is the present value of its future income. Three methods consistent with the income approach are: the free cash flow method (a.k.a. discounted cash flow method), the capitalized cash flow method, and the residual income or excess earnings method.

### The Free Cash Flow Method

Once free cash flows have been estimated as we have done previously, they are discounted by a rate that reflects their risk. Typically, there is a series of discrete cash flows and a terminal value that reflects the value of the business as a going concern at some future date. The terminal value is calculated for a point of time in the future, at which the growth rate is expected to level off and remain constant. In practice, most analysts estimate the terminal value five years out.

The terminal value can be calculated using a constant growth model (e.g., dividend discount model). Some analysts use a price multiple approach to estimate a firm's terminal value. Note, however, that if the price multiple is for a firm in a high growth industry, the price multiple applied will often reflect both high growth and normal growth. In this case, the high growth is double counted, once in the price multiple and once in the periodic cash flow forecasts.

 *Professor's Note: The free cash flow method here is a two-stage model. The capitalized cash flow method described in the following is a single-stage model.*

### The Capitalized Cash Flow Method

This method is also known as the capitalized income method or the capitalization of earnings method. Under this method, a single measure of economic benefit is divided by a capitalization rate to arrive at firm value, where the capitalization rate is the required rate of return minus a growth rate. This is a growing perpetuity model that assumes stable growth and is, in effect, a single-stage free cash flow model. It is most often used for small private companies. It may be suitable when no comparables are available, projections are quite uncertain, and stable growth is a reasonable assumption.

If growth is non-constant, the capitalized cash flow method (CCM) should be avoided in favor of the free cash flow method. The CCM could be used to back out the discount rate or growth rate implicit in market data.

Valuing the firm as a whole using the CCM:

$$\text{value of the firm} = \frac{\text{FCFF}_1}{\text{WACC} - g}$$

where:
FCFF$_1$ = expected free cash flow to the firm over the next year
WACC = weighted average cost of capital (assuming a constant capital structure)
g = sustainable growth rate in free cash flows

To estimate the value of the equity, the market value of the firm's debt is subtracted from firm value. Alternatively, the value of firm equity can be estimated by discounting the free cash flows to equity by the required return on equity ($r$):

$$\text{value of equity} = \frac{\text{FCFE}_1}{r - g}$$

The denominator in both the FCFF and FCFE equations is the capitalization rate of the CCM.

---

**Example: Calculating firm value using the capitalized cash flow method**

Given the following figures, calculate the value of the firm and equity using the CCM.

| | |
|---|---|
| FCFF in one year | $12,100,000 |
| Growth rate of FCFF | 4.0% |
| WACC | 15.0% |
| Market value of debt | $4,000,000 |

**Answer:**

*Step 1:* Calculate the value of the firm.

Using the FCFF formula:

value of firm = ($12,100,000) / (0.15 – 0.04) = $110,000,000

*Step 2:* Calculate the value of the equity.

Subtract the debt value from firm value:

value of equity = $110,000,000 – $4,000,000 = $106,000,000

Note that the capitalization rate in this example is 11% (15% – 4%). The WACC will be greater when more (relatively expensive) equity and less debt are used, resulting in lower estimates of firm and equity values.

---

## The Excess Earnings Method

Under the excess earnings method, the analyst starts with the earnings that *should* be generated by working capital and fixed assets based on an estimate of the required return. Excess earnings are firm earnings minus the earnings required to provide the required rate of return on working capital and fixed assets. The value of intangible assets can be estimated as the present value of the (growing) stream of excess earnings (using the excess earnings and the growing perpetuity formula from the CCM). This value for the intangible assets is added to the values of working capital and fixed assets to arrive at firm value.

The excess earnings method (EEM) is used infrequently but can be used for small firms when their intangible assets are significant. However, the required return for working capital and fixed assets is subject to estimation error.

---

**Example: Calculating firm value using the excess earnings method**

Given the following figures, calculate the value of the firm using the EEM.

| | |
|---|---|
| Working capital | $300,000 |
| Fixed assets | $1,000,000 |
| Normalized earnings (year just ended) | $130,000 |
| Required return for working capital | 6% |
| Required return for fixed assets | 10% |
| Growth rate of residual income | 5% |
| Discount rate for intangible assets | 14% |

**Answer:**

*Step 1:* Calculate the required return for working capital and fixed assets.

Based on the required rates of return for working capital and fixed assets, the required earnings are:

working capital: $300,000 × 6% = $18,000
fixed assets: $1,000,000 × 10% = $100,000

*Step 2:* Calculate the excess earnings.

excess earnings = $130,000 − $18,000 − $100,000 = $12,000

*Step 3:* Value the intangible assets.

Using the formula for a growing perpetuity, the discount rate for intangible assets, and the growth rate for excess earnings:

value of intangible assets = ($12,000 × 1.05) / (0.14 − 0.05) = $140,000

*Step 4:* Sum the asset values to arrive at the total firm value.

firm value = $300,000 + $1,000,000 + $140,000 = $1,440,000

*Professor's Note: In the excess earnings method, the FCFF may be given in place of the normalized earnings. The growth rate in free cash flow may be given in place of the growth rate of residual income. After these substitutions, the calculations are identical to those above.*

---

## LOS 37.g: Explain factors that require adjustment when estimating the discount rate for private companies.

*CFA® Program Curriculum, Volume 4, page 438*

Estimating the discount rate in a private firm valuation can be quite challenging for the following reasons.

*Size premiums:* Size premiums are often added to the discount rates for small private companies. Estimating this premium using small public firm data may be biased upward by the fact many of the small firms in the sample are experiencing financial distress.

*Availability and cost of debt:* A private firm may have less access to debt financing than a public firm. Because equity capital is usually more expensive than debt and because the higher operating risk of smaller private companies results in a higher cost of debt as well, WACC will typically be higher for private firms.

*Acquirer versus target:* When acquiring a private firm, some acquirers will incorrectly use their own (lower) cost of capital, rather than the higher rate appropriate for the target, and arrive at a value for the target company that is too high.

*Projection risk:* Because of the lower availability of information from private firms and managers who are inexperienced at forecasting, that analyst should increase the discount rate used.

Management may not be experienced with forecasting and may underestimate or overestimate future earnings, requiring adjustment by the analyst. Such adjustments are highly subjective, however.

*Lifecycle stage:* It is particularly difficult to estimate the discount rate for firms in an early stage of development. If such firms have unusually high levels of unsystematic risk, the use of the CAPM may be inappropriate. Although ranges of discount rates can be specified for the various lifecycle stages, it may difficult to classify the stage a firm is in.

## LOS 37.h: Compare models used to estimate the required rate of return to private company equity (for example, the CAPM, the expanded CAPM, and the build-up approach).

*CFA® Program Curriculum, Volume 4, page 438*

Using the CAPM, the expanded CAPM, and build-up methods to estimate discount rates for private firms may not be as straightforward as that for public firms.

*CAPM:* Typically, beta is estimated from public firm data, and this may not be appropriate for private firms that have little chance of going public or being acquired by a public firm. Due to the differences between large public firms and small private firms, some U.S. tax courts have rejected the use of the CAPM for private firms.

*Expanded CAPM:* This version of the CAPM includes additional premiums for size and firm-specific (unsystematic) risk.

*Build-up method:* When it is not possible to find comparable public firms for beta estimation, the build-up method can be used. Beginning with the expected return on the market (beta is implicitly assumed to be one), premiums are added for small size, industry factors, and company specific factors.

---

**Example: Private equity valuation methods**

An analyst is examining a private firm under consideration as an acquisition and determines the following:

- The current capital structure is non-optimal because the owner avoids the use of debt.
- A small stock premium and company-specific risk premium are determined because the private firm is much smaller and much less diversified than the public firms that beta is estimated from.
- The industry risk premium reflects the additional risk in this industry compared to the broad market.

The relevant figures are listed below.

| | |
|---|---|
| Risk-free rate | 3.6% |
| Equity risk premium | 6.0% |
| Beta | 1.3 |
| Small stock premium | 3.0% |
| Company-specific risk premium | 2.0% |
| Industry risk-premium | 1.0% |
| Pretax cost of debt | 9.0% |
| Debt/total cap for public firms in industry | 30% |
| Optimal debt/total cap | 12% |
| Current debt/total | 3% |
| Tax rate | 30% |

a. Calculate the required return on equity using the CAPM, the expanded CAPM, and the build-up method.

b. Calculate the WACC using the current capital structure and the optimal capital structure, assuming a cost of equity of 16%.

c. Comment on the appropriate capital structure weights.

---

**Answer:**

a.  The required return on equity using the CAPM is: 3.6% + 1.3(6%) = 11.4%.

Using the expanded CAPM, a small stock premium and company-specific risk premium are added: 11.4% + 3% + 2% = 16.4%.

Using the build-up method, beta is omitted, but an industry risk premium is added to the risk-free rate, the equity risk premium, the small stock premium, and a company-specific risk premium: 3.6% + 6% + 3% + 2% + 1% = 15.6%.

b.  The WACC, using the current capital structure, factors in the debt to total capitalization, the cost of debt, the tax rate, and the given cost of equity:

$$[3\% \times 9\% \times (1 - 30\%)] + [(1 - 3\%) \times 16\%] = 15.7\%$$

The WACC, using the optimal capital structure, is:

$$[12\% \times 9\% \times (1 - 30\%)] + [(1 - 12\%) \times 16\%] = 14.8\%$$

c.  The current capital structure reflects the current owner's conservative use of debt. The optimal capital structure can be determined through discussions with financiers. The optimal capital structure should be used to calculate the (lower) WACC for the acquisition, given that the firm can support this level of debt.

The capital structure for public firms in the same industry should not be used because public firms are likely to have better access to debt financing. A public firm could likely take on more (less expensive compared to equity) debt than a private company. For this reason, a private firm will likely have a greater WACC than a public firm in the same industry would have.

---

LOS 37.i: Determine the value of a private company based on market approach methods, and describe advantages and disadvantages of each method.

*CFA® Program Curriculum, Volume 4, page 446*

Market approaches to valuing private firms use price multiples and data from previous public and private transactions. The three methods discussed in the following are the guideline public company method (GPCM), the guideline transactions method (GTM), and the prior transaction method (PTM).

Many practitioners prefer market approaches to valuation over income and asset approaches because actual sales data are used. Although U.S. tax courts accept both market and income approaches, they usually prefer market approaches.

As discussed previously, private firms may have risks not common to public firms, such as greater company risk and illiquidity. Therefore, it is important that the public comparables be chosen carefully. Furthermore, price multiples reflect both risk and growth. Each of these should be extracted from the price multiple and compared to the subject private firm to decide what adjustments might be made. When choosing the comparables, commonalities in industry, operations, size, and lifecycle are desired.

Although public firms are often valued on the basis of price-earnings ratios, large private firm valuation is usually based on EBIT or EBITDA multiples. The numerator would be the market value of invested capital (MVIC), from which the market value of debt could be subtracted when examining equity value. Because the market value of debt is often hard to ascertain, the book value can be used if the firm has low financial leverage and is stable. If the firm has high debt levels or volatility, an analyst could use matrix pricing, where the prices of similar debt are used to infer a value for the subject's debt.

For small private companies with limited assets, net income multiples might be used instead of EBITDA multiples. A revenue multiple might be used for extremely small firms, given the greater likelihood and impact of discretionary expenses such as owner compensation.

Nonfinancial measures may be appropriate in some industries. For example, a hospital's price per bed could be used. These measures should be accepted in its industry and accompanied by financial measures.

In the following discussion, we will see that the advantage of each of these methods is that the comparable data are usually available. The disadvantage, however, is that the comparable transactions may not be similar to the subject transaction. The issues of comparability are discussed for each of these methods in the following sections.

## Guideline Public Company Method

The guideline public company method (GPCM) uses price multiples from trade data for public companies, with adjustments to the multiples to account for differences between the subject firm and the comparables. Although there are usually numerous public company transactions available, the data should be checked to see that they are comparable.

When evaluating a controlling equity interest in a private firm, the control premium (i.e., the value of control) should be estimated. The control premium equals the difference between the pro rata value of a controlling interest and the pro rata value of a noncontrolling interest. Most public share trades are for small, noncontrolling interests; therefore, the price multiple does not reflect a control premium.

To estimate a control premium, a public transaction should be used where a firm was acquired. When estimating a control premium, the following issues should be considered:

*Transaction type:* Recall that a transaction may be either strategic or financial (nonstrategic). A strategic buyer is one who will have synergies with the target, and a financial buyer is one who is buying the firm for its stand-alone value. A financial transaction typically has a smaller price premium.

*Industry conditions:* Periodically, there is a flurry in industry acquisition activity, driving up acquisition prices. In such markets, share prices of public companies may already reflect some premium for control, and adding a standard control premium to such share prices may overstate the appropriate premium for control.

*Type of consideration:* Some historical acquisitions involve the acquirer's stock rather than cash. Estimates of the control premium when acquisitions are made with shares that are at higher temporary or "bubble" values will be overstated.

*Reasonableness:* The use of control premiums and price multiples can quickly result in significant differences in valuations from historical pricing. For example, suppose a 20% historical control premium is estimated on top of a 6 price multiple. If the price multiples from public comparables at the valuation date are 10, a price multiple of 12 (10 × 1.2) is applied to the private firm. The price multiple of 12 is substantially different than the 6 estimated earlier. The 12 multiple should be investigated for reasonableness.

**Example: Valuation using the guideline public company method**

An analyst, Natalie Hoskins, is valuing a private firm, Rensselaer Components, using the GPCM and MVIC to EBITDA multiples. Hoskins has gathered data for comparable public firms; however they are larger in size than Rensselaer. Hoskins decided to deflate the average public company multiple by 20% to account for the higher risk of Rensselaer.

A premium of 30% was paid for a firm by an acquiring firm in the same industry. The acquirer exchanged stock for the target.

Other data are as follows:

| | |
|---|---|
| Market value of debt | $1,100,000 |
| Normalized EBITDA | $12,800,000 |
| Average MVIC/EBITDA multiple | 8.0 |

a. Comment on the relevance of the information above for the valuation of Rensselaer.

b. Calculate the equity value of Rensselaer using the GPCM.

**Answer:**

a. The application of control premiums is difficult and requires subjective judgment. The control premium of 30% is probably not relevant for the valuation of Rensselaer. The premium for the prior acquisition likely contained some value for synergies since it was a strategic transaction, and because stock was used for the purchase, there is also the possibility that the stock value at the time was inflated, adding to the estimated premium.

The adjustment to the public company multiple of 20% is appropriate because growth and risk may differ between public comparables and private firms.

b. The adjustment to the MVIC/EBITDA multiple for the higher risk of Rensselaer is:

$$8.0 \times (1 - 0.20) = 6.4$$

No control premium is applied, for the reasons mentioned above.

The adjusted multiple is applied against the normalized EBITDA:

$$6.4 \times \$12,800,000 = \$81,920,000$$

Subtracting out the debt results in the equity value:

$$\$81,920,000 - \$1,100,000 = \$80,820,000$$

Control premium adjustments are made only to the equity portion of the firm's value. There are two ways to incorporate control premium under a guideline public company method:

1. Use the raw multiple to estimate firm value (without control premium) and estimate the equity portion (by subtracting debt). Apply the control premium to the equity portion as estimated.

2. Adjust the multiple by:

$$\text{adjusted multiple} = \text{raw multiple}\left[1 + \frac{\text{control premium}}{1 + D/E}\right]$$

   where:
   $D/E$ = firm's normal debt-to-equity ratio

## Guideline Transactions Method

When using the guideline transactions method (GTM), prior acquisition values for entire (public and private) companies that already reflect any control premiums are used, so no additional adjustment for a controlling interest is necessary.

Although data on the sale of public companies are readily available, the data on the sale of private firms are more limited and not always accurate. When using multiples from historical transactions, several issues should be considered.

*Transaction type:* As mentioned previously for the GPCM, a prior transaction may be a strategic transaction where firm value was based, in part, on perceived synergies. If the subject transaction is nonstrategic, the analyst may need to adjust the historical multiple.

*Contingent consideration:* Contingent consideration refers to that part of the acquisition price that is contingent on the achievement of specific company performance targets, such as receiving FDA approval for a drug. As contingent consideration increases the risk to the seller, transactions with contingent consideration should be scrutinized before they are compared to transactions without such contingencies.

*Type of consideration:* As noted previously, some transactions are for stock rather than cash. Comparing transactions of different consideration type may not be relevant.

*Availability of data:* The historical data for comparables that are relevant and accurate may be limited.

*Date of data:* If the sales of the comparable companies were very long ago, the prices and estimated premiums may not be relevant to the extent that macroeconomic and industry conditions have changed.

**Example: Valuation with the guideline transactions method**

Natalie Hoskins is valuing a private firm, Lafayette Furniture, for acquisition using the GTM and MVIC to EBITDA multiples. Hoskins deflates the average public company multiple by 30% to account for the higher risk of Lafayette.

Other data are as follows:

| | |
|---|---|
| Market value of debt | $1,400,000 |
| Normalized EBITDA | $18,200,000 |
| Average MVIC/EBITDA multiple | 7.2 |

 *Professor's Note: Recall that in the GTM, historical transactions are not adjusted for control premiums because the transactions are for the acquisition of entire companies.*

Calculate the equity value of Lafayette Furniture using the GTM.

**Answer:**

The adjustment to the MVIC/EBITDA multiple for the higher risk of Lafayette Furniture is:

$$7.2 \times (1 - 0.30) = 5.0$$

The adjusted multiple is applied against the normalized EBITDA:

$$5.0 \times \$18,200,000 = \$91,000,000$$

Subtracting out the debt results in the equity value:

$$\$91,000,000 - \$1,400,000 = \$89,600,000$$

## Prior Transaction Method

The prior transaction method (PTM) uses transactions data from the stock of the actual subject company and is most appropriate when valuing minority (noncontrolling) interests. The valuation under this method can be based on the actual transaction price or multiples derived from such transactions.

Ideally, the previous transactions would be arm's-length, of the same motivation (strategic or financial) as the subject transaction, and fairly recent.

## LOS 37.j: Describe the asset-based approach to private company valuation.

*CFA® Program Curriculum, Volume 4, page 453*

The asset-based approach estimates the value of firm equity as the fair value of its assets minus the fair value of its liabilities. It is generally not used for going concerns. Because it is easier to find comparable data at the firm level compared to the asset level, the income and market approaches would be preferred when valuing going concerns. Additionally, it is difficult to find data for individual intangible assets and specialized assets.

Of the three approaches, the asset-based approach generally results in the lowest valuation because the use of a firm's assets in combination usually results in greater value creation than each of its parts individually.

The asset-based approach might be appropriate in the following circumstances:

- Firms with minimal profits and little hope for better prospects. In this situation, the firm might be valued more highly for its liquidation value rather than as a going concern by a firm that can put the assets to better use.
- Finance firms such as banks, where their asset and liability values (loan and security values) can be based on market prices and factors.
- Investment companies such as real estate investment trusts (REITs) and closed-end investment companies (CEICs) where the underlying assets values are determined using the market or income approaches. Management fees and the value of management expertise may result in values different from net asset value.
- Small companies or early stage companies with few intangible assets.
- Natural resource firms where assets can be valued using comparables sales.

## LOS 37.k: Explain and evaluate the effects on private company valuations of discounts and premiums based on control and marketability.

*CFA® Program Curriculum, Volume 4, page 454*

In general, adjustments are required when the liquidity or control position of an acquisition differs from that of the comparable companies. If, for example, the comparable firm values are for the purchase of an entire public company and we wish to value a minority stake in a private firm, we would need to apply discounts for both a lack of control and a lack of marketability (liquidity).

The variability of estimated discounts varies with the following:

- The data used to estimate them and the analyst's interpretation of them.
- The perceived importance of the invested position.
- The allocation of shares and the resulting effect on control.
- The relationships between various parties.
- The protection provided to minority shareholders by state laws.
- The likelihood of an IPO or sale.
- The payment of dividends.

## The Discount for Lack of Control

Minority shareholders are at a disadvantage relative to controlling shareholders because they have less power to select the directors and management. Without a voice, they cannot determine the investment and payout policies that affect the value of the firm and the distribution of earnings.

Controlling shareholders can also enjoy excessive compensation and other perquisites to the detriment of minority shareholders. However, firms that will experience an IPO or sale are less likely to pursue actions that damage minority shareholders.

The factors for determining a discount for lack of control (DLOC) are the same as those for the control premium discussed earlier. Because it is difficult to measure the disadvantage from a lack of control, the discount is usually backed out of the control premium.

$$\text{DLOC} = 1 - \left[ \frac{1}{1 + \text{control premium}} \right]$$

For example, if the control premium is 25%, the DLOC is 20%:

$$\text{DLOC} = 1 - \left[ \frac{1}{1 + 0.25} \right] = 20\%$$

To calculate control premiums, data from the acquisitions of public companies are typically used.

The table below summarizes when control premiums or discounts are appropriate.

**Figure 1: Premiums (Discounts) for Controlling Interest**

| Scenario | Comparable Data | Subject Valuation | Adjustment to Comparable Data for Control |
|---|---|---|---|
| 1 | Controlling interest | Controlling interest | None |
| 2 | Controlling interest | Noncontrolling interest | DLOC |
| 3 | Noncontrolling interest | Controlling interest | Control premium |
| 4 | Noncontrolling interest | Noncontrolling interest | None |

An example of Scenario 2 would be when the GTM is used for valuing a noncontrolling interest. Recall that in the GTM, the comparable price multiple data is for the sale of entire firms where control is acquired.

An example of Scenario 3 would be when the GPCM is used for valuing a controlling interest. Recall that in the GPCM, the comparable price multiple data is from noncontrolling interests.

The use of discounted cash flow methods such as the FCF and CCM could also require adjustments, depending on whether the estimated and subject cash flows were on a controlling or noncontrolling interest basis.

## The Discount for Lack of Marketability

If an interest in a firm cannot be easily sold, discounts for lack of marketability (DLOM) would be applied (sometimes termed a discount for lack of liquidity). It is often the case that if a DLOC is applied, a DLOM will also be applied. For example, if a controlling shareholder believes that a private firm should not be sold, minority shareholders both lack control and lack the ability to sell their position.

The DLOM varies with the following:

- An impending IPO or firm sale would decrease the DLOM.
- The payment of dividends would decrease the DLOM.
- Earlier, higher payments (i.e., shorter duration) would decrease the DLOM.
- Contractual restrictions on selling stock would increase the DLOM.
- A greater pool of buyers would decrease the DLOM.
- Greater risk and value uncertainty would increase the DLOM.

To estimate the DLOM, an analyst can use one of three methods. In the first method, the price of restricted shares is used. As an example, SEC Rule 144 may restrict the sale of shares acquired in a firm prior to its IPO. In this case, the price of the restricted shares is compared to the price of the publicly traded shares.

In the second method, the price of pre-IPO shares is compared to that of post-IPO shares. One complicating factor is that post-IPO firms are generally thought to have more certain cash flows and lower risk, so the estimated DLOM may not purely reflect changes in marketability.

A third method would estimate the DLOM as the price of a put option divided by the stock price, where the put used is at-the-money. The time to maturity of the valued option could be the time to the IPO. The volatility used could be based on the historical volatility of publicly traded stock or the implied volatility of publicly traded options. The advantage of this approach over the other two DLOM estimation methods is that the estimated risk of the firm can be factored into the option price. The drawback of this approach is that a put provides a certain selling price, not actual liquidity.

Although these methods provide a basis for calculating the DLOM, it is often challenging to implement them. The data may be limited, the interpretation of the data will vary, and the magnitude of the DLOM applied to a company will vary by analyst. In addition to the DLOC and DLOM, other discounts could be applied, such as key person discount.

Because they are applied in a sequential process, the DLOC and DLOM are multiplicative, not additive. So if the DLOC is 20%, and the DLOM is 13%, the total discount is:

total discount = 1 − [(1 − DLOC)(1 − DLOM)]
total discount = 1 − [(1 − 0.20)(1 − 0.13)] = 30.4%

This is not the 33% found when using an additive calculation.

 *Professor's Note: This point seems very testable.*

### Example: Calculating the value of a minority interest

Assume that a minority shareholder holds 15% of a private firm's equity and that the CEO holds the other 85%. There are two possible scenarios.

In Scenario 1, the CEO will likely sell the firm very soon. In this case, valuation discounts will be very small. A DLOM of 5% will be applied and a DLOC will not be applied under the assumption that all selling shareholders will receive the same price. The value of the firm's equity is estimated at $10 million.

In Scenario 2, the CEO has no plans to sell the firm, and the minority shareholder cannot sell its interest easily. A DLOM of 20% will be applied. A DLOC will be estimated by using reported earnings instead of normalized earnings to provide an estimated firm equity value of $9 million.

Given these figures, calculate the value of the minority shareholder's equity interest under both scenarios.

**Answer:**

The following provides the calculations under each scenario.

| Scenario 1: Assuming sale is likely | |
|---|---|
| Firm's equity value | $10,000,000 |
| Minority interest | 15% |
| Value of minority interest without discounts | $1,500,000 |
| minus DLOC of 0% | 0 |
| Value of interest if marketable | $1,500,000 |
| minus DLOM of 5% | $75,000 |
| Value of minority interest | $1,425,000 |

| Scenario 2: Assuming sale is unlikely | |
|---|---|
| Firm's equity value | $9,000,000 |
| Minority interest | 15% |
| Value of minority interest without discounts | $1,350,000 |
| minus DLOC of 0% | 0 |
| Value of interest if marketable | $1,350,000 |
| minus DLOM of 20% | $270,000 |
| Value of minority interest | $1,080,000 |

The smaller value of the minority interest in Scenario 2 is due to the higher DLOM and the DLOC (as reflected in the lower firm equity value of $9,000,000). The $9,000,000 value assumes that certain firm inefficiencies (e.g., above-market compensation for the owner) cannot be corrected without a sale of the firm.

## LOS 37.l: Describe the role of valuation standards in valuing private companies.

*CFA® Program Curriculum, Volume 4, page 460*

There has been an increased focus on the valuation of private companies, in part due to the use of fair value estimates for financial reporting. As a result, a number of valuation standards have been developed, which specify the formation and dissemination of the valuation. There is no single valuation standard.

In response to the U.S. savings and loan crisis in the late 1980s and early 1990s, the Uniform Standards of Professional Appraisal Practice (USPAP) were created by the Appraisal Foundation. These standards cover real estate, fixed income, and private business valuations. Although the Appraisal Foundation is a congressionally authorized provider of standards, business appraisers are not required to adhere to the standards.

The International Valuation Standards Committee (IVSC) has created the International Valuation Standards, covering businesses, real estate, and tangible assets. These standards have been adopted in 53 countries.

The American Institute of Certified Public Accountants (AICPA) Consulting Services Executive Committee has put forth the Statement of Standards on Valuation Services (SSVS), which must be adhered to by members but not by nonmembers.

Fair value estimates (and their methodology) are reviewed by the auditors and possibly by the SEC, in the case of companies registered with the SEC.

Standards for private equity valuation have been developed by the International Private Equity and Venture Capital Valuation Board, as well as the Private Equity Industry Guidelines Group.

There are many challenges involved with the implementation of appraisal standards:

- The compliance with these standards is usually at the discretion of the appraiser because most buyers are still unaware of them.
- Because most valuation reports are private, it is very difficult for the organizations to ensure compliance to the standards.
- Although the organizations provide technical guidance on the use of their standards, it is necessarily limited due to the heterogeneity of valuations.
- Valuation will depend on the definition of value used. Some valuation methods are required because of the specific definition of value, whereas in other cases an appraiser will use several definitions to show a range of values.

# KEY CONCEPTS

### LOS 37.a

Both company-specific and stock-specific factors distinguish private and public companies. Company-specific factors for private firms may include the degree to which they:

- Are less mature.
- Have less capital.
- Have fewer assets.
- Have fewer employees with less depth of management.
- Are riskier.
- Have higher managerial ownership.
- Have a longer-term focus.
- Provide less disclosure of information about the firm.
- Have greater tax concerns.

Stock-specific factors for private firms may include the degree to which they:

- Have less liquidity in the equity interests.
- Often have restrictions on liquidity.
- Have concentration of control to the possible detriment of noncontrolling shareholders.

Company-specific factors can have positive or negative effects on private company valuations while stock-specific factors are usually negative. There is more heterogeneity in private firm risk, discount rates, and valuation methods.

### LOS 37.b

Private company valuations are used for transactions, compliance, and litigation. Transaction-related valuations are performed when there is venture capital financing, an IPO, a sale of the firm, bankruptcy, or performance-based managerial compensation. Compliance-related valuations are performed for financial reporting and tax purposes. Litigation-related valuations may be required for shareholder suits, damage claims, lost profits, or divorces.

### LOS 37.c

The definition of value will affect estimated asset value, and a valuation should only be used for the purpose it was generated. The main definitions of value are:

- Fair market value: used for tax purposes in the United States and based on an arm's length transaction.
- Fair value for financial reporting or litigation: similar to fair market value and used for financial reporting or legal purposes.
- Market value: used in real asset appraisals for a particular date characterized by well-informed parties.
- Investment value: in contrast to the previous definitions that were market based, this is the value to a particular buyer.
- Intrinsic value: the "true" value derived from investment analysis.

## LOS 37.d

The three major approaches to private company valuation are the income approach, the market approach, and the asset-based approach. The valuation should consider the firm's operations, lifecycle stage, size, risk, and growth.

## LOS 37.e

Normalized earnings are calculated by adjusting for:
- Nonrecurring and unusual items.
- Discretionary expenses.
- Non-market levels of compensation.
- Personal expenses charged to the firm.
- Real estate expenses based on historical cost.
- Non-market lease rates.

The normalized earnings for a strategic buyer incorporate acquisition synergies, whereas a financial (nonstrategic) transaction does not.

When estimating free cash flow to value the firm or equity, the following issues should be considered:
- Estimates may vary for controlling and noncontrolling equity interests.
- Several scenarios of future cash flows should be examined.
- The scenarios should consider the lifecycle stage of the firm.
- Management biases should be anticipated.
- FCFF would be used when there will be capital structure changes.

## LOS 37.f

The three methods of valuation using the income approach:
- Free cash flow method: discounts a series of discrete cash flows plus a terminal value. It is a 2-stage model.
- Capitalized cash flow method: discounts a single cash flow by the capitalization rate. It is a single-stage model.
- Excess earnings method: values tangible and intangible assets separately and is useful for small firms and when there are intangible assets to value.

## LOS 37.g

Estimating the discount rate in a private firm valuation should factor in the following elements:
- Size premiums: the appraiser may use data from small cap public firms, but these may include a distress premium not applicable to the private firm.
- Availability and cost of debt: compared to a public firm, a private firm may not be able to obtain as much debt financing or at as cheap a rate.
- Acquirer vs. target: the WACC used should be that for the target, not the acquirer.
- Projection risk: projecting cash flows for private firms is riskier given the lower availability of information and reliance on management for projections.
- Lifecycle stage: it is difficult to estimate the discount rate for early stage firms.

LOS 37.h
Using discount rate models for private firms includes the following:
- CAPM: may not be appropriate for private firms because beta is usually estimated from public firm returns.
- Expanded CAPM: adds premiums for size and firm-specific risk.
- Build-up method: adds an industry risk and other risk premiums to market rate of return and is used when betas for comparable public firms are not available.

LOS 37.i
The three market approach methods are as follows:

1. The *guideline public company method* (GPCM) uses price multiples from traded public companies with adjustments for risk differences. The advantage is that there are usually numerous public company transactions available, but the public firms may not be comparable. When estimating a control premium for a controlling interest, the transaction type, industry conditions, type of consideration, and reasonableness should be considered.

2. The *guideline transactions method* (GTM) uses the price multiples from the sale of whole public and private companies with adjustments for risk differences. The following issues regarding the comparable data should be considered: transaction type, contingent consideration, type of consideration, availability of data, and date of data.

3. The *prior transaction method* (PTM) uses historical stock sales of the subject company and is best when using recent, arm's-length data of the same motivation.

LOS 37.j
The asset-based approach is usually not used for going concerns but is used for troubled firms, finance firms, investment companies, firms with few intangible assets, and natural resource firms. It values equity as the asset value minus the debt value of a firm.

LOS 37.k
The application of discounts and premiums to comparable company values depends on differences between the characteristics of the interest in the comparable company (companies) that serves as the benchmark value and the characteristics of the interest in the target company to be valued. A discount for lack of control (DLOC) is applied when the comparable values are for the sale of an entire company (public or private), and the valuation is being done for a minority interest in the target company. A control premium is added when the comparable company values are for public shares or other minority interests, and the target company valuation is for a controlling interest.

A DLOC can be estimated using valuations based on reported earnings rather than normalized earnings or as:

$$DLOC = 1 - \left[ \frac{1}{1 + \text{control premium}} \right]$$

Discounts for lack of marketability (DLOM) are applied when the comparables are based on highly marketable securities, such as public shares, and the interest in the target company is less marketable, as in the case of a minority interest in a private firm. The DLOM can be estimated using restricted share versus publicly traded share prices, pre-IPO versus post-IPO prices, and put prices. It can be challenging to implement these methods.

The DLOC and DLOM are applied multiplicatively using:

total discount = 1 − [(1 − DLOC)(1 − DLOM)]

## LOS 37.l
The challenges involved with valuation standards are:
- There are many different valuation standards.
- Compliance is at the appraiser's discretion.
- It is difficult to ensure compliance to the standards.
- Technical guidance on the use of standards is limited.
- Valuation will depend on the definition of value used.

## CONCEPT CHECKERS

1. Compared to public firms, private firms *most likely* have:
   A. fewer tax concerns.
   B. a longer-term focus.
   C. less managerial ownership.

2. Which of the following *best* describes the process of valuation in venture capital financing?
   A. Valuations are usually based on negotiation.
   B. Discounted cash flow and price multiple analysis are typically used.
   C. The appraiser estimates value using comparable company values and the prices of recent IPOs.

3. An appraiser is working for a large multinational that is considering buying a privately held firm in the southeastern United States. The multinational believes that the acquisition would allow it to realize cost savings in its production process. Which of the following is the *most likely* standard of value the appraiser will use?
   A. Fair value.
   B. Market value.
   C. Investment value.

4. An analyst is valuing the equity of a firm that has been experiencing financial distress for several months. Which of the following is the *most likely* valuation approach the analyst will use?
   A. The market approach.
   B. The income approach.
   C. The asset-based approach.

5. Given the following figures, calculate the normalized EBITDA for a financial and strategic buyer.

   | | |
   |---|---|
   | Reported EBITDA | $6,700,000 |
   | Current executive compensation | $800,000 |
   | Market-based executive compensation | $650,000 |
   | Current SG&A expenses | $8,100,000 |
   | SG&A expenses after synergistic savings | $7,300,000 |
   | Current lease rate | $200,000 |
   | Market-based lease rate | $250,000 |

   The normalized EBITDA for each type of buyer is:

   | | Financial buyer | Strategic buyer |
   |---|---|---|
   | A. | $6,800,000 | $7,600,000 |
   | B. | $6,900,000 | $6,800,000 |
   | C. | $6,900,000 | $7,700,000 |

6.  Given the following figures, calculate the FCFF. Assume the earnings and expenses are normalized and that capital expenditures will equal depreciation plus 4% of the firm's incremental revenues.

| | |
|---|---|
| Current revenues | $10,000,000 |
| Revenue growth | 5% |
| Gross profit margin | 20% |
| Depreciation expense as a percent of sales | 1% |
| Working capital as a percent of sales | 12% |
| SG&A expenses | $1,600,000 |
| Tax rate | 40% |

The FCFF is:
A. $157,000.
B. $277,000.
C. $407,000.

7.  Using the following figures, calculate the value of the equity using the CCM, assuming the firm will be acquired.

| | |
|---|---|
| Normalized FCFE in current year | $2,200,000 |
| Reported FCFE in current year | $1,800,000 |
| Growth rate of FCFE | 6.0% |
| Equity discount rate | 18.0% |
| WACC | 14.5% |
| Risk-free rate | 4.2% |
| Cost of debt | 11.0% |
| Market value of debt | $3,000,000 |

The value of the equity is:
A. $15,900,000.
B. $19,433,333.
C. $27,435,294.

8.     Using the following figures, calculate the value of the firm using the EEM.

| | |
|---|---|
| Working capital | $400,000 |
| Fixed assets | $1,800,000 |
| Normalized earnings | $235,000 |
| Required return for working capital | 4% |
| Required return for fixed assets | 12% |
| Growth rate of residual income | 3% |
| Discount rate for intangible assets | 16% |

The value of the firm is:
A.  $2,223,077.
B.  $2,223,769.
C.  $4,061,923.

9.     Which of the following *best* describes the appropriate approach to estimating the WACC for a private company acquisition? The WACC should be:
A.  the target's WACC.
B.  the acquirer's WACC.
C.  a weighted average of the target's and acquirer's WACC that factors in financing arrangements.

10.    Which of the following models is recommended for estimating the discount rate for a private company if there are no comparable public equity firms?
A.  The CAPM.
B.  The build-up method.
C.  The expanded CAPM.

**Use the following information to answer Questions 11 and 12.**

| | |
|---|---|
| Income return on bonds | 5.7% |
| Capital return on bonds | 1.1% |
| Long-term Treasury yield | 4.8% |
| Beta | 1.5 |
| Equity risk premium | 5.5% |
| Small stock premium | 3.8% |
| Company-specific risk premium | 2.5% |
| Industry risk-premium | 2.0% |
| Pretax cost of debt | 10.0% |
| Optimal debt/total cap | 15.0% |
| Current debt/total | 4.0% |
| Debt/total cap for public firms in industry | 40.0% |
| Tax rate | 35.0% |

11. Calculate the cost of equity for a mature private firm of similar size and firm-specific risk as its public comparable. The cost of equity is:
    A. 13.1%.
    B. 15.1%.
    C. 19.4%.

12. Calculate the WACC for the acquisition of a small private firm with a high degree of firm-specific risk. The firm is dissimilar to public firms. The WACC is:
    A. 12.1%.
    B. 16.8%.
    C. 17.4%.

13. An analyst is valuing a private firm on the behalf of a strategic buyer and deflates the average public company multiple by 30% to account for the higher risk of the private firm. Given the following figures, calculate the value of firm equity using the GPCM.

    | | |
    |---|---|
    | Market value of debt | $2,600,000 |
    | Normalized EBITDA | $27,100,000 |
    | Average public company MVIC/EBITDA multiple | 9.0 |
    | Control premium from past transaction | 25% |

    The value of the firm's equity is:
    A. $168,130,000.
    B. $210,162,500.
    C. $214,090,000.

14. Which of the following would *least likely* be valued by the asset-based approach?
    A. A natural resource firm.
    B. A financial firm such as a bank.
    C. A firm with significant intangible assets.

15. Which of the following would result in a larger DLOM, other things equal?
    A. An IPO.
    B. Lower asset risk.
    C. A longer asset duration.

16. An analyst determines that a control premium of 18% is included in the acquisition prices of the comparable firms used for valuing a minority interest in a private company. If she also determines that a discount for lack of marketability of 22% is appropriate for the private company interest, what is the total adjustment she will make to the value of the comparables when valuing the private company interest?
    A. 33.9%.
    B. 36.0%.
    C. 40.6%.

17. Which of the following *best* describes the implementation of valuation standards?
    A. Technical guidance is limited.
    B. Appraisal organizations periodically review valuations for compliance.
    C. The U.S. government mandates the use of AICPA standards for appraisals.

## ANSWERS – CONCEPT CHECKERS

1. **B** Private firms can take a longer-term view because their managers/owners do not have to focus on the short-term needs of external shareholders. Private firms, however, are more concerned with taxes because of the impact of firm policies on the taxation of the firm's owners. In most private firms, management has substantial ownership.

2. **A** In venture capital financing, the private company valuations are usually subject to negotiation and are informal due to the uncertainty of future cash flows.

3. **C** The appraiser will most likely use investment value. This valuation provides value to a particular buyer. In this case, the multinational may place a higher value on the private firm due to the perceived synergies.

4. **C** The analyst will most likely use the asset-based approach which values a firm as its assets minus liabilities. The firm's future cash flows are uncertain, and it may have to be liquidated given its distress. Therefore, the income approach should not be used, and the firm should not be compared to other firms that are going concerns, as in the market approach. The amount that equity holders could reasonably expect is their claim after liabilities have been satisfied.

5. **A** Both strategic and financial buyers will attempt to reduce executive compensation to market levels by $150,000 ($800,000 – $650,000). They will also have to pay a higher lease rate of $50,000 ($250,000 – $200,000). So the initial adjustment for both buyers to generate normalized EBITDA is $6,700,000 + $150,000 – $50,000 = $6,800,000.

   However, only a strategic buyer will be able to realize additional synergistic savings of $800,000 ($8,100,000 – $7,300,000). So normalized EBITDA for a strategic buyer is $7,600,000 and for a financial buyer it is $6,800,000.

6. **A** The answer is calculated as follows.

| Pro Forma Income Statement | |
|---|---:|
| Revenues | $10,500,000 |
| Cost of goods sold | $8,400,000 |
| Gross profit | $2,100,000 |
| SG&A expenses | $1,600,000 |
| Pro forma EBITDA | $500,000 |
| Depreciation and amortization | $105,000 |
| Pro forma EBIT | $395,000 |
| Pro forma taxes on EBIT | $158,000 |
| Operating income after tax | $237,000 |
| | |
| *Adjustments to obtain FCFF* | |
| Plus: depreciation and amortization | $105,000 |
| Minus: capital expenditures | $125,000 |
| Minus: increase in working capital | $60,000 |
| FCFF | $157,000 |

The following provides a line by line explanation for the previous calculations.

| Pro Forma Income Statement | Explanation |
|---|---|
| Revenues | Current revenues multiplied by the growth rate: $10,000,000 × (1.05) |
| Cost of goods sold | Revenues multiplied by one minus the gross profit margin: $10,500,000 × (1 − 0.20) |
| Gross profit | Revenues multiplied by the gross profit margin: $10,500,000 × 0.20 |
| SG&A expenses | Given in the question |
| Pro forma EBITDA | Gross profit minus SG&A expenses: $2,100,000 − $1,600,000 |
| Depreciation and amortization | Revenues multiplied by the given depreciation expense: $10,500,000 × 0.01 |
| Pro forma EBIT | EBITDA minus depreciation and amortization: $500,000 − $105,000 |
| Pro forma taxes on EBIT | EBIT multiplied by tax rate: $395,000 × 0.40 |
| Operating income after tax | EBIT minus taxes: $395,000 − $158,000 |
| *Adjustments to obtain FCFF* | *Explanation* |
| Plus: depreciation and amortization | Add back noncash charges from above |
| Minus: capital expenditures | Expenditures cover depreciation and increase with revenues: $105,000 + (0.04 × $10,500,000 − $10,000,000) |
| Minus: increase in working capital | The working capital will increase as revenues increase 0.12 × ($10,500,000 − $10,000,000) |
| FCFF | Operating income net of the adjustments above |

7. **B**   To arrive at the value of the equity using the CCM, it can be estimated using the free cash flows to equity and the required return on equity (r):

$$\text{value of equity} = \frac{\text{FCFE}_1}{r - g}$$

$$\text{value of equity} = \frac{\$2,200,000 \times (1.06)}{0.18 - 0.06} = \$19,433,333$$

Note that we grow the FCFE at the growth rate because the *current* year FCFE is provided in the problem (not next year). We use normalized earnings, not reported earnings, given that normalized earnings are most relevant for the acquirers of the firm. The relevant required return for FCFE is the equity discount rate, not the WACC.

An alternative approach to calculate the value of the equity would be to subtract the market value of the firm's debt from total firm value. However, the FCFF are not provided, so a total firm value cannot be calculated.

8. **B**   The answer is calculated using the following steps.

*Step 1:* Calculate the required return for working capital and fixed assets.

Given the required returns in percent, the monetary returns are:

working capital: $400,000 × 4% = $16,000

fixed sssets: $1,800,000 × 12% = $216,000

*Step 2:* Calculate the residual income.

After the monetary returns to assets are calculated, the residual income is that which is left over in the normalized earnings:

residual income = $235,000 – $16,000 – $216,000 = $3,000

*Step 3:* Value the intangible assets.

Using the formula for a growing perpetuity, the discount rate for intangible assets, and the growth rate for residual income:

value of intangible assets = ($3,000 × 1.03) / (0.16 – 0.03) = $23,769

*Step 4:* Sum the asset values to arrive at the total firm value.

firm value = $400,000 + $1,800,000 + $23,769 = $2,223,769

9. **A**   The private target's WACC should be used. It may be much different than the acquirer's, given that acquirers are usually larger and more mature than targets.

10. **B**   If there are no comparable public firms with which to estimate beta by, then the build-up method can be used where various risk premiums are added to the risk-free rate.

11. **A**   The CAPM will be used because the private firm is mature and of similar size and firm-specific risk as the public comparable. The expanded CAPM is not used because premiums for size and firm-specific risk are not needed. The build-up method is not needed because the private firm has a public comparable.

The CAPM calculation uses the risk-free rate, the beta, and the equity risk premium: 4.8% + 1.50(5.5%) = 13.1%.

The risk-free rate is the Treasury yield, not the returns for bonds in general.

12. **B**   The build-up method is used when there are no comparable public firms with which to estimate beta. Because the firm is small with a high degree of firm-specific risk, risk premiums will be used for these. An industry risk premium is used in the build-up method but not beta.

Because the firm is being acquired, we assume the new owners will utilize an optimal capital structure and weights in the WACC calculation. The capital structure for public firms should not be used because public firms have better access to debt financing.

Study Session 12

The resulting calculations are as follows.

Using the build-up method: the risk-free rate, the equity risk premium, the small stock premium, a company-specific risk premium, and an industry risk premium are added together:

4.8% + 5.5% + 3.8% + 2.5% + 2.0% = 18.6%

The WACC using the optimal capital structure factors in the debt to total cap, the cost of debt, the tax rate, and the given cost of equity:

[15% × 10% × (1 − 35%)] + [(1 − 15%) × 18.6%] = 16.8%

13. **B**   The adjustment to the MVIC/EBITDA multiple for the higher risk of the private firm is: $9.0 \times (1 − 0.30) = 6.3$.

The adjusted multiple is applied against the normalized EBITDA:

6.3 × $27,100,000 = $170,730,000

Subtracting out the debt results in the equity value:

$170,730,000 − $2,600,000 = $168,130,000

Since the buyer is a strategic buyer, a control premium of 25% is added:

168,130,000(1.25) = $210,162,500

14. **C**   It is difficult to find comparable data for individual intangible assets, so the asset-based approach would not be used. Natural resource firms and finance firms where their asset values can be determined by examining market prices would be easier to value using the asset-based approach.

15. **C**   An IPO would increase liquidity and decrease the DLOM. Lower asset risk would result in less value uncertainty and a lower DLOM. A longer asset duration (later, lower payments) would result in reduced liquidity and a higher DLOM.

16. **A**   The discount for lack of control (DLOC) can be backed out of the control premium:

$$DLOC = 1 - \left[\frac{1}{1 + \text{control premium}}\right]$$

$$DLOC = 1 - \left[\frac{1}{1 + 0.18}\right] = 15.25\%$$

The total discount also uses the discount for lack of marketability (DLOM):

total discount = 1 − [(1 − DLOC)(1 − DLOM)]
total discount = 1 − [(1 − 0.1525)(1 − 0.22)] = 33.9%

17. **A**   Although various organizations provide technical guidance on the use of their valuation standards, it is limited due to the heterogeneity of valuations. It is very difficult for the organizations to ensure compliance to the standards because most valuations are confidential. There is no single mandated valuation standard.

**Use the following information to answer Questions 1–6.**

VisionLink is a U.S.-based producer of flat-panel televisions. The company is known for its low cost products, which are primarily sold through retail electronics stores and discount super stores. While the design work is handled in house, production is outsourced to a Taiwanese electronics manufacturer, ElectroTech, which manufactures televisions for several other major television brands.

ElectroTech is just one of three companies that actually manufacture televisions. The major brands primarily handle design, marketing, and product distribution and leave manufacturing and assembly to ElectroTech and its competitors.

VisionLink's CFO, David Lewis, is concerned about VisionLink's position in the consumer television industry and the profitability of the industry in general. Lewis consults with Roger Diltz, the director of VisionLink's marketing department, regarding his concerns and requests that Diltz identify the major factors that will affect the long-term profitability of the consumer television industry. Since VisionLink has positioned itself as a low cost provider of televisions, Lewis is concerned about the potential for rampant price-cutting by the other competitors, which will erode VisionLink's profits and market share. Lewis asks Diltz to identify the factors that would contribute to rivalry among existing competitors.

VisionLink is interested in the development and incorporation of 3D technologies into consumer televisions and has been discussing internally the possible entry into the 3D television market. Jonathan Levy, head of research for VisionLink, has done some initial research on what it would take to develop a line of 3D televisions and writes an email to VisionLink's CFO, David Lewis. In his e-mail, Levy notes that while some initial R&D will be required to enter into the 3D market, the costs are minimal, and VisionLink will not be required to pay any royalties or fees to patent holders. Levy also believes that as new content is developed specifically for 3D viewing, the demand for 3D televisions will continue to grow.

VisionLink is looking at different options on how it might expand into the 3D market. Right now, there are few competitors, and one of the strategies being reviewed is an acquisition of one of the leading brand names of 3D televisions. There is currently internal debate within VisionLink regarding the short-term versus long-term benefits of such an expansion strategy.

Lewis is also concerned about the threat of substitutes to consumer televisions. Specifically, Lewis believes that computers will be used more frequently for viewing television content over the internet as will portable devices such as tablets and mobile phones. While discussing the threat of substitutes with Lewis, Levy suggests that VisionLink could respond by increasing functionality in its televisions to include web surfing and viewing of internet videos. Levy also suggests that VisionLink could offer a line of computer monitors that provides a superior viewing experience to customers that decide to use computers as substitutes to televisions.

1.   Given the structure of the television industry, the bargaining power of suppliers is:
  A.  high, leading to higher long-term profitability for VisionLink.
  B.  low, leading to higher long-term profitability for VisionLink.
  C.  high, leading to lower long-term profitability for VisionLink.

2.  Which of the following would Diltz be *most likely* to identify as a determinant of long-term profitability for the consumer television industry?
    A.  Industry structure.
    B.  Supply and demand.
    C.  Eliminating competitors through an acquisition or merger.

3.  Which of the following is *most likely* to increase rivalry and price competition among existing competitors in the consumer television market?
    A.  High brand identity within the industry.
    B.  High degree of operating or financial leverage.
    C.  Threat of forward integration.

4.  Based on Levy's analysis, the innovation and development of 3D televisions will *most likely* cause profits in the consumer television industry to:
    A.  permanently increase.
    B.  temporarily increase.
    C.  remain at current levels.

5.  If VisionLink goes forward and acquires a leading manufacturer of 3D televisions, how would this strategy be *best* characterized?
    A.  The strategy is risky because it may attract more competitors.
    B.  The strategy is preferred because changes to industry structure will improve the company's competitive position.
    C.  The strategy is preferred, since it will reduce competition longer term.

6.  Levy's suggested ideas regarding the threat of substitutes would *best* be described as:
    A.  altering the firm's existing position.
    B.  creating changes in the industry structure.
    C.  capitalizing on changes in the industry.

**Use the following information to answer Questions 7 through 12.**

Charles Porter, a CFA Level II candidate, is a junior analyst for ValueSegment, an independent provider of equity analysis and valuations. Porter has been tasked with valuing four different firms and has questions regarding the valuation models and techniques to apply to each. The firms that he has been assigned to value are described in the following:

*   Firm 1 is a publicly traded retail fashion store that has been in operation for more than 70 years. The firm has a consistent dividend policy with a target dividend growth rate of 3.5% per year. Additionally, its earnings are projected to steadily increase in the near future. A ValueSegment customer who is looking to become the majority shareholder of the firm requested the independent valuation of this firm.
*   Firm 2, a software manufacturer, has a consistent track record of paying dividends that is related to its earnings. The firm is projected to have a growth rate of 25% for the next five years and has an estimated required rate of return of 14%. The valuation of Firm 2 will be included in a ValueSegment research report targeted toward common investors.
*   Firm 3 is a steel manufacturer that has been in business for more than 50 years. The firm has a stable dividend history with a historical growth rate of 7.5% over the last 10 years. The most recent dividend per share was $2.25. Porter has estimated that the required rate of return (r) for Firm 3 is 12%.

- Firm 4 is an upstart internet retailer that is growing at an extremely fast rate. The firm's guidance suggests that the dividend growth rate will be high during the next year, and then gradually decline over the next five years to a lower, more sustainable rate. The most recent earnings per share (EPS) was $3.25, and Porter estimates that EPS next year will be $3.90. The estimated required rate of return is 10.25%.

After collecting information on his assigned firms, Porter believes that he will need to use the Gordon growth model (GGM) to value at least one of the firms. Since he is concerned about using the model, he decides to consult a coworker, Albert Huang, about the strengths and weaknesses of the GGM. Huang makes the following statements to Porter regarding the GGM:

- **Statement 1**: The Gordon growth model is simple to use and discuss and can be applied to stable, dividend-paying firms.
- **Statement 2**: The Gordon growth model is sensitive to estimates of the required rate of return but is insensitive to estimates of the dividend growth rate.

7. The type of valuation model that is most appropriate for Porter to use to value Firm 1 is a:
   A. dividend discount model.
   B. free-cash flow model.
   C. residual income model.

8. Would it be appropriate for Porter to use a dividend discount model (DDM) to value Firm 2?
   A. Yes.
   B. No, the DDM should only be used when an investor takes the perspective of a majority shareholder.
   C. No, the dividend growth rate is higher than the required rate of return.

9. If the current stock price of Firm 3 is $34.50, the growth rate implied by the Gordon growth model would be:
   A. 5.86%.
   B. 5.14%.
   C. 7.50%.

10. The valuation model that would be *most appropriate* to value Firm 4 would be the:
    A. two-stage DDM.
    B. three-stage DDM.
    C. H-model.

11. If Firm 4's shares trade at $45, then the present value of growth opportunities (PVGO) for Firm 4 is *closest* to:
    A. $13.29.
    B. $31.71.
    C. $6.95.

12. Are Huang's statements to Porter regarding the Gordon growth model accurate?
    A. No, one of the statements is inaccurate.
    B. No, both statements are inaccurate.
    C. Yes, both statements are accurate.

# SELF-TEST ANSWERS: EQUITY INVESTMENTS

1. **C**   Since there are a limited number of suppliers (three) that actually manufacture and assemble televisions, there is a high concentration of suppliers, meaning that the suppliers have higher bargaining power. Since the major brands team with manufacturers to produce all of their televisions, there would be a high cost to switch their line to another manufacturer. Additionally, there is a high threat of forward integration as a manufacturer like ElectroTech could develop their own line of televisions to sell direct to consumers.

2. **A**   Supply and demand is a determinant of short-term rather than long-term profitability. Long-term profitability is determined by industry structure, which is determined by Porter's five forces: threat of new entrants in the industry, threat of substitutes, bargaining power of buyers, bargaining power of suppliers, and rivalry among existing competitors. While it is tempting to eliminate rivals through a merger or acquisition, the resulting increase in profits may be short-term, since increased profits could attract more competitors, including online competitors, which would serve to reduce profitability in the long-run.

3. **B**   This relates to Porter's Force Five—the degree of rivalry among existing competitors. A high degree of operating/financial leverage increases the likelihood that participants in this market space will price cut in order to defend their market share and attempt to cover their fixed costs. Brand identity within an industry is associated with product differences. Product differences make it more difficult to compete directly on price, therefore reducing the strength of this force. The threat of forward integration relates to the bargaining power of suppliers.

4. **B**   Innovation and technology may affect an industry on a temporary basis but do not determine long-term profitability unless the change in technology affects one of Porter's five forces. In this case, the barriers to entering the new 3D market segment are low, indicating that television producers that adopt the technology early, may initially be able to charge higher prices and earn higher profits. The higher profits will cause the other competitors to adopt the technology, resulting in profitability returning to normal levels.

5. **A**   While eliminating a major competitor may appear to be an attractive proposition at first, the increased profits will only be temporary as the profits will entice new competitors to enter the market.

6. **C**   Lewis is projecting changes in the threat of substitutes, while Levy is suggesting ways to exploit these changes. This is best described as capitalizing on changes in the industry.

7. **B**   Because the valuation is being done on the customer's behalf, Porter will need to use a model that accounts for the perspective of a majority shareholder. The free cash flow model is the best choice because it can be used to value a firm when the perspective is that of a controlling shareholder.

8. **A** The dividend discount model (DDM) is an appropriate valuation methodology to use when:
   - The company has a history of dividend payments.
   - The dividend policy is clear and related to the earnings of the firm.
   - The perspective is that of a minority shareholder.

   Based on the information provided, the firm meets the requirements of a dividend discount model. The fact that the current growth rate is higher than the required rate of return means that the single-stage Gordon growth model could not be applied, but a multiple stage dividend discount model may be appropriate.

9. **B** We start with the standard Gordon growth model (GGM) and input the known variables: $P_0 = \dfrac{D_0(1+g)}{r-g} = \dfrac{\$2.25(1+g)}{0.12-g} = \$34.50$.

   Then, we rearrange the terms and solve for g as follows:
   $$\$2.25 + \$2.25g = \$34.50 \times 0.12 - \$34.50g$$
   $$\$1.89 = \$36.75g$$
   $$g = 0.0514 = 5.14\%$$

10. **C** The dividends for Firm 4 start out high and then linearly decrease over time to a constant future rate. The two-stage and three-stage DDM models are inappropriate because they assume that dividend growth remains constant during a phase and then immediately changes at the start of the next phase. The H-model, on the other hand, assumes that dividends start out at a high rate and then gradually decline to a lower, constant rate.

11. **A** The present value of growth opportunities can be calculated as follows:

   $$V_0 = \frac{E}{r} + PVGO \Rightarrow PVGO = V_0 - \frac{E}{r}$$
   $$PVGO = \$45 - \frac{\$3.25}{10.25\%} = \$13.29$$

   Current earnings should be used instead of next year's earnings because the current earnings represent the no-growth earnings level.

12. **A** Statement 1 is correct. The Gordon growth model is easily communicated and explained, and it is applicable to stable, mature, dividend-paying firms. Statement 2 is inaccurate. The Gordon growth model is sensitive to estimates of both the growth rate and the required rate of return.

# FORMULAS

## STUDY SESSIONS 10, 11, & 12: EQUITY

Holding period return: $r = \dfrac{P_1 - P_0 + CF_1}{P_0} = \dfrac{P_1 + CF_1}{P_0} - 1$

Gordon growth model equity risk premium:

$$\begin{pmatrix} \text{GGM equity} \\ \text{risk premium} \\ \text{estimate} \end{pmatrix} = \begin{pmatrix} \text{1-year forecasted} \\ \text{dividend yield on} \\ \text{market index} \end{pmatrix} + \begin{pmatrix} \text{consensus long-term} \\ \text{earnings} \\ \text{growth rate} \end{pmatrix} - \begin{pmatrix} \text{long-term} \\ \text{government} \\ \text{bond yield} \end{pmatrix}$$

Adjusted beta = (2/3) × (regression beta) + (1/3) × (1.0)

Weighted-average cost of capital:

$$WACC = \dfrac{\text{market val. of debt}}{\text{market val. of debt \& equity}} \times r_d \times (1 - \text{tax rate}) + \dfrac{\text{market val. of equity}}{\text{market val. of debt \& equity}} \times r_e$$

Gordon growth stock valuation model: $V_0 = \dfrac{D_0 \times (1+g)}{r-g} = \dfrac{D_1}{r-g}$

Two-stage stock valuation model: $V_0 = \left[ \displaystyle\sum_{t=1}^{n} \dfrac{D_0(1+g_S)^t}{(1+r)^t} \right] + \left[ \dfrac{D_0 \times (1+g_S)^n \times (1+g_L)}{(1+r)^n \times (r-g_L)} \right]$

Value of perpetual preferred shares: $V_P = \dfrac{D_P}{r_P}$

Present value of growth opportunities: $V_0 = \dfrac{E}{r} + PVGO$

**H-model:** $V_0 = \dfrac{D_0 \times (1 + g_L)}{r - g_L} + \dfrac{D_0 \times H \times (g_S - g_L)}{r - g_L}$

**Sustainable growth rate:**

$$g = \left(\dfrac{\text{net income} - \text{dividends}}{\text{net income}}\right) \times \left(\dfrac{\text{net income}}{\text{sales}}\right) \times \left(\dfrac{\text{sales}}{\text{total assets}}\right) \times \left(\dfrac{\text{total assets}}{\text{stockholders' equity}}\right)$$

**Value with free cash flow models:**

firm value = FCFF discounted at the WACC

equity value = FCFE discounted at the required return on equity

**Free cash flow to the firm and free cash flow to equity:**

FCFF = NI + NCC + [Int × (1 − tax rate)] − FCInv − WCInv

FCFF = [EBIT × (1 − tax rate)] + Dep − FCInv − WCInv

FCFF = [EBITDA × (1 − tax rate)] + (Dep × tax rate) − FCInv − WCInv

FCFF = CFO + [Int × (1 − tax rate)] − FCInv

FCFE = FCFF − [Int × (1 − tax rate)] + net borrowing

FCFE = NI + NCC − FCInv − WCInv + net borrowing

FCFE = CFO − FCInv + net borrowing

FCFE = NI − [(1 − DR) × (FCInv − Dep)] − [(1 − DR) × WCInv]

**Weighted average cost of capital:** WACC = $(w_e \times r) + [w_d \times r_d \times (1 - \text{tax rate})]$

**Single-stage FCFF model:** value of the firm $= \dfrac{FCFF_1}{WACC - g} = \dfrac{FCFF_0 \times (1 + g)}{WACC - g}$

**Single-stage FCFE model:** value of equity $= \dfrac{FCFE_1}{r - g} = \dfrac{FCFE_0 \times (1 + g)}{r - g}$

## Price multiples:

$$\text{trailing P/E} = \frac{\text{market price per share}}{\text{EPS over previous 12 months}}$$

$$\text{leading P/E} = \frac{\text{market price per share}}{\text{forecasted EPS over next 12 months}}$$

$$\text{P/B ratio} = \frac{\text{market value of equity}}{\text{book value of equity}} = \frac{\text{market price per share}}{\text{book value per share}}$$

$$\text{P/S ratio} = \frac{\text{market value of equity}}{\text{total sales}} = \frac{\text{market price per share}}{\text{sales per share}}$$

$$\text{P / CF ratio} = \frac{\text{market value of equity}}{\text{cash flow}} = \frac{\text{market price per share}}{\text{cash flow per share}}$$

where:
cash flow = CF, adjusted CFO, FCFE, or EBITDA

$$\text{EV/EBITDA ratio} = \frac{\text{enterprise value}}{\text{EBITDA}}$$

$$\text{trailing D/P} = \frac{4 \times \text{most recent quarterly dividend}}{\text{market price per share}}$$

$$\text{leading D/P} = \frac{\text{forecasted dividends over next four quarters}}{\text{market price per share}}$$

## Justified P/E multiples:

$$\text{justified trailing P/E} = \frac{P_0}{E_0} = \frac{D_0 \times (1+g) / E_0}{r - g} = \frac{(1-b) \times (1+g)}{r - g}$$

$$\text{justified leading P/E} = \frac{P_0}{E_1} = \frac{D_1 / E_1}{r - g} = \frac{1 - b}{r - g}$$

## Justified P/B multiple:

$$\text{justified P/B ratio} = \frac{\text{ROE} - g}{r - g}$$

**Justified P/S multiple:**

$$\text{justified } \frac{P_0}{S_0} = \frac{(E_0/S_0) \times (1-b) \times (1+g)}{r-g}$$

**Justified P/CF multiple:**

$$V_0 = \frac{FCFE_0 \times (1+g)}{r-g}$$

**Justified dividend yield:**

$$\frac{D_0}{P_0} = \frac{r-g}{1+g}$$

**PEG ratio:**

$$\text{PEG ratio} = \frac{P/E \text{ ratio}}{g}$$

**Weighted harmonic mean:**

$$\text{weighted harmonic mean} = \frac{1}{\sum\limits_{i=1}^{n} \dfrac{w_i}{X_i}}$$

**Residual income:**

$$RI_t = E_t - (r \times B_{t-1}) = (ROE - r) \times B_{t-1}$$

$$V_0 = B_0 + \left[ \frac{(ROE - r) \times B_0}{r-g} \right]$$

$$g = r - \left[ \frac{B_0 \times (ROE - r)}{V_0 - B_0} \right]$$

**Economic value added:**

EVA = NOPAT – $WACC

NOPAT = EBIT × (1 – t) = (sales – COGS – SGA – dep) × (1 – t)

$WACC = WACC × invested capital

invested capital = net working capital + net property, plant, and equipment
= long-term debt + stockholders' equity

# INDEX

# Notes

**Notes**

# Notes

# Notes

# Notes

# Notes

# Notes

# Notes

# Notes